To Katie,

May you cont...

to dare your audien...

to think big + past

themselves!

Hilary Corna

ONE WHITE FACE

She dared to discover Asia,
and ended up discovering herself

Hilary Corna

Hilary Corna

Publisher's Note
This is a work of nonfiction. The events and experiences detailed herein are all true and have been faithfully rendered as the author has remembered them, to the best of her ability. Some names, identities, and circumstances have been changed in order to protect the privacy and/or anonymity of the various individuals involved. Others have vetted the manuscript and confirmed its rendering of events.

One White Face

To Ren,

For being so darn cute that I had to say, "Konnichiwa."

Hilary Corna

One White Face

Contents

Hilary Corna

One White Face

Year III.
July 2009 – August 2010

Hilary Corna

"Life is a daring adventure or nothing at all"
-Helen Keller

Hilary Corna

ONE WHITE FACE

Hilary Corna

Year I.
July 2007 — June 2008

Chapter 1
May Be Crazy

One thing I've always loved to do is imagine myself, where I am at that moment, on a world map. On the day I interviewed at Toyota Motor Asia Pacific, I pictured my home state of Ohio in the United States all the way to the west, and to the far east, me sitting there on a leather couch in the Lexus room of the Centennial Tower, in the city-state of Singapore, looking out on a stunning view of Marina Bay, and listening — or should I say, not listening — to my prospective boss's question.

"Tell me more of your thoughts on this," Kimura-san said.

I looked up, trying not to panic, begging my mind to replay any portion of the past two minutes. In Japanese manner, the three businessmen sat expressionless, waiting for me to reply.

When I graduated from college, sold my '95 Jeep Wrangler, and moved to Singapore in hopes of pursuing a pipe dream, I had no idea what I would gain and lose. As it turns out, I gained a serendipitous highly esteemed position with the world's largest car manufacturer, a room at the Shangri-La Resort, and dozens of stamps in my passport. Along the way, I lost the girl I used to be. I lost friendships, the support system of my Italian family, any chance at ever feeling normal again, and a boy named John.

My Italian heritage came from my dad's side. All my relatives were very close and spent every major holiday together, which made for a room full of lasagna, red wine, babies, gossip, and a whole lot of love. When my twin brother and I were eight months old, our father passed away in car accident, leaving my mother to raise five children alone. She struggled to make ends meet, but instead of complaining, she persevered and took good care of the children she loved. Mom was the hardest working person I knew, and she taught me to work hard too. As a kid, I picked out my own outfits from a pile of laundry four feet high. I packed my own lunch for school and arranged my own rides to sports practices. At times, I resented this responsibility. I wanted the things the other kids at school had, and I wanted them to come easily. But my self-reliance also meant I began setting goals at a young age, and achieving them.

One goal I always had was to travel. My mother had spent several years of her childhood in Japan, where her father served as a sergeant in the US army, and my curiosity about this far-off place grew as I flipped the pages of her black-and-white photo album. During their time in Japan, my grandmother had learned many of her domestic skills from Japanese women: housekeeping, sewing, quilting, and gardening. Grammy always kept her home immaculately clean and required guests to remove their shoes at the entrance. Temple rubbings, ornate Japanese furniture, and silk screens decorated her home — there was even an oil painting from the Honda family, with whom she was very close.

So when I got the scholarship letter awarding me enough funds to study abroad in Japan during my junior year of college, the words were almost illegible from my shaking hands. I had been studying over two years and couldn't wait to fully immerse myself in Japanese culture.

While in Japan, I lived with a homestay family, indulged in home-cooked Japanese dinners prepared by my *okaasan* (host mom), and ate sushi with local businessmen who wanted to practice their English. These businessmen also gave me tours of their offices and even invited me into their homes to meet their families. Surrounded by faces and languages from around the world, I sang karaoke and guzzled whiskey in local bars. It was five of the best months of my life.

During this time, I also spent tireless hours studying Buddhism and foreign currency. My class visited shrines and temples as well as modern landmarks like the Kyoto Tower. My language teacher was the hardest I'd ever encountered, and together with my homestay family, helped skyrocket my Japanese language skills. I knew I'd never see the world the same way again.

Sure enough, when I returned home, I felt different around the other students at my university. My curiosity had blossomed; I had developed a taste for the unknown. Asia had reinvigorated my senses. I wanted to hear new things, taste new things, and touch new things. I wanted experiences outside of the ordinary, but these desires set me apart from my peers. They winced when I told them I preferred to eat a whole fish down to its spine because it had more flavor than a breast of fish. I couldn't stop thinking about Asia and what else it had to offer. For the first time, I wondered if I could work abroad. But there was someone else in my life whose feelings I had to consider.

I had been dating John long-distance throughout college. He was a few years older, living in Chicago, and was an accountant. By the end of my

3

study abroad trip, we were counting down the days until we could see each other again, but then something happened—I got an opportunity to stay.

One of my business contacts offered me a summer internship in Tokyo. I was shocked and ecstatic, but knowing that it meant another three months in Japan, I became skittish at the thought of bringing it up to John. With only a week left to make the decision, I finally did it.

"John, I need to tell you something," I said one night over Skype. "I've been offered an internship."

"That's amazing!" John said. "When? Where?"

"It's this summer, here in Japan." A space of time passed. I started to think something had happened with the computer connection.

"You mean you would stay?" he asked.

"I don't know. I just wanted to throw it out there and see what you thought."

"I can't do it, Hilary. It's been long enough. I'm tired of not having my girlfriend around. I want a normal relationship."

I knew then that I wasn't ready to have that discussion, so I changed the subject quickly. After that, I was afraid to even mention the internship. It was difficult enough to get a job in Japan, much less as a young American woman, but I knew what John would say. And the idea of losing John frightened me. He was my first real boyfriend, my first love. I cared deeply for him and couldn't imagine not being with him. So I passed up a once-in-a-lifetime opportunity.

John and I continued talking about the summer ahead of us and how wonderful it would be to finally be back together. I already had an internship lined up in Chicago so I could spend a few months with him before returning to North Carolina for my senior year of college.

But things weren't the same. I kept thinking about what I had given up for John and wondering if I'd made the right decision. By the end of the summer, I couldn't fight my instinct any longer. I was too young to forgo an amazing life experience for a man. I loved John, but I was barely twenty-one. I wondered what other opportunities I'd miss because I had chosen to be with him. These thoughts had haunted me all summer, and I felt weary and discontent. I knew what I needed to do.

The day I broke up with John, a fall wind blew through the leaves of the acorn trees on campus. My final year at school had just begun, and it was John's first weekend trip down from Chicago to visit me. We sat on the edge of my bed, talking about our plans for the weekend. I gathered my strength to get up and shut the door, then sat down next to him again.

"John, I need to be honest with you," I said.

He looked confused.

"I don't think we should be together anymore."

My heart felt like someone was squeezing it in a fist. John's eyebrows creased over the big blue eyes that I loved. He sunk into the bed, and I watched him try not to cry.

"I know it's been hard since you've come home from Japan, but we can work through it," he said. "We've made it this far." His voice softened and he reached for my hands.

"There's nothing wrong with us, John. This is a personal decision. I need to do this for myself right now." I said, ignoring the feeling of his balmy hands in mine.

Nothing I could say could ease what felt like an overwhelming unfairness to him. John had taught me more about myself than anyone else. He was honest with me, challenged me. He was my best friend. Having him in my life made me a better person. I had nothing but high regard for him, and the hardest part of breaking up was knowing that there wasn't anything wrong with our relationship, other than the timing. We were in love, but at that point, I just wasn't willing to give everything else up for it.

As graduation approached, everyone asked about my future plans. The job market was great at that time, and my grades were impressive. The offers were streaming in, but I didn't feel my blood boiling in anticipation for any of them. Friends and family kept advising me, "Accept any job out of college, no matter what. You can't be picky," but that thought process always stupefied me. On the cusp of graduation—*that* is when a young adult *should* be picky. You're uncommitted, unencumbered, and have little to lose. It's one of the best times to pursue your passions.

I knew my passion: to return to Asia. As the school year came to a close, I proposed the idea to my professors, mentors, and friends.

"You want to do what?" they'd ask.

"I may be crazy," I said.

Most people, including my family, were unsure of what to do other than offer encouragement. They smiled and wished me luck. To this day, I can remember the five individuals who actually supported my wishful thinking. I moved forward with the decision anyway—a decision ruled by instinct and my heart. I graduated jobless with two bachelor degrees, and an excitement that was immeasurable.

Over a few weeks time, I had several leads and contacts in Asia, but all of them said the same thing: "You have a great resume, and we'd love to have you, but it just doesn't make sense to hire you from the U.S. if we've never met you in person." Skype call after Skype call, e-mail after e-mail, my head hung low after another long day of rejections and cynicism.

One evening, I found myself sitting on a crooked stool at the local campus bar, battling disappointment and wondering whether or not I had set the bar too high for myself this time. Then everything started to make

5

sense. I saw an old friend, Brian. Drinking one-dollar beers in plastic mugs, I told him my plight, and he proposed a plan. Suddenly, my pipe dream of working in Asia actually seemed like a viable post-graduation option.

"My dad lives in Singapore," he began. "I'm probably going out there after graduation. You're more than welcome to stay with us until you can find a job and get up on your own two feet."

Brian was a drinking buddy. By that, I mean that I really only saw him when we happened to be at the bar on the same night. Our conversations rarely reached higher than a recount of the recent drama among mutual friends. Needless to say, this offer immediately deepened our acquaintance.

"Typical American," I thought as I realized that I couldn't even locate Singapore on my mental world map. I began asking Brian questions to hide my ignorance. He described the hot, humid weather of Singapore, the air-conditioned shopping malls, and the nightlife that kept people out until the sun rose. I was not hard to convince; what started out as chitchat between friends in a bar quickly turned into a catalyst that would enable my return to Asia.

Immediately, I contacted everyone I'd been in touch with to let them know I was coming. Like a viral social media community, connections started springing up. I liquefied my only asset into cash — my pride and joy, a '95 Sahara Jeep Wrangler.

When the time came to purchase my flight, I was staying at my mom's house. She had turned my middle school bedroom into her office. Behind the computer screen, a window overlooked my childhood backyard. A maple tree had grown taller and broader, shading Mom's garden. I took a breath and remembered how easy life had been, playing in the yard with friends, helping Mom plant tomatoes.

Upstairs, I began searching for flights online. Mom was downstairs, clinking dishes and silverware as she set the table for dinner. I was all alone. My hand shook as I touched the mouse and watched the arrow hover over the "BOOK FLIGHT" button beneath the itinerary. I was still shaking moments later when my mother came up the stairs calling my name.

"Dinner's ready," she said.

"I'm in here," I said in a hushed voice.

Mom stood in the doorway. I was still sitting at the computer, looking outside. Summer had just begun. The sun was shining.

"Are you hungry?" she asked.

"I just booked my flight."

"You what?"

"I told you I was going."

"I kind of thought you would back out," she said, her voice louder, more urgent. "Hilary, you don't even have a job. What happens if you get there and it doesn't work out?"

"I don't know. I'll figure it out." My endeavors in the past had been ambitious, but this was by far the most ruthless. I was just as frightened as she was, but I couldn't show it. "I have to go, Mom."

"I can't believe you are doing this. You've been gone for four years already! I was finally excited about having my daughter back in my life!"

I pushed the chair back and stood up, taking a step or two closer to her. "That's ridiculous. I've always been in your life!"

"Seeing you for a few weeks throughout the year is being in my life? You've spent nearly every summer with John. It's like you just stop in to say hello."

"Mom, you can't say that."

"I can too. I am your mother. This is unbelievable, Hilary . . . You've really done it this time."

"It'll all work out."

"I can't talk to you until you have a job." She disappeared from the doorway and walked with loaded footsteps down to the kitchen.

Leaning my hands on the desk, I peered back at the maple tree. Mom had taught me the most important things in life—strength, resiliency, determination. But for the first time, Mom didn't support what I was doing. It felt like a bad omen. Had I made the wrong decision?

My flight was scheduled to arrive in Singapore on July 5. As a new graduate, I had an allowance of cash from graduation gifts, the money from my Jeep, and $7,000 in school debt. I made a budget, gave myself two months in Singapore, and promised my mother that if either the money or the time ran out before I had a job, I would come home. I didn't know if I would succeed or fail. I didn't know if my plan was actually feasible or just plain crazy. But my heart dominated over all logic. All I could be certain of was this: I had to try.

Chapter 2
You Are Brave

As the floor-to-ceiling glass doors opened at the arrival platform of the airport, a gush of sultry air seared my sinuses. Black darkness hovered over the palm trees allowing only glimpses of their human-sized leaves. I remember thinking how quiet it was.

After three flights and thirty-six hours, I had landed in Singapore. It was 11:00 p.m., which meant it was 11:00 a.m. back home. Brian had arranged for a driver to pick me up, and I had wondered the whole flight how he would identify me. It all made sense when I saw the driver standing with my name printed on a piece of paper: HILARY CORNA.

"That's me!" I said, as giddy as ever to find him.

"Nice to meet you, Hilary."

"Nice to meet you too!"

As the driver drove into the city, I rolled down the window and watched the endless palms lining the highway. The air softly brushed my strained eyes. Although I couldn't see the ocean, I could hear its waves. I'd made it safely.

When I opened the doors to my temporary home, I didn't expect to find one of the most lavish condos in Singapore — River Place — which overlooked the Singapore River that ran through the middle of the city. Brian had just returned from a vacation in Thailand.

"Welcome!" he greeted me.

"Wow, this is stunning." I said, trying to acknowledge my friend while staring in awe around the penthouse. The interior design of the three-bedroom penthouse was simplistic in style with dark mahogany wood furniture. Oil paintings covered the tan walls with primary-colored illustrations of Vietnamese farmers tending rice paddies.

"Yeah, it is pretty sweet," he nodded. "Here's your room. I recommend we get up at a normal time tomorrow so you can adjust to the time zone. You don't want to sleep during the day."

"Sure! I can't wait to see what this city is all about." It had taken me two weeks to adjust when I first went to Japan. Someone told me that it takes a day of recovery for every time zone passed. Yet even though I knew I needed rest, I stayed up with Brian for a little while, chatting about life since college.

"Life is amazing here."

"I just hope I can find something to allow me to stay."

"Well, you've got ninety days." The tourist visa gives Americans this length of time before they need to leave or renew the visa.

"If it takes me that long," I said, "I'll take it as a sure-fire sign that this whole thing just wasn't a good idea. I only budgeted two months, anyway."

"You'll make it happen. I have no doubt about that."

Not long after that, we wished each other good night. I was wide awake since it was midday back home, but Brian had already switched his internal clock to "Asia time." Lying in bed, I stared up at the air-conditioning unit on the wall — decentralized cooling, just like Japan. I smiled with the confirmation that I had, in fact, returned to Asia like I promised I would. Now I just needed to find a way to stay.

Bright sun in my eyes woke me up the next morning. I rolled over and pulled the curtain back. The view overlooked the condo pool, which was surrounded by tall palm trees and bright green grass. The sky was baby blue and clear of clouds. It was the perfect day.

"Good morning!" I said, coming out of the room to find Brian already awake.

"Good morning. Do you want watermelon juice?" he asked.

"Watermelon juice?" I had heard of many juices but not this one. "What's in it?"

He chuckled. "Um, watermelon?"

"Weird. I've never heard of that. But sure."

The taste of watermelon juice became one of my favorite things in Singapore. Just like the fruit, it was crisp and refreshing, coating my throat and cooling it from the heat outside.

"This stuff is incredible."

Brian laughed. "All right, let's go." Brian was only in Singapore a couple days before going on a three-week vacation. Upon return, he'd start his job.

Walking out of the condo door was like leaving the airport. I would never forget that blast of heat.

"This is insane."

"Wait until we start walking," he said with a sigh. "I go through deodorant here like it's my job."

We exited the condo from the back gate that opened onto the Singapore River.

"A lot of people run out here," he explained. "It's beautiful on the river."

"Run? I can't even breathe."

"Yeah, give it a few weeks before you try that."

We walked along the river, lined with shopping malls, restaurants, and bars. Only a few hundred feet after starting, I could feel sweat beads down my lower back and forehead, my long hair sticking to my shoulders.

Everything was shockingly clean. There wasn't a piece of litter in sight.

"So, Singapore is famous for their laws," Brian said.

"I heard someone from Ohio got caned for chewing gum?"

"You can chew it, but you just can't sell or spit it," he clarified. "That guy was an idiot . . . I think he spit it and then made a scene of it or something." This concerned me a bit because I chewed gum a lot. My mom would have to send it by mail to me later. Although such laws appeared strict, they created a clean living environment for Singapore's citizens.

Men and women with short black hair and eclectic styles surrounded us.

"This reminds me of Japan."

"You'll get used to it," Brian said.

"It's kind of nice."

9

"We live in Robertson Quay," Brian said. "As you go toward the city, the Quay changes at every bridge." We walked under one bridge and came out on the other side. "This is called Clarke Quay. It's where most of the expatriates go out at night."

"Awesome. Do you come here?"

"Sometimes, but the clubs can be very touristy. I like the lounge bars better."

I've always had a good sense of direction, but after walking under a few more bridges, I was lost. "Where are we?" I asked.

"There is no grid system here. The streets wind in circles so don't worry, it's not just you. Giving directions here is difficult."

As we strolled down the brick-paved path along the river, one building in particular made me feel disoriented. Advertisements covered curved panels of glass windows across a huge shopping mall. The retail brand's name was written in capital letters on top of a photo of models. Not a single one of them was Caucasian.

"It's so weird to see an advertisement with no white people," I whispered to Brian.

"Yep." We walked across the bridge and stopped. He said, "Let's go back. I think that's enough for one day."

"Great. Because I have no idea where we are."

He pointed back the way we'd come. "If you keep walking, that is Raffles Quay." In the distance, a clump of monstrous buildings towered over green trees.

"That is the financial district where most people work. Suntec City is across from Raffles Quay. That's where more of the corporations are located." I felt like Dorothy cresting the hill and seeing the Emerald City all spread out before her. Excitement thundered in my chest.

"Suntec is actually five buildings," he continued. "The architect designed the building in the shape of a hand. Each one's height is comparable to the one next to it — just like your fingers."

"I don't get it," I said.

"It's feng shui. There's a huge fountain in the middle called the Fountain of Wealth."

"You're joking."

"Nope. It's Chinese architecture. By designing it this way, they believe it will bring wealth for the companies in the Suntec City buildings. This is a very popular place to have an office for Chinese companies."

"Wow, that's wild. Could you imagine someone wanting to do that in the U.S.?"

"Never. Hey, are you hungry?"

"Yes!" I was excited to try some local food — some kind of noodles or fish — but instead Brian took me to an Italian restaurant across the street from River Place. It was the last thing I imagined would be my first meal in Singapore, but I didn't want to complain.

The bill came, and my portion was SG$15. "How much is that in US dollars?" I asked.

"About twelve."

That was more expensive than I had anticipated. I had brought only US$2,000 with me from home and needed to make it last as long as possible.

We returned to the condo to take a nap. "You'll meet my dad tonight," Brian said. "It's his fifty-first birthday so we're going out for a nice dinner. Do you like duck?"

"Duck? Never had it." I'd never been a big fan of red meat. In fact, I liked to claim that I was Japanese at heart because I preferred fish.

"It's delicious. I promise you'll like it. It's one of Singapore's specialties."

Duck is expensive and the dinner celebrated a special occasion. I was nervous about meeting Brian's dad. We had spoken over the phone and he was kind, but his financial wealth and professional success intimidated me.

Brian and I were sitting at the kitchen table when Mr. Drucker came home, dressed in a striking black suit. He'd just flown back from Hong Kong for work.

"He had to fly on his birthday?" I whispered to Brian, who laughed in response.

"He always flies. Dad, this is Hilary."

"Hi, Mr. Drucker. I cannot say thank you enough for what you have done."

"Oh, there's no need for that. It's my pleasure to have you. You are doing something great and unique from your peers. I'm glad to support it."

"I really owe you so much. I hope to one day repay you for your help."

"It's not necessary at all. Now, I have a question. Are you hungry?"

"Yes."

"Great, because this restaurant is one of my favorites."

We drove to the establishment called Mia Jiang in a shiny black BMW. Cars were not a common luxury in Singapore, but Brian's father was high up in his company and had lived in Asia for many years. I later found out that the restaurant we were going to was one of the most expensive in Singapore and one of the finest places to have duck. We sat at a round table with a crisp, white tablecloth amid lush tropical trees. The restaurant was full of foreigners, mostly Caucasians wearing white linen, designer handbags and diamonds on multiple pieces of jewelry.

The duck was stupendous. They brought out several, freshly cooked, with all of their limbs still visible. They allowed us to choose which one we wanted, like fish at a proper seafood restaurant. I'd learned how to tell a difference in fish from Japan but could not tell any difference with duck. They smelled like sweet barbeque, and the waiters served us the meat in three different forms over the course of the next two hours. They provided two dips: one sweet and one spicy. The server stood between Brian and me as I watched him sliced the duck with a large knife. My stomach rumbled. First, we dipped it in our preferred dipping sauce. Then the server presented us bread-like tortillas to wrap the duck in, followed by lettuce wraps. I never knew I liked duck so much.

Brian's dad asked me about my family and background, concluding the discussion with, "Why Singapore?"

"Well, as I mentioned, my family has a connection with Japan. I adore the country. But after passing up the internship, I thought I would use this opportunity to see more of Asia. I was considering Hong Kong or Singapore, and here just made the most sense. It's hot, the locals speak English, and the immigration laws are the most welcoming for Americans."

"It sounds like you did your homework."

"A little."

"So, what is your week like? Do you have some interviews scheduled?"

"Yes. Two interviews, but they're more like introductions. I have several lunch and coffee meetings, too."

"Well, I wish you the best of luck, my dear."

"Thank you, Mr. Drucker."

For the next three weeks, I spent every daylight hour researching the Singapore job market, writing cover letters, revising my resume, and e-mailing complete strangers in hopes of convincing them of my worth as an employee. During the day, I met a variety of people for lunch and coffee from HR reps to hotel managers to Americans who had lived in Singapore for over ten years—all referrals. At night, I crashed networking events.

Brian's father and his Filipino girlfriend treated me to a homemade dinner every night. Friends and family back home bombarded me with requests to send pictures, but I had to constantly re-inform them this was not a vacation. This was work, and I had a mission to accomplish.

The majority of the time, I was too busy to doubt my success, and too determined. My growing knowledge and love for Singapore motivated me to realize my dream. At first, I used taxis to go everywhere because they were significantly cheaper than in the States. It wasn't until I realized how efficient the public transportation system was that I changed my mode.

In Singapore, the train stations have flat-screen TVs at each platform showing the number of minutes until the next train, which is always on time. I was used to the Chicago train which bears no information and can leave a person waiting anywhere from one to twenty minutes. The Singapore train stations, like the streets, are spotless and have signs announcing SG$500 fines for drinking or eating while riding. There is even a fine for bringing a certain fruit called a Durian on board due to its notoriously appalling smell.

People generally abide by these rules, but there are a few rebels. I almost always carried water with me because it was so hot outside. I would take a tiny sip on the train, and seconds later, a computer voice would boom over the train speakers, "Please note, no drinking or smoking is permitted on the train. Doing so will result in a fine." I swore to friends that someone was watching the passengers through cameras and that the announcement served as a first level of warning. When I heard it, I stopped drinking. A fine was the last thing I needed, especially when I was on such a tight budget.

To make phone calls, I purchased a basic Nokia phone from the 7-Eleven and a SIM card from the local telecommunications company. I couldn't get a contract until I had a green card, which meant I needed a job. Until then, I was paying for every single minute and text.

My fortitude suffered during this period. I wasn't receiving the response I had expected from employers. Many of them commented on my age and lack of experience; e-mail after e-mail, I faced the rejection that everyone warned me about. But I didn't tell anyone at home. I didn't want them to worry, but I also didn't want to confirm that their suspicions were true, that I couldn't actually find a job. Positivity was the only thing I had left going for me. If someone had pulled me aside at that point and told me how my job search would end, I would have never believed it.

One day, I took a break from the relentless hunt and treated myself to a swim at the River Place pool. With slow breaststrokes, I drifted around the circular pool and propped my elbows up on the edge overlooking the Singapore River. What was I thinking? How could I fight the sinking reality that I might not find a job? Taking deep breaths, I tried to calm my mind enough to appreciate the beauty of the lush Singaporean greens around me.

Suddenly, I was distracted by a young boy swimming in floaties nearby. He was protected from the sun in a bodysuit and a sun hat that disrupted his visibility as he reached out with his little arms. His skin was so smooth, his eyes a bottomless brown. He was precious.

"Konnichiwa," I said. When I lived in Japan, I'd learned to tell Japanese people from other Asians. The little boy said nothing but looked as if he was wondering how such a familiar word could come from such an unfamiliar face.

"Genki desu ka?" I tried again, asking how he was, but he remained silent. I decided then to use actions rather than words and began playing the only universal children's game I knew — Peek-a-boo. I was able to make him laugh, and the sound of that laugh made me forget all about the daunting job search waiting for me upstairs.

"Kare wa Ren desu," I heard a woman's voice say. From behind him, his mother moved slowly through the water and introduced the boy as her only child, Ren. She thanked me for playing with Ren and asked my name. We carried on our conversation for several minutes when a deep but kind voice asked Ren's mother who I was. I looked past her shoulder to see a short but muscular man in his late forties.

After she responded to his question, I greeted him: "Yoroshiku onegaishimasu." It's very nice to meet you.

He was surprised that I spoke Japanese and said, "How cool!" This was the typical response I received when a Japanese person discovered that I, a young white woman, could speak their language. It caught me off guard initially, but I secretly adored the pleasant surprise in their voice and took pride in showing that not all Americans are the same. I stood up straighter in the water and smiled, but without revealing my teeth to remain modest.

The man's name was Sato-san. He was Ren's father and the former owner of one of the most successful Toyota dealerships in Tokyo. He had recently been hired as a consultant for Toyota's Asian regional office in Singapore. He was the last person I expected to meet while swimming in the River Place pool.

"What are you doing here in Singapore?" he asked.

"I just arrived a couple weeks ago to look for a job."

"A job all the way over here? Why?"

I reiterated my story which, after explaining to so many people, had become rehearsed.

"You are brave," Sato-san said.

"I have nothing to lose."

"What did you study?"

"I have two degrees, one in international business and the other in Asian/Pacific studies."

"You understand where your passion is. Do you know *kaizen?*"

"Yes, of course! Operations management was one of my favorite classes in college. We studied kaizen at Toyota often." I splashed the water with my hands in excitement.

"I don't know, but I think I may have an opportunity for you."

"Excuse me?"

He started to exit the pool and said, "Please, follow me." His wife Keiko and Ren stayed in the pool, playing. Sato-san went over to their things on a pool chair and pulled out a business card. He offered me a towel to dry my hands.

"There may be an opening in my new department. I cannot guarantee it, and it depends on many things, but please e-mail me. I will inquire with HR."

14

I tried to keep my jaw from dropping. I hesitated to let my hopes rise. I couldn't imagine Toyota, of all companies, hiring me. Yes, I had passion for Japan and its culture, and I knew the language, but this was the famous Toyota—the world's largest car manufacturer and leader in quality. Why would they want to hire a young American, fresh out of college?

It was time to do my homework, again. I needed to learn more about the Singapore office, kaizen, and research Toyota's activities and direction for Asia.

Chapter 3
It's Just a Little Rain

In the meantime, Brian returned from some travels, and I needed to find another place to stay. Even though Toyota sounded like a promising opportunity, I felt skeptical. I had no place to live, and I was quickly running out of cash.

Through another school introduction, I met Amanda. She was a year younger than me and just arrived for a summer internship. Her parents lived in Singapore and welcomed me into their home temporarily.

Although I felt like a burden to them, I had to do whatever it took to launch my career in Asia. I'd never felt more determined about anything in my life; I wonder now how I kept that level of resiliency afloat.

That weekend after I moved in with Amanda, we went down to the beach for the day to hang out at a famous bar. I was getting low on cash so I didn't even order a drink. We sat on beach beds with white cushions only a few feet away from the ocean. Techno music blared from speakers courtesy of the in-house DJ. Below him, a round, swim-up bar sat waist-high in a long pool of good-looking people.

"This is our new home," Amanda said. "Pretty sweet, huh?"

"Yeah, pretty sweet." As much as I wanted to think positively about the situation, I was also trying not to get too excited about life in Singapore just in case things didn't go as planned. Looking back, I wish someone had told me to relax and live in the moment. In the end, that was the key to making the plan work.

Katie was another new friend scheduled to meet us that day. Mutual friends from school in North Carolina had put us in touch with one another since we were both moving to Singapore at the same time. Amanda was just saying something about not meeting many Americans when Katie walked up.

"Katie?"

"Hilary?"

"Hi! I recognize you from the photos online."

"Yeah, same here. It's nice to finally meet you in person! This is Amanda."

Katie joined our conversation easily.

"We were just talking about how few American are abroad. How long are you staying here?" I asked Katie.

"It's just a one-year work assignment. My college has a joint alliance with a school here to build a new medical facility."

Admittedly, I was jealous. "How did you get that job?"

"I was nominated for it out of college. It was totally sudden, but I just felt like I couldn't turn it down — like I would never be able to do it again." I knew right then that Katie and I were going to get along.

Amanda was with her family the following weekend, so Katie and I went out by ourselves. Our plan was to check out one of the most famous clubs in Singapore, called Ministry of Sound.

We had both downed several cocktails and were dancing along with the crowd when I looked down and realized that my pocketbook was unzipped. Something was missing from inside.

"My camera! It's gone!" After searching the floors of the club for a while, we gave up looking for the camera and went elbowed our way through the crowd to the long, skinny bar. As I recovered from two lemon-drop shots, I looked down and saw a plastic sword on the ground; it looked like it was from a costume. I pointed at it to Katie questioningly.

"Only in Asia would you randomly find a sword in a club!" she yelled across to me, laughing. I picked up the sword and began swinging the light plastic around, already feeling the impact of the shots, when I caught eyes with someone staring at me in amusement. He looked to be over six feet tall with black wavy hair, dark skin, and big lips that led me to believe he was of Filipino descent. He was dressed like a rocker, with chains and necklaces hanging on his chest, bangles on his wrists and a black vest over a white cotton t-shirt.

"You!" I said, striking the sword at his chest. I attempted a playfully demanding voice. "What is your name?"

His chuckle exuded confidence but not in a haughty way. "Peter," he said. I was enthralled when his bright green eyes reciprocated interest.

"Peter?" I said.

"Yes, Misses. May I ask who you are?" His words exposed a strong British accent, making me practically collapse in my heels.

"Are you British?"

"Yes," he laughed. "And your name is?"

"Hilary."

"Well, Ms. Hilary, it's lovely to meet you. Might I ask why you're stabbing me with your plastic sword?"

16

I later confessed to Katie and Amanda that Peter's appearance was what attracted me to him initially, but there really was more to it than that. He made me jumble my words and stumble over my feet. He made me stab him with a plastic sword. His presence instigated a smitten feeling that enveloped my entire body in our few moments together. With a few words, I felt like I knew him, and he knew me.

"It's not something I can explain," I said to them as we prepared for another night out.

"What does he do here?" Katie asked.

"I didn't get much information from him that night, but I know that his parents live here. He goes to college in England and is only here for the summer."

"So, how old is he?" Amanda asked a warning in her voice.

"I don't know . . . Definitely a senior, though."

"Cradle rocker!" she teased. "When are you going to see him again?"

"He's coming to SINGfest tonight." SINGfest was one of Singapore's biggest music festivals, and Amanda had gotten free tickets from her rich British friend. I attempted to keep Peter out of my thoughts, but failed. I couldn't wait to see him.

When we got to the festival and found a spot on the hill overlooking the crowd, I couldn't stop thinking about what I was going to say to him.

"Don't be so nervous," Amanda laughed. She'd already made fun of me for taking such a long time to figure out what I was going to wear.

I saw Peter walking up the hill with his friend. His hair was practically waving in the wind while a childlike crush came over me.

"Hilary, my dear," Peter said. He hugged me with his long, strong arms and I nearly lost control of my feet again.

I'm never shy with people and can talk to anyone, generally. But Peter was different. I lost all common sense with him.

We sat down on the hill overlooking the band. Tall, flat-topped trees lined the park like in an African safari skyline. The air was humid but cooled as the sun set over the trees. We were the perfect distance from the music to listen yet still carry on a conversation.

"So how did you end up in Singapore, anyway?" he asked.

My intention was not to tell him my entire life story but the narrative just came out. I told him about my giving up an internship in Japan, about realizing that I was too young to be making such sacrifices, about my dream to work abroad, and eventually my arrival to Singapore with two months to find a job. He devoted his full attention the entire time.

"I've had two job offers," I said, "but I'm waiting now to hear back from Toyota."

"That was so bold of you," he said.

"It'll be bold when I get a job."

"Even that you've tried is bold."

I should have given myself a break and accepted his encouragement, but I only felt embarrassed that I still didn't have the job I wanted. Talking about my situation was exhausting and made me desperately want to change the subject.

"What do you study at school?" I asked, regaining my composure.

"Film."

"Wow, that's cool!" I sat up in the grass. It wasn't something I heard very often.

"I adore it."

"What about it do you adore?" I asked.

"Seeing things through different lenses. I think it's fascinating."

I was never a very creative or artistic person, so his perspective deeply intrigued me. He began to tell me about different approaches of films, their stories and the styles of different directors.

"I don't think I've ever held a conversation with someone about this," I said. He smiled. "Wait, so how old *are* you, anyway?"

"How old do you want me to be?" he said.

"No, really," I said with a giggle.

"I'm nineteen."

It was like waking up from a deep, wonderful sleep to a bucket of water in the face. "You're *what?*" Between his accent, British etiquette, and overall appearance, I would have never guessed he was younger than me, much less by three years.

"How old do I appear?"

"Not nineteen," I admitted. But our conversation continued; I didn't care. I kept reminding myself that a marriage was not in prospect and that I could be attracted to someone younger than me. I certainly was.

With rock 'n' roll music playing in the background, we sat on that hill for hours, talking about life abroad, school, and love. Our exchange deepened quickly. I even revealed the fact that my father had passed when I was a child.

"I'm sorry," he said in reply.

"Thank you." That should have been the end of it, but tears suddenly welled up in my eyes. I didn't know why. "This is so weird," I told him. "I never cry about my dad."

"It's okay."

"No, really. I never get upset."

"It is beautiful."

I immediately felt comfortable with Peter. I didn't need his approval to open up or let go.

One White Face

While Peter and I sat talking, Amanda and the others were off dancing. When they asked us if we wanted to go out after the concert, it wasn't a surprise to anyone that we refused the invitation.

"I'll take her home, Amanda," Peter said. Conveniently, his parents lived down the road from Amanda's house.

We continued talking even when the taxi came to a halt at Amanda's house.

"Do you want to go for a walk? I want to show you something," he said, and of course I said yes. He led us in the opposite direction of Amanda's house. A few minutes later, I found myself standing in a vast plot of green land, surrounded by what looked like a tropical forest. Seeing a lush, natural landscape was strange after spending weeks in the city.

"My house is over there," Peter said, pointing to the other side of the grass. "This is one of my favorite places to come. It's away from the streets, so it's quiet, and you can see stars. Come."

I felt like I was in an enchanted fairytale. My prince was sweeping me off my feet.

We lay in the itchy grass and watched the stars. I was wearing a white sundress that I knew was probably getting ruined, but it was worth it just for a few more minutes with Peter. I was waiting for him to kiss me. Instead, it started raining.

"Oh no," I groaned.

"It's just a little rain," he assured me. Peter was laid-back. To him, everything just was.

"Just a little rain," I repeated with a nod. Right as the words left my mouth, he rolled over in the grass, held my cheek, and kissed me. His round lips that I'd been admiring for hours felt every bit as sensual as I'd imagined. Everything, every thought of expatriates and job-hunts and deadlines and resumes and disapproving family members left my mind. Everything except him.

The rain came then. It poured as if from a hose, drenching our bodies with warm water. My dress was definitely ruined now if it hadn't been before, but even that seemed irrelevant. We just held each other, unsure of where the attraction came from, what it meant, or what was going to happen next. That moment in time was something I would never forget.

My fantasy with Peter lasted for another month. We hung out almost every day. His return to school at the end of the summer, however, tore me apart. Dating abroad was never my intention. Now, I'd met someone and couldn't deny my feelings for him, yet pursuing him was simply impossible. For the first time since John, I felt like I was in love—but I couldn't do anything about it.

About two weeks after my night with Peter, I had my first professional meeting with Sato-san. I took this as a good sign but it was difficult for me

19

to discern the feasibility of the opportunity with Toyota. I kept in touch with my other contacts, just in case.

I met Sato-san for lunch at a café called Simply Sandwich located just below the Toyota office. I was so nervous that I worried that my internal organs would suddenly malfunction. I wore the first suit I ever owned — one I bought in high school for the interview portion of a pageant; it was outdated, but made up for that in quality. Like the company itself, my outfit was classic and traditional. I had multiple copies of my resume ready and a leather paper pad from my internship in Chicago, the one I took in place of the Tokyo internship I had sacrificed for John.

It was about 11:45 a.m. I watched the early birds flock out of the office on their way to lunch and tried to picture myself in the crowd, part of the corporate world, a team member adding value to the world's most renowned car company and to the societies of Asia.

I knew then, if I didn't know already, that I was prepared to do almost anything to make this vision a reality.

I had a surprisingly easy time relaxing when Sato-san, jovial yet humble and certainly not the typical composed Japanese man, entered the sandwich shop. One of the other general managers walked with him. Bustling high heels and ties produced a loud eatery. I barely had time to touch my chicken sandwich because they asked me so many questions about what I had studied in school, my family, and my love for Japan. We actually talked very little about work, and they didn't ask to see any copies of my resume. We ate and finished the conversation in less than forty-five minutes.

"We've got to get back to the office," Sato-san said.

"Thank you for your time, Sato-san," I said. "It was a pleasure."

They left the shop. I lingered for a few minutes at the small table where our conversation had just taken place. I had expected a grueling recount of my professional history and experience, to be tested on the history of Toyota and my knowledge of the Toyota Production System. Here I was, in my suit with my resume and support papers ready, and all they wanted to know was if I'd eaten natto when I was in Japan — a type of fermented soybean that usually repulses foreigners. This meeting was the beginning of my journey in understanding the Toyota Way and conducting business with the Japanese. Sato-san wanted someone else to meet me prior to the interview so that he could confirm his impression.

I left the shop unsure of what to do next. Sato-san said that the HR staff would contact me for an interview. Patience would be key. I finally received the call about a week later after a long chain of e-mails between HR and myself. I was scheduled for an interview on the following Monday at 10:00 a.m. I couldn't have imagined a more perfect way to start the week.

Chapter 4
Indefinitely

"Centennial Tower, please," I said to the taxi driver.

"Where-lah?"

"Cen-tenn-i-al To-wer," I tried again, enunciating even though I knew the problem wasn't my accent. He wasn't familiar with the building. Amanda had warned me that the country was constructing buildings so fast that it was hard for the taxi drivers to keep up.

The taxi was an old stick shift Toyota Crown, ironically enough, from the early '90s. These were the most common in Singapore because of their reliability. There were advertisements both in and outside of the car for products like Chrysanthemum Tea and SingTel, and there was a horrible stench that I later found out was some kind of prayer incense. For my entire time in Singapore, I prayed not to get taxis with that smell. If I did, I would always have to hold my nose.

The taxi driver nodded and I assumed he understood. It started to rain right as he put the car into drive, and the clouds were so dark that you couldn't see the tops of the buildings.

"Which one is Centennial Tower?" I asked.

"Don't know-lah. I'm just a taxi driver."

"Yes, and that's your job, isn't it?" He didn't respond. This was the most important meeting of my life, and I had to be on time for it, regardless of how fast the buildings were being built.

"Here-lah," I told him, handing him the money. I had adjusted to the local "Singlish" already. They often add *lah* to the end of words.

The office was in the middle of Suntec City — the corporate area that Brian had pointed out was in the shape of a hand. I had no idea where in the hand I was. I frantically ran around in my suit and high heels, grasping my umbrella, asking people every one hundred feet, "Centennial Tower, where-lah?" No one knew.

"How do you not know?" I asked one innocent woman at the 7-Eleven. It turns out, the place where the taxi dropped me off was just around the corner from the office, but I had no way of knowing. By the time I arrived, I was a discombobulated mess, but I was still on time.

The security guard explained that he had to hold my ID in exchange for a guest pass, which made me nervous — the only ID I could give him was my passport. A US driver's license would not suffice here. I took the elevator to the thirteenth floor. The big red Toyota sign above the receptionist made the breath catch in my throat.

"Good morning. My name is Hilary Corna. I'm here for an interview."

"Good morning. Yes, I see. Please, have a seat."

She directed me to the waiting chairs where I sat alongside two other candidates interviewing for the same position. They were both Asian, but after taking a quick glance, I remained steadfast. One lady appeared very young and wore a short skirt with a designer bag perched on top. The other candidate had plenty of notes and a pad of paper sitting upright in a grey suit.

The American candidate sat up straight, shoulders back, in a traditional but classy grey suit that successfully disguised her age. She wore hose and heels that were an appropriate two inches high. The research and notes she had prepared beforehand sat on her lap in a leather notebook. She was as ready as she'd ever be. This was the moment for which she had sacrificed convention, support, security, friendship, love, everything. There was nothing that could stop her now.

The assistant approached me just five minutes later and said, "They are ready for you, Miss Hilary."

She led me to the door of the room entitled "Lexus," furnished with four leather couches in the shape of a square. A beautiful Japanese circular dish graced the center. I noticed a large world globe standing in the corner and thought about how I had always wanted one. The air smelled clean, like a new car, and I let myself marvel at the stunning view of the Marina Bay and Indonesian Islands visible from the couches. I felt perfectly calm during these moments, strangely enough. It wasn't until after the interview started that I began to get nervous. There were three men waiting for me, including Sato-san and his friend from our lunch meeting. The third was Kimura-san, the general manager of RDSD, the Retail Development Support Department.

They were exceptionally polite, and we carried on some small talk before easing into broader questions about me. I kept reminding myself to be calm, to remember that I was not answering technical questions or being drilled on material that I'd had to stay up studying all night. This was not a skill-measuring test; it was just me. They wanted to know about me, and I was more than capable of telling them. I knew why I was there. I knew what I wanted. It was time to let this fierce awareness of myself do its job.

This was the point where one of Kimura-san's questions dragged on for a couple minutes, and my mind began to wander. I started to examine the sheen of the leather seats, the view of the sea, and the enchanting globe. This was a mistake.

As Kimura-san's voice lulled me into a daydream, I imagined myself again on the world map. I suddenly realized the impossibility of this scenario, of this dream of mine. Everyone at home certainly thought it was impossible, didn't they? That one thought bored a hole in my confidence, and the reality of the situation began to overwhelm me. What on earth was

I doing here? What was I thinking? Did I really think that Toyota would hire *me*, a young, white American woman just out of college?

"Tell me more of your thoughts on this," Kimura-san said in my direction.

Thankfully, I remembered an interviewing technique for just such a situation. To buy more time, the interviewee can ask for clarification of the question. Granted, these men were unbelievably intelligent, and every second that ticked put a bigger spotlight on my silence, but it was all I could do.

"Excuse me, but could you expand a bit further on your question and what you mean by it?" My voice sounded confident and composed, but I felt like a particularly vital organ was trying to jump out of my mouth. I was terrified that Kimura-san would criticize me for not listening, that I had ruined everything, that I'd lost my chance and the interview was over and I would have to go home to America with my head hung — all because I was imagining my stupid map.

Kimura-san smiled and repeated his question. He'd certainly noticed that I was daydreaming but appreciated my professionalism in handling the situation. I later asked him if he remembered this moment in the interview. He said he didn't.

I pushed the sight of the leather couches, the view, the globe, and my map out of my mind and answered his question. I continued being honest, being myself. I was back on board. The interview only lasted twenty minutes, but it had gone superbly.

"It was very nice to meet you, Hilary," Kimura-san said to me. He had a grin on his face, and I felt like he was telling me something without saying anything at all.

A week passed.

"Let's go shopping," Amanda said. I didn't have any money to go shopping, but I did want to get out of the house. All I could do was sit around and crave the immense relief I would feel once I heard the result of the interview — for better or for worse.

Amanda went to the dressing room of an expensive retail store to try on an armload of clothes. I meandered through the racks and tables of clothing, listening to the horrendously loud music, observing the ridiculously priced items. It was rare for me to buy new things after wearing hand-me-downs from my sisters my whole life, and I definitely couldn't condone it when I didn't have a job. But I made a promise to myself that I would treat myself to one of those dresses when I did finally get employed.

My cell phone rang. I nearly jumped out of my skin.

"Miss Corna, this is Yun from Toyota Human Resources," began the feminine voice on the other end.

"Yes. Hi, Yun."

"Thank you for taking the time to interview with Kimura-san's department, RDSD. We would like to proceed to offer you a position as Executive Officer within this department."

I began jumping up and down frantically in the middle of the store.

"Miss Corna? Are you there?"

"Yes! Sorry!"

"You have been short-listed."

I stopped jumping. This didn't sound good. "Short-listed?"

"Yes, short-listed. We have narrowed you down from a longer list of candidates." Oh, so that's what it meant. She must have taken my question for disinterest because she asked, "Were you still interested in the position?"

"No, of course I am! Sorry, I'm just not used to that word."

"Good," she answered. "We will need some more information from you. I will follow up with you by e-mail. Can you reply there?"

I was still jumping up and down. I was holding my hand over my mouth, trying to hold in the scream of excitement threatening to burst out of me. "Yes, of course."

"Okay then. I'm looking forward to seeing you again, Miss Hilary."

"Just one thing!" I said, trying to catch her before she hung up. "How long will the employment last?"

Most expatriates only lived in Asia on a time-bound contract that generally lasted one to two years, but I wasn't technically an expatriate because Toyota wasn't hiring me in my home country and relocating me. I honestly didn't know what details to expect in the contract.

"Indefinitely," she responded.

My eyes must have doubled in size. "Indefinitely?"

"Yes."

Something about that word startled me. This adventure wasn't just for the sake of traveling anymore. Now I could actually live in another country. Everything became more real to me in that moment, the moment I realized that I was about to make a promise to serve a company. There was certainly no going back now, and, for the first time, I was confident I could look forward and begin my professional life. Yet, I still wondered what was going to happen in this indefinite period of time.

"So, if this is not a time-bound contract like a regular expatriate would have, what is it?" I asked.

"Upon acceptance of our offer, you would be what we call a local hire."

That seemed like strange terminology considering I wasn't from Singapore, but later I found that this situation was relatively common. All of the other Asian nationalities working for Toyota came to Singapore on their own in search of employment; they were also called local hires.

"Wonderful," I said, nodding. "I'm looking forward to seeing you again, Yun."

"Same, Miss Hilary."

As soon as I hung up the phone, my knees buckled beneath me, and I collapsed to the cool marble floor of the air-conditioned store. I was laughing so hard that I could barely speak. Amanda must have heard me from the dressing room because she suddenly appeared beside me.

"Oh my God, what happened?" she asked. I just kept laughing. "Hilary? What? Did you get the job?"

I leapt to my feet and hugged her as tight as I could. "I got the job, Amanda. I did it! I got the job with Toyota!"

We held each other's hands and jumped wildly around the store like monkeys in a zoo. I kept saying, "I did it! I did it! I did it!" She echoed, "You did it! You did it! You did it!"

I had achieved the impossible.

I called my mom as soon as we returned to Amanda's house, not caring that it was 2:00 a.m. in Ohio.

"What?" Mom mumbled on the other line. "Hilary, I'm sleeping."

"Mom, I got the job with Toyota!"

"Hmm?"

"The job! I got the job!"

"The job?" she groaned, obviously still asleep. I waited a moment for it to register with her. "The job! Oh my Lord! Hilary, that's wonderful!"

"Sorry for waking you!"

"Don't be silly! This is amazing!"

"Okay, go back to sleep," I told her. "I'll call you tomorrow. I love you, Mom!"

The next morning, I received an e-mail from my mom that was also addressed to my four siblings:

HILARY GOT THE JOB WITH TOYOTA HILARY GOT THE JOB WITH TOYOTA HILARY GOT THE JOB WITH TOYOTA HILARY GOT THE JOB WITH TOYOTA HILARY GOT THE JOB WITH TOYOTA! I'M SO PROUD! SHE'S EMPLOYED!

Details later she goes in to sign her package tomorrow- she'll be teaching Southeast Asia dealerships how to implement their strategies of keeping the Toyota proactive in their product and sales (JUST THE REASON TOYOTA'S SO HOT RIGHT NOW)

PROACTIVE NO RESIDUE:) IF YOU KNOW WHAT I

MEAN PROACTIVE PROACTIVE GO HILARY GO
HILARY GO HILARY IT
IS A GOOD DAY PLEASE LET HER KNOW THAT YOU
KNOW

WHEW
LOVE YOU!
MOM

Chapter 5
One White Face

"Nice top," one of the girls in my orientation group said. We were sitting in one of the main meeting rooms doing paperwork with the human resource staff. The room was just next door to the room I'd been interviewed in, where I'd pictured my location on the map and had no idea that that location would be indefinite.

"Thanks!" I said. "I just wanted something new to wear on the first day."

"It's strange," she added.

I tilted my head. "Strange?"

"Yes, Japanese mostly wear black and gray. None wear purple on work's first day," she giggled. "But it's nice."

"Oh, I didn't know," I answered, but the more I thought about it, the more I remembered seeing that pattern in Japan. I had noticed that people riding the train to work or school always wore dark, dull colors. I had assumed it was because of the weather but found out it had more to do with not wanting to stand out.

"It's not bad," she assured me. "It's just different."

Over the prior weeks, Amanda had returned to the United States for her senior year. The Singapore government had approved my green card, and I could finally get my own contracted cell phone and begin searching for an apartment. My life as an expatriate had officially begun. I no longer felt like I belonged to any one country, but to the entire world.

"Now, we'll go for an office tour," Yun announced. During the interviewing process, I had asked if I could view the office, but HR had refused. Apparently, this is forbidden until employees report to work their first day. I had no idea what to expect.

The office was in the shape of a big circle with doors permitting entry to either side. As the new hires walked through one of the entryways, Sato-san appeared. I couldn't hide my grin. He wore a silver pinstriped suit paired with a purple tie. On his shirt pocket, his initials were embroidered, also in purple.

"Sorry!" he said to Yun. "May I interrupt?" She nodded, without having much choice.

He turned to me and said, "Hilary-chan!" The two of us hugged while the rest of the group looked on, confused at how I'd already befriended one of the managers.

"Good morning, Sato-san," I said, smiling.

"Is everything okay? You found the office okay and on time?"

"Yes, of course. Thank you."

"And how is today?"

"Just fine. We are going for the tour now."

"Okay, then. I have to go to the airport now. I will be in touch to check in on you," he said.

"Thank you!" I said. His concern shocked and flattered me, but I tried not to show it.

"Sumimasen, Yun-san," he apologized.

"It's okay, Sato-san," she replied.

I gave Sato-san a little wave as he left, and the tour continued. "This side contains all of the departments," Yun began. "The other side is where I sit, with the administrative resources."

As soon as we entered the room, the older employees' eyes shifted in our direction. I just smiled, thinking it was normal to want to see the latest hires, but the employees were used to new people coming through the office on a regular basis and usually ignored them. My skin color, however, called for a different reaction.

Yun explained each department and its general responsibility. I was anxious to see the one to which I had been assigned, but I was a little concerned that the people I interviewed with wouldn't recognize me. Since the interview, I'd cut my long hair to my chin after losing patience with the scorching heat and the humidity that made my hair go flat no matter how I styled it.

There were no cubicles in sight. Rather, several small tables connected like the outline of a hopscotch game drawn in chalk. Employees faced each other, and the general manager, or GM, of the department sat at the end square, facing down the line at his team.

Each member had the same sized desk, including the GM, and they were only slightly bigger than the desks at my middle school. Coming from the United States where employees had not only their own desks but also entire cubicles to themselves, I was shocked at their small size. A plastic nameplate—pink for women and blue for men—rested at the corner of each desk with the member's picture and extension.

The only people with standard-sized corporate desks (as Americans know them) were the top management above GMs. Of these, there were only a handful, including the president, and none of them had nameplates.

Everyone knew these executives by sight, and knew their extension, and knew that they were male.

All of the staff had the same kind of chair, unstylish and grey, like the ones on clearance in an office store. The thought of sitting in it for hours at a time made me wince, but I found out later that, if you became a manager, your chair upgraded from a short back to a tall back — a subtle but significant sign of authority. No one told me this directly. I had to ask months later when I noticed.

As we walked along the length of the office, we eventually came to RDSD.

"This is your department, Hilary," Yun said. Kimura-san sat at the end of the hopscotch line of tables, smiling at me. Everyone else sneaked a glance at me. I wasn't sure if it was culturally appropriate to smile at them or not, but I did anyway. The team sat in order of their level of position, downwards from Kimura-san. My desk was at the end.

The desk consisted of very few items, and Yun wasted no time in clarifying the company's policy on office supplies. "HR will give you a list. Each item on your desk has a code. Please write down the code of the item correlated to the list. This is for documentation and tracking purposes."

I didn't think much of this at first, but my eyes widened when I saw that the list included everything from my desk to my assigned hole puncher and stapler. Everything had a code. This level of control startled me, but I certainly wasn't going to complain.

One of the items on the list was the desk phone, which resembled something from the 1950s. It was off-white with what looked like hundreds of buttons, and no one had voicemail. A colleague later explained, "If the phone rings, someone in your department should pick up and take a message for you," but he didn't explain why, so I eventually developed two hypotheses: either (1) Toyota saw the act of taking a message and calling back as wasteful or (2) it encouraged team members to work quickly for customers. Either option displayed Toyota's attempt at efficiency and customer satisfaction. Having to take other people's calls was aggravating at first, but eventually its value became clear.

At first, the open-air environment intimidated me, but it didn't take long for me to realize the benefits of this office style. It encouraged positive behavior by making information and resources easily accessible, and as a result, fostered better work relationships.

Toyota Motor Asia Pacific (TMAP) had only been in operation for ten years when I joined. It was established for the first time as a regional office for the South Pacific Asian countries because their markets were emerging so rapidly. The office was divided by distributor or country, and each department handled basic functions such as pricing, distribution, product, and supply and demand. Because the markets were growing so quickly and the office was so new, there were constant changes to our procedures.

Most people know Toyota for high quality and reliability. This reputation is due to Toyota's founding strategy, The Toyota Way, which has two pillars: continuous improvement and respect for people. Using this management style, the company created the Toyota Production System, which is a series of techniques used to improve quality and efficiency in their production procedures. In the past, Toyota only applied these techniques to the manufacturing side of the business, but within the past ten years, the company has made an initiative to apply them to the retail side, the dealership operations, as well. This is where my job came in.

Kaizen is a Japanese word that means "change for the better." Back home, we call it continuous improvement. Kaizen involves consistently working together to identify problems and develop solutions to them. My new job would be collaborating with each distributor to work in one dealership at a time to conduct a new kaizen activity. These projects would typically last one year. First, the team spends several months studying the dealership operations, and then we identify problem areas, prioritize one, and select a theme. After improving the problem through standardizing the process and achieving good results, we share the best practices with other dealerships and establish a standard for the country operation. I only understood a glimpse of this on the first day from a colleague's explanation.

We met again after the tour and more paperwork. Kimura-san shook my hand and said with a grin, "I'm honored you accepted the position. We are excited to have you here."

In Japan, Toyota accepts new graduates in batches — or "classes" — every year after graduation season. Even the bosses in the company refer to other top management as being "in my class" or "after my class." This tradition imposes seniority, subtly communicating based on age what managers have authority over others.

Kimura-san attended high school and college in the United States. Once admitted into a class at Toyota, he was sent back to be a part of the first manufacturing plant in America, located in Kentucky. Because of his experience in my home country, we immediately got along. His English was nearly perfect compared to the other bosses and over the years, my office friends repeatedly told me, "You have no idea how lucky you are that Kimura-san is your boss."

On casual Fridays, all the other bosses at Kimura-san's level continued to wear business formal attire, including ties. Kimura-san wore jeans and a polo shirt. From a career that began in the United States, moved to the Philippines, and then Singapore, he developed a westernized style apparent not only in his clothing, but his management approach as well.

The other bosses were less social; they kept their opinions to themselves and reported straight back to their desks after meetings. Kimura-san spoke freely about his opinions, shared stories about his family, and loved a casual chat between meetings. He greeted us every morning with a smile and an *ohayou gozaimasu* — "good morning."

I couldn't wait to tell Katie about my first workday. She was fast becoming my closest friend, and I cherished her support and encouragement in the absence of my family.

Katie greeted me, "Well, hello, Miss Professional!" at the entrance of the hotel where her father, who happened to be in Singapore on business, was staying.

"Same to you!" I said. I was still grasping the fact that we were both fresh out of college, starting our careers abroad. She'd started her job only a couple of weeks earlier.

That night we ate at an American restaurant which Katie's father chose. The dinner out represented my first in a while given my tight budget. After the hostess ushered us to a table, Katie introduced me to her father and, without hesitating, I began spewing out all my observations from the day, from the gender-colored nameplates to the height of the seatbacks that indicated authority level.

"Wow, that is intense," Katie said. "My office is nothing like that."

"You certainly have a challenge ahead of you, Hilary," her father said. "It seems your journey is only now beginning. But a wonderful journey! Try to relish in your success. You have done something remarkable."

Being in an entirely new society freed me of all expectations. Even if Toyota hadn't hired me, I had nothing to lose by coming to Singapore; I would have accepted another job or gone home with invaluable business contacts and friendships, and an understanding of other cultures. I had taken my first gasp of air in this new world, and it only furthered my belief in determination, resiliency, and serendipity.

The next week, I attended my first official meeting with RDSD in a room filled with people with light skin, dark hair, and briefcases. An eerie calmness filled the room. I sat wearing a bright red dress in a sea of black, grey, and white outfits as though superimposed into one of those cartoons in the business section of the newspaper.

At one point, one of the vice presidents entered the room and interrupted our discussion. I noticed that he had stern eyes that vanquished his soft skin and silver hair; he was one of the few in the building that had a high-back chair and no nameplate. Everyone else stood up immediately, so I did too. The boss looked directly at me, and I glanced around in confusion. My heart began to thump in my ears as he walked to my chair. He bent at the waist, and I followed, but my bow probably looked every bit as awkward as it felt.

He murmured, "I hope you realize you are the one white face of the company."

All I could think to say was, "Thank you". Had it been three years later, I would have just nodded in acceptance.

I took my seat again and tried to focus as the meeting continued, but his comment had put a splinter in my heart. Did he not want me there? Was this whole thing a bad decision after all? What was I thinking, moving halfway across the world to work for a foreign car manufacturer?

As the meeting progressed, I plucked the splinter and attempted to think more positively. The big boss wasn't telling me he didn't want me there. He was making a statement to help me understand my situation. The company had taken a risk in hiring me; it was up to me to prove I was worth it. I would have to overcome the barriers of race, gender, and nationality. I would have to show I could successfully conduct business for Toyota in Asian countries.

This notion of 'one white face' would underscore not only my career in Asia, but my life there as well. I vowed to succeed in living on my own as a foreigner. My attempt to understand what it means to be a minority and a global citizen would consume my thoughts for the next three years.

As a kid, I always desired to be normal and accepted but found myself doing things that set me apart. Moving to Singapore was no different, and it would take me several years of living there before I'd know if it was all worth it, especially, as friends and family back home remained the same. In my attempt for normalcy and acceptance, I'd become more and more abnormal.

Chapter 6
You are Funny Corna-san

I'd been reporting to Centennial Tower for over a month when they finally updated the organizational chart. I didn't know this when I interviewed at Toyota, but there was actually a number of different nationalities in my department, including Indian, Singaporean, Chinese, Thai, Filipino, and Japanese. My heart inflated with pride when the new chart displayed RDSD's the one American as a new member with the other cultures.

"Welcome to TMAP," a younger man said as he tapped me on the shoulder from behind. He was short and cute, with a caramel skin color. I could tell he was not Japanese.

I stood up to greet him, as I did for everyone. "Thank you."

"My name is Kom."

None of my other Asian colleagues explained to me that Thai people had nicknames because their real names were so long. His last name was Panthuvichien.

"Nice to meet you, Kom."

"Have you ever been to Thailand?" he asked.

"I have, actually!" I had treated myself to a weekend in Bangkok after I'd found out I got the Toyota job.

"Oh, you went to my country!" Kom said. "Where did you go?" Asians were always very proud when they heard you'd visited their country. They seemed to adore their countries but didn't understand why Americans felt the need to vacation abroad. "But you have America!" they would say in disbelief.

"I flew into Bangkok, but we spent the weekend in Koh Samet," I told Kom.

"Wow, no one knows Koh Samet. That is a very quiet and beautiful island."

"It was perfect," I said.

"Well, where will you take your lunch today?"

"Take? I didn't pack my lunch."

"Pack? No, where will you take your lunch?"

"I'm sorry?" I'd never heard anyone describe a lunch as something you take.

"Do you have anyone to eat lunch with?" he asked a third time, patiently.

"Oh! No. I don't have any plans."

"You should take lunch with Pong and me. We have a lunch group with two other guys from the country departments. We can show you where the good lunch places are."

"That'd be great. Thank you."

When noon came, I went to the elevator to meet my new friends. I stood against the wall, waiting as the herds of people exited the main doors of the office. Behind them hung a mural-size photo of a Tundra truck, with red letters across the top: TOYOTA. No one looked at the photo because it was always there, but I would always try to give it the same awe-filled attention that I did the first time I saw it.

As I waited for Kom, I noticed some beautiful Asian girls dressed in stylish business attire, standing tall with their arms down or crossed in front of them. They smiled and giggled with their chins down as they looked at the white girl standing alone.

"I like your dress," I said to one girl.

"Thanks!" she responded, seeming surprised.

"I noticed everyone wears dresses."

"Yeah-lah. Because it's so hot."

"That makes sense."

"My name is Yui." I had noticed Yui in the office already. She was a stunning local Chinese Singaporean: tall, skinny, with beautiful black hair. Apparently, everyone loved her in the office. She intimidated me at first until I realized how friendly she was.

"You're the new girl from the States right?" she continued.

"Yes, America. Why does everyone call it the States?"

"Don't know-lah! That's just what we call it. America is too long."

"My name is Hilary."

"Want to take lunch with us?" she asked.

"Aw, thank you. I'm having lunch with Kom and a few other guys—I guess from . . . Area Operations?" I said, hoping I didn't misunderstand.

"Sure, Pong and their lunch group. Well, join us anytime."

"Thank you!" I was wondering when Kom was going to show up. The HR rep had told me we were only given forty-five minutes for lunch.

"Can I ask you something?" Yui asked.

"Of course."

"Why do you have your purse with you?"

"What do you mean?"

"Are you going somewhere?"

"To lunch."

"So why do you need your purse?" she asked.

I looked around and noticed that no one else had their large purse they usually hauled around. The women were either holding a coin purse or a small clutch.

"I don't know."

She laughed. "Then no need to bring-lah."

This instantly made sense to me.

"Sorry! Got caught up in a meeting!" Kom said, coming from behind me.

"Ready for lunch?" I asked him.

"Yes!"

The other colleagues arrived, and we jumped in the nearly full elevator before the doors closed.

"So, where are we going for lunch?" I asked Kom. He stood upright with his head turned slightly to avoid the black hair of a woman standing in front of him. He nudged his head a bit forward, as if to say that we'd talk when he got out of the elevator. I suddenly realized the entire elevator was silent.

"Oops, sorry." I whispered, blushing. He just grinned. Asians are generally very private people. They rarely make conversation about their families or personal drama at work, and my bosses never even spoke on their work phones in public or in front of others. They were apparently also silent in elevators. A few years later, I would begin to notice how loud and public westerners boast their personal information. They talk about new hires or fires, figures and earnings, even office love affairs.

When we got off the elevator, Kom told me, "We are going to go for chicken rice. Have you had it yet?" I had, but I didn't want to mention it because he seemed very excited to share it with me. "This is the best chicken rice in town. Do you know how they make chicken rice? They take the fat of the chicken and boil the rice in it. It is the perfect combination."

I really didn't want to try the fat soaked rice again, but I just couldn't turn him down. "Sure, that sounds nice."

"Can-lah!" Kom said. Even though he wasn't Singaporean, he'd adjusted. *Can* was another strange thing about Singlish; people used the word by itself instead of placing it in a full sentence, saying "can" or "cannot" and adding the typical *lah* ending. It was irritating at first, but I was beginning to get used to it.

Over lunch, Kom and his friends didn't ask me about how I liked the company or how I was adjusting to my new job, but more about my overall reason for moving abroad and my interest in Japan. I was beginning to get tired of telling everyone the story.

"So who is the woman that walks around serving tea?" I asked once I'd finished.

"Auntie?"

"I'm not sure. Whose Aunt is she?"

All the guys laughed, pushing me in the shoulder as if I had told the funniest joke they'd heard all day.

"No one's Aunt. We call the tea lady Auntie." They also called older men "uncle." It's was similar to a "mister" or "miss."

"Ok," I said. "Auntie. And the Auntie just serves tea?"

"Yeah-lah! She serves tea for the bosses and when there are guests. She also manages the pantry."

"The what?"

"The pantry-lah!" They pushed me again, as if I were giving them a hard time. "Where did you come from?"

"Where I come from," I said, chuckling, "a pantry holds food, like a cupboard. But are you referring to the kitchen?"

"A kitchen is in someone's home," Kom clarified. "This is the office. That is why it's a pantry."

I waved my hands, exasperated. "I'm just going to eat my chicken rice."

They all laughed at how lost I was in their Singlish. "You are funny Corna-san."

When I got back to the office, Pong gave me another set of presentations to review. It was all I had done for the first few weeks.

"Please review the project's past history," he'd say. They wanted me to review the progress reports of the major activity in Thailand and Malaysia.

I suspected the famous quality control company would have had a strict education program, but there was nothing. Formal training in kaizen is quite a misconception outsiders have about Toyota. The manufacturing employees receive a lot of training, but in the sales area, on-the-job experience is the best teacher. Unlike in the west, Toyota uses less training certifications because the objective of learning becomes lost in the desire to simply have the piece of paper.

Kimura-san also allowed me to sit in on a few meetings so I could see the company in action. There was a department meeting every month where RDSD discussed the progress of each project. For my first meeting, I went to the meeting room early to prepare my things. A nameplate on the door titled it "Camry." As you walked down the hallway, other nameplates designated the "Corolla," "Prius," and "Lexus" meeting rooms. It was the Lexus room, I remembered, where I had zoned out in nervousness during my interview.

The Camry room was perfectly square with light gray carpet and dark wood interior. Shelves lining the wall held ornate objects gifted to the company from regional distributors and partners. The gold-plated bowl with a floral design always caught my eye. It sat on the six-foot-tall windowsill, peering over a river. In the distance, Indonesian islands were so visible it looked like I could simply reach out and touch them. The water shone as the sun rose over the east. The East Coast Park freeway, the road that led to and from the airport, ran directly in front of the window, and I remembered how, on the night of my arrival, I had gazed at the Singapore skyline from that freeway, never imagining that my office at Centennial Tower would be the entryway to the city.

The door to the room closed promptly at 10:00 a.m., and everyone sat quietly as Kimura-san began the meeting. Even though I had already met everyone, my formal introduction would take place here.

Kimura-san began, "We welcome a new team member to RDSD. Hilary Corna. She is from the United States and studied kaizen in college. She will mainly be working with Pong-san and Kom-san."

With that said, the meeting continued as normal. New members could not interrupt the flow of work.

About halfway through the meeting, the discussion revolved around choosing the location of a kaizen conference. I felt an anxious desire to make a comment. I wanted to prove my interest and show I had an opinion. As I raised my hand like a kindergartner in class, a feeling of discomfort overshadowed my desire to speak. The other eyes peered at me, curious of what I could possibly have to say.

"Before we raise such logistical questions, should we not identify clearly what the purpose of the forum is and our expectation for the distributors after they attend the forum?" I recommended.

I felt my ego inflate, but then later pop when one of the managers scolded me. "First input, then output," he said, reminding me of my position as a newcomer. This notion was drastically different from my Western upbringing, where I'd been taught to prove my worth from the beginning. Now, I needed to listen first.

That same week, one of our team members, Adeline, had a birthday. Adeline was quiet but elegant, with big eyes—rare in Asia—and fair skin. I always admired her graceful way of doing things and her modest but impressive work ethic. However, Adeline avoided speaking to me unless it was absolutely necessary, and if she did, she would not look me in the face.

"Does she have a problem with me?" I once asked Kimura-san.

"Well, have you tried to get to know her?" he said.

I had not, which put me in the wrong. But at the same time, I felt that she wasn't making any effort either. She wasn't very approachable and, given my fresh presence in the company, I felt reluctant to push a friendship on anyone.

Adeline blew out the candles on her twenty-seventh birthday cake in the Prius conference room. After eating a small slice, I left the room to return to my desk; later, Sato-san came up.

"Can you please go back to Prius and help the other girls clean up?" he said. The men had already left and had gone back to their desks to work. Meanwhile, the three women in the department were cleaning up the plates. I stood for a moment, watching them, my jaw dropping. Surely . . . surely this was not some kind of gender stereotype? I instantly felt distraught and wondered what other situations I might face because of my gender. I had joined a masculine-run industry, company, and profession.

It seems strange to the American sensibility, of course, but I eventually learned to admire the way the Japanese view the role of women. Toyota actually taught me how to be a lady, and the minute cultural difference at Adeline's birthday party was only the beginning. Whenever I felt uncomfortable, I reminded myself that it was my decision to put myself out of context. It was up to me to adapt.

Chapter 7
No Warm Water

"Margaret! Margaret! Margaret!" I yelled to my new roommate, jumping onto my desk chair to avoid a two-inch long cockroach on the floor. I had been cleaning my new room when it secretly crawled out of the corner.

"What are you screaming about?" Margaret yelled back from her bedroom.

"Cockroach! Cockroach! Cockroach!" I'd only ever seen small ones, maybe the size of a fingernail. This monster was the size of my entire finger.

I heard her sigh from her bedroom. "Oh, geez."

I screamed again as the insect took flight and landed in the creases of my curtains.

"Oh, God!" I yelled again. "They fly? What in the world?" I jumped off the chair and ran to the doorway. Margaret walked into the room with a black bottle labeled "Bug Killer."

"Yes, they fly. They're cockroaches. This is the South Pacific, Hilary." She was inches away from the insect, poised like a hero about to slay the villain at the climax of a cartoon.

"Don't spray it! I won't have curtains!"

But it was too late. The smell of repellent filled the room.

"It's dead," Margaret said dryly.

"That was repulsive," I said, my eyes peeled for any friends of the deceased. "Ugh! Is that normal?"

"Do you not have those back home?" she asked.

"Gross. No!"

"I grew up with them. We'd chase them and collect them as kids." Margaret was a local hire like me; she came to Singapore on her own from the Philippines. She was raised on a farm in a working family, so she was able to get an education and travel abroad, although she was far from rich. She was a rare example of the tiny Filipino middle class.

"You collected them?" I said.

"Yes. It's just a bug."

"Disgusting. Margaret, how I am supposed to sleep knowing that was in my room?"

"There are probably more," she shrugged. She had an odd sense of humor that sometimes made me feel like I annoyed her, but that was just her way of being funny. It made her a little bit socially awkward too, but in a cute way.

I groaned. "Great, thanks."

"It's true. All the more reason to keep the place clean. In these old HDBs, they live in the trash shoots under the sink. Therefore, they don't build them like that anymore."

HDB stood for the Housing Development Board, which was Singapore's government-subsidized housing. Singapore is one of the only countries in the world to successfully execute this kind of housing with at least eighty percent of the citizens living in it. The luxury condominiums being built around the city, like River Place, were for a different part of the community — the expatriates.

"Sorry, you probably wouldn't have to deal with this if you had chosen to live in a condo," she said. It was uncommon for a foreigner to live in an HDB.

"I couldn't help myself. I just liked you too much," I said. We both smirked.

It had taken three months and six moves to finally find the apartment with Margaret, who would be my roommate for the next two years. With my new entry-level salary, I didn't want to spend a lot of money on an expatriate-style apartment that included a pool, gym, and other amenities. And besides, all of my friends had pools and gyms anyway. River Place was always my favorite, and I would eventually meet more friends that lived there other than Brian and Sato-san.

Our HDB stood tall over the Tanjong Pagar train station in the developing neighborhood. Only a ten-minute bus ride separated me from my office. We lived next to a Singaporean family that had owned the unit since the 1960s. The entire family lived in a three-bedroom HDB, including their fragile and quaint grandmother. In Asia, families still take care of their elders, even though nursing homes are slowly evolving in popularity. When I returned home from work every evening, I would see the Grandma through the front door that they kept wide open because of the heat. She couldn't have weighed more than eighty pounds and always sat gracefully in the same part of a lacquered, wood-carved couch. She reminded me of my grandmother who had lived in Japan, not only because she was just as petite, but also because of her immaculate home filled with priceless heirlooms, antiques, and ornate artifacts.

Our apartment was spacious and combined the living room with the dining area at its entry. The refrigerator stood in the dining area, but it was shorter than me, about half the size of an American fridge, so it didn't take up much space. We had a small kitchen, and given my lack of cooking skills, it would certainly suffice. When I used the sink to wash my first set of dishes, I spent twenty minutes trying to run warm water.

"Margaret, I think there's something wrong with the sink. I can't get warm water," I said.

"Nope. There is no warm water in the sink," she answered.

A miniscule washing machine was also located in the kitchen, but there was no dryer, as they are not common in Singapore. It just didn't make sense to use energy to dry clothes when there was free access to the unlimited natural heat outside. So, we clipped our clothes to bamboo poles that hung outside the kitchen window. When I first arrived, it looked strange to see everyone's clothes hanging out there, and sometimes an intimate piece would fall to the sidewalk, causing a tongue-tied moment among the pedestrians.

When I went to take my first shower, I asked Margaret why the toilet was in a separate room from the shower.

"I don't know. Ask the architect," she replied. I was already getting used to her sarcasm. "But, if you think about it, isn't it a little weird to have the toilet and shower in the same room?"

"I've never really thought about it before," I admitted.

Inside the shower, a mounted water heater hung on the wall. I was looking at it when all of the sudden a gush of blue water began to pour onto my feet. I danced from one foot to the other, hopping out of the shower.

"Margaret, I think there's something wrong with the shower or pipes or something!" I yelled, standing in my towel inside the bathroom.

"I forgot to tell you. That's the washing machine."

"What?"

"When we run the washing machine, the water gets drained into the shower."

"Why is it blue?" I asked.

"I'm washing my jeans."

I let the rest of the water drain before getting back in. I eventually got used to taking showers while the washer was running. However, some days it would make me jump just as much as it did that first day.

After my shower, it was time to set up my room, hopefully clean of cockroaches. It had once belonged to a child, so it came with a blue star night-light, which became a constant reminder that I had grown from adolescence to adulthood.

My favorite thing about the room was the view. From the seventeenth floor, peering over Chinatown, I could see HDB neighborhoods and their drying clothes to the left and the financial district with its skyscrapers to the right. Below my window, streets curved through a jumble of retail shops, all covered with Chinese-style red roofs.

Peter helped me every time I moved, comforting me with his company in the process. When I finally settled in Tanjong Pagar, he said, "At school in England, I have a wall in my apartment that I post things on to remember all the beautiful moments I've experienced. It started small, but it grew." He showed me a photo of his room; all four walls were covered in posters, tickets, and Polaroid photos.

"You should do the same here. You are starting your life. It will help you keep aware of all the lovely things you were able to see and do."

"Isn't that just like a corkboard?" I asked.

"Corkboard? You silly Americans. Why limit yourself?"

"Well, what should I start with?"

"Where is your train map?" he asked. I pulled out the paper train map that I'd picked up from the station when I first moved to Singapore. It folded into a square to fit in my pocket, so several creases were ripped. Dirt and oily hands made certain parts of the map illegible from many lost moments navigating the city.

"Perfect. You know the train stations now. You don't need this anymore. Post it. It represents so much."

Strangely, a feeling of pride and accomplishment welled up inside me when I did.

"Now post anything that has meaning to you. Do you still have the SINGfest ticket from when we first hung out together?" A huge smile graced my face.

"Of course you do," he said. "Post that too. I mean, if you want to remember me." He winked and kissed me on the cheek.

I was beginning to like Peter's idea more and more. I loved my apartment and my new roommate Margaret. For the first time in almost three months, I could unpack my things from my suitcase and feel settled. My life in Singapore had begun.

Chapter 8
You Must Eat the Eyeball

In our first few months working in the real world, Katie and I went out a lot at night. From Oktoberfest to Halloween parties to even running a local 10K race, we had no problem keeping busy. Amanda had returned to the States for college and Peter left for England. I was looking forward to seeing Peter again, but meanwhile had my job to focus on. At work, I was eager to start something and be a part of a project. I wanted to travel. One day, I was reading through the sales material from India when Kimura-san approached me.

"Have you ever filed for a visa before?" he asked.

I jumped from my short-back chair. "No, but I can find out how." Most Americans think of a credit card when they hear the word "visa," but expatriates think of the passport sticker that some foreign countries require for entry.

"Please ask Ajay to help you to get an India visa. I want you to come see Galaxy Toyota in Delhi," Kimura-san said. Ajay was from Toyota's Indian headquarters in Bangalore, Toyota Kirloskar Motor (TKM). He had been working in our office for two years, helping run the kaizen activity with Kimura-san and Sato-san at Galaxy Toyota in India.

"Okay. Pong-san gave me some of the Galaxy Toyota presentations and business trips reports," I said.

"Wonderful. I want it to be your first dealership visit, because it is so different and important for Toyota. It is our second biggest market behind Brazil."

I nodded.

"This is also a very good opportunity for you to have access and exposure to the top management. They are all heavily involved and interested in India," Kimura-san said. At the time, I didn't understand the significance of "being exposed to the top management," but later projects helped me realize its role and power within Toyota.

Three weeks and another filled passport page later, I was on my way to India. Exiting immigration at the airport, my colleagues and I were bombarded with Indian drivers holding signs with the names of passengers and hotel guests. The drivers hid their shyness and giggles behind the signs as we looked for our names.

"Mr. Hilary Corna," a sign read.

"Well, hello, Mr. Corna," my colleague said jokingly.

"I'd like to just assume it's because they probably see more men than women here," I laughed.

The cost of hotels in India was astronomical, and the company spent roughly US$400 a night for us to stay in the Shangri-La Resort. I was anxious to see what all the hype was about for this five-star hotel I had heard so much about.

The von Trapp-style gate opened graciously, allowing us onto the grounds of the hotel. We entered a low-ceilinged lobby, wide and vast with an exotic bouquet of flowers in the center. The hotel staff changed the bouquet once a week and I always wondered what they did with the thousands left over.

The concierge carried my bag to the room, and I was shocked by its beauty. I thanked him and shut the door quickly before jumping up and down in excitement.

"Holy crap," I said out loud, to the silent room. "How in the world did I get here?" The room was almost the size of my entire apartment in Singapore, rectangular in shape with a bathroom with a window that opened up to the living area. Mahogany furniture and shiny masonry exuded a sense of high class.

Immediately, I hooked up my computer to the Internet and called my mom through Skype to tell her about my fancy new apartment. I carried my computer around the room using the video feature to show her where I was staying.

"That is so cool, Hilary," she said.

"I know! I just graduated college! Now I'm traveling and staying in world-renowned hotels. This is awesome."

"Toyota obviously thinks highly of your potential. I just hope you won't be gone forever," she said.

I hadn't set a time on how long I wanted to work abroad. When I was still searching for jobs, Amanda's mom had told me about the standard two-year mark, which is when most expatriates either decide they miss home or decide they never want to leave. I'd have to wait until then to see how I felt.

The next morning, we met Kom and Kimura-san in the hotel lobby where a driver waited to take us to Galaxy, an hour away. We'd arrived at night, so this was my first time seeing India during the day. Our morning commute down the brown, dusty highways revealed homeless people in clusters on the streets, free of any belongings, some even without shoes. We were stopped by traffic at one intersection, and multiple women approached our van with infants in their arms. Their clothes were covered in dirt, and whatever skin wasn't covered was black from the sun. Their babies lay naked in their mom's arms, asleep from hunger.

"Just don't look," Kom said, sitting next to me. "You will get used to it."

I took his advice and looked down at my lap. I sat in black slacks, the purple blouse that I'd bought for my first day at Toyota, and high heels, and thought: everything I have on at this moment probably equals in money what one of these women would need to live for her entire life. I couldn't help but feel guilty.

Over time, seeing this kind of third-world poverty became normal, and I learned not to think twice about it.

Sato-san stood at the entrance of the dealership proudly waiting for our arrival. He gave us a tour of the office and introduced us to his team members.

It happened to be an Indian holiday that week, so the dealership was covered in blossoming white and pink flowers; incense filled the air. My colleague captured the only picture I took that business trip as I stood in front of three Toyota cars with three Indian saleswomen dressed in saris. They stood tall with their arms crossed in front of them, each a foot away from each other. Only one of them smiled. I stood in the middle with my computer bag over my shoulder and a huge grin across my face.

Within a few days of returning from India, Kimura-san and I left for another one of many business trips together. This time, we were visiting Taiwan. When we arrived at the airport, I began walking to the check-in desk for economy seats.

"Just follow me," Kimura-san said, gesturing toward the business class desk.

"Sorry? I'm not business class, though," I protested.

"Trust me. It's okay," he said. I shifted my bags and followed him.

The man working the desk reached his hand out. "Passport?"

"Oh, yes. Here you go." I was nearly shaking when I pulled it from my bag.

"All set," he answered after a moment.

We walked away, and I whispered, "How did you do that?" as if Kimura-san had just figured out the numbers to a winning lottery ticket.

"Don't worry about it. But you're fine. It's allowed." I later found out that when you reach "Gold Class" with an airline, one perk is the ability to bring another guest to check in with you. You can also bring your guest into the lounge.

"She's with me," Kimura-san would say.

My eyes opened wide that first time I entered the airline lounge. Leather couches lined the walls facing flat-screen TVs, and there were tables with every business magazine imaginable. At the back of the room, a long bar with mirrors behind it entertained lounge patrons. I tried not to gawk at the free buffet offering gourmet cheese and crackers, Chinese noodles, and curry chicken. I'd become a global business traveler.

We sat down next to each other in two navy blue leather chairs and Kimura-san began to talk about Hotai, the Taiwanese distributor.

"The country is considered to be advanced with kaizen. They set the best practices in the region. India is new to kaizen, so now you can see both sides."

I felt immediately at home when we landed in Taiwan. It reminded me of Japan. There was even an airplane that landed next to us with giant Hello Kitty characters painted all over it.

The Toyota staff paid full attention to us during our entire visit. They picked us up from the airport, escorted us to the headquarters, and immediately took us to meet their top management. Their respectful efforts superseded other countries.

Our business trip only lasted two and a half days. We spent the first day entirely with Hotai. They accompanied us for lunch at a quaint little restaurant only a few hundred feet from the headquarters.

The street was narrow and crowded with people wearing black or gray business-casual attire. Looking around, I considering dying my hair back to brown, as the fake highlights made me stand out.

"We'll just stay for a smoke," Kimura-san said outside the restaurant. He gestured for me to follow the kaizen leader inside. Ducking under the cloth that hung from the doorway, I entered into the miniscule restaurant, and immediately my nose was filled with exquisite smells.

The restaurant reminded me of my favorite eateries in Japan—a locally owned shop with a low ceiling, a tiny kitchen against the back wall, and a handful of tables with just enough space to comfortably fit the maximum amount of guests. I had to raise my voice to my colleague over the din of the lunch crowd.

We sat at a small table for six people. I had to hold my elbows in so I wouldn't intrude on the person sitting next to me. The waitress poured us tea without asking if we wanted it. I wondered if that meant we were automatically charged or whether it was free because everyone drank it.

No one moved the napkins or flatware on the table as we waited for Kimura-san and the other boss to finish their smoke.

"So I hear you lived in Japan?" one of the staff members asked me. "How did you like it?"

"Yes, in college I studied there. I adore Japan," I said, speaking slowly. "Your country actually reminds me a lot of it."

"Well, you know, many ancestors in Taiwan can speak Japanese because of the history of immigration," he explained. I didn't know this. "But it's very rare now in my generation."

The bosses finally arrived from outside. Just as the manager sat down, he immediately cut off the work chat they'd obviously been having outside, picked up his utensils — everyone else followed — and struck up a conversation with me.

"You! Okay to eat fish?" the boss asked me.

"Hai," I said. Yes, of course.

"Ohhh!" Everyone at the table shifted their heads back and forth at each other, like puppets, surprised both that I responded in Japanese and that I liked fish.

The manager continued his business talk with Kimura-san during the entire lunch break while I spoke with the local kaizen leader. Despite the restaurant being busy, our food came out on time, prepared flawlessly. My stomach was rumbling when they brought out an entire white fish that looked over a foot long. It was served in whole, raised up on a platter with several green garnishes about it. Back home with my Italian family, we would have just welcomed ourselves from the start; in this setting, I waited for the bosses. They ended up serving me first because I was the only woman at the table.

"This is what you eat in America?" my kaizen counterpart asked me.

I thought about soup and sandwich combos at home and, unable to hold in a laugh, I chuckled, "Nope, not at all." I wondered how my friends in the United States would handle the situation if asked to eat fish from its bone. I loved being faced with the challenge, though, and having lived in Japan, I knew how to eat it. Taking pieces of fish meat off bone is a very finicky process, one that only improves with practice.

"Corna-san, you must eat the eyeball. It is the most good for women's skin," the kaizen staff said.

If they expected me to be disgusted, the grin on my face certainly confused them. I'd been in this situation before when I was in Japan at a dinner with a local businessman. I wasn't much of an explorer when it came to food—especially meat—but I'd eaten a fish eye before, so I had no problem doing it again. If swallowed whole, you didn't taste anything. The worst thing you could do was to chew.

I picked up my spoon and scooped the eyeball from its socket, accepting their challenge without words.

"Oh, really?" they all exclaimed. We suddenly became the loudest table in the restaurant. Leaning my head back, I dropped it in my throat, swallowed, and smiled victoriously. They stood out of their chairs and clapped.

We returned to the office and finished our first day in Taiwan. The next morning, we took a bullet train to a local dealership an hour away. The train was, again, just like Japan—clean and sleek. It overlooked a vast, grain-colored countryside. It was chilly outside, but the sun was beaming. The last time I had been on a bullet train was when John had come to visit me in Japan. It was a strange déjà vu; I missed him, but tried to appreciate the moment.

Kimura-san and I spent a full day at the rural dealership, and when we finally dispersed for a smoke break, the quiet loyal kaizen staff took me inside since we didn't smoke. Most Taiwanese, like the Japanese, smoke; I noticed it was common in a lot of Asian cultures.

We sat on black leather couches in what appeared to be a room, though it had no walls and had been sectioned off from the rest of the dealership by bookshelves. The kaizen staff spoke no English, so I remained hushed sitting upright on the couch. From under the table, he pulled out a large wooden platter and began to prepare formal Chinese tea. The man walked me through the process in silence and prompting me to follow each step. The fragrant aroma from the tea filled our makeshift room. Caught up in the ceremony of the act, I almost forgot to drink the tea itself.

Kimura-san returned from his smoke break, and we departed from the dealership, giving thanks and multiple farewells to the staff that had hosted us. Good-byes in Japan and Taiwan can sometimes last minutes because people say thanks to everyone repeatedly as to not miss anyone and to show proper gratitude. I bowed good-bye to my tea ceremony instructor. He turned his body to me and bowed back, without looking me in the eye.

Chapter 9
Ma'am Corna

"I want to take you to one more country," Kimura-san said, "the Philippines."

"Of course!" I said, still eager to travel.

"They have been doing some kaizen, but it's slowed. They are facing some new obstacles, though, so it could be the best time to do kaizen."

Kimura-san had spent five years working for the Philippines office in Makati, which was the central business district of the country's capital, Manila. He knew the market and the management well, so he thought it would be a good starting point for my first official project.

With kaizen, the most important part of the project is the beginning: establishing relationships and winning the management's confidence. These are the most important foundations on which to build. If top management doesn't support the project's direction, it becomes impossible to implement the recommended changes in the distributor's operation. We would later face these issues and more. On top of the fact that this was my first project for the company, it was Kimura-san's first time conducting kaizen on a dealership operation. It resulted in a major learning experience for both of us.

Arriving in the Philippines was entirely different from arriving in India and Taiwan. The airport was old and slow, and Kimura-san told me to pay extra close attention to my belongings. Manila's immigration lines were among the worst I'd ever seen. We stood there for thirty minutes while the VIPs and diplomats flew through their separate lines. It didn't matter if we had priority luggage tags.

We stayed in a plush Shangri-La Resort again. The structure stood powerfully in the middle of Makati. There was no gate, but guards carrying large guns patrolled the driveway with bloodhounds by their side. They stopped every car before allowing it to enter the main lobby's overhang.

Two women with white gloves opened the car doors, greeting us. "Welcome to Shangri-La, Ma'am." After my fourth or fifth trip to the Philippines, these same women would come to greet me by name.

Upon entering the lobby, two more women stood in stunning matching dresses of silk material. With sharp shoulders, the silk cusped their miniscule waists and flowed into floor-length gowns. Combined with three-inch heels, their dress permitted them to take steps no larger than their shoe size. Their hair clinched around an elegantly styled bun, slicked back so tightly that not one hair flew loose.

Their elegance and sophistication struck me. They represented the quintessential Asian beauty.

With one month to go until Christmas, the hotel displayed a Christmas tree in the lobby instead of a floral bouquet. It stood at least ten feet tall, towering over the Filipino guests. While most Asian countries are predominately Buddhist, the Philippines is a Christian nation. I was surprised to hear that almost eighty percent of its citizens are Christians, because of the country's history of foreign control by the Spanish and the United States. It was incredibly comforting to see my first Christmas tree in Asia, yet it made me long for the warmth of home.

To my shock, the rooms at the Makati Shangri-La were even larger than in India—twice the size. The bathroom alone was practically the size of my bedroom in Singapore. The main room contained a king-size bed, desk, couch, and table. Floor-to-ceiling windows overlooked either Makati, the business district, or the newly built shopping hub.

In the morning, I always met Kimura-san at the Circles Restaurant for breakfast. "Ma'am Corna," the hostesses called me as I approached their podium. The Filipinos were always sweet, even at 7:30 in the morning.

The first day in the Philippines, we left the hotel full and caffeinated promptly at 8:00 a.m., heading for Toyota Motor Philippines, with the car and driver TMP supplied for us. This was common of the distributor for the TMAP visitors.

"Good morning, Sir, and Ma'am," the driver said. He had soft tanned skin and a shaved head. His belly was large and round, typical of Filipinos in their mid-thirties with their diet of mostly pork dishes and fried rice with every meal.

"Good morning, Carlos-san," Kimura-san said. He'd known Carlos from his past work in Manila. "This is Hilary. She will be working here a lot now."

"Nice to meet you," I said, shaking Carlos's hand. I didn't know that drivers would become like friends to us. They saw us when we were still waking up and when we were dead tired at the end of the day. We'd grow especially close during traffic jams.

"Please, let me help you," he said, taking my computer bag, purse and bottled water from my hands and loading them in the trunk.

"Thank you, sir." I nodded.

At TMP, we spent all morning simply making introductions. Kimura-san took me first to the heads of departments. The head of operations was a skinny Japanese man, energetic and infamous for spending late nights partying at clubs with Filipino ladies. The Filipino marketing head towered in height compared to everyone else at over six feet all. His conversations always stimulated deep thought, yet his personality was incredibly goofy. Finally, we met Christian-san, a short, quiet Filipino man who was the boss of them all, the head of sales.

"Well, it is nice to meet you Ms. Hilary. We've heard much about you," he said slowly while looking down at the ground. He seemed strange to me, stern and intimidating, as if he was hiding his real thoughts.

"It is a pleasure to meet you. Thank you for having me," I said.

Kimura-san nudged me and looked down at one of my bags. I'd forgotten to give the gift we'd brought.

"Oh, this is for you, from us." I pulled out a box of pineapple tarts decorated with Singapore branding that we'd bought in the airport. With both hands, I held the box toward Christian-san and bowed confidently, as if I'd done it before. But I hadn't. I'd just watched Kimura-san do the same thing in India and Taiwan.

"My, thank you," Christian-san said. Coming up from the bow, we caught eyes and I saw a softer side to him hidden behind the stress of his position. Even though he wasn't Japanese, we treated all the top management within the company with this kind of respect.

On that first trip, we briefly met with our soon–to-be team: Noelle, Gio, and Francis, the manager. They had a good amount of experience with kaizen but we were all new to kaizen in the sales area. Francis stood in front as Noelle and Gio stood behind.

"Great to meet you!" Francis said, shaking my hand with excitement. I noticed that his hands were incredibly soft. He had a huge smile of big teeth that stood out against his dark skin.

"Nice to meet you too, Francis." I said. Francis was older than me, probably in his mid-thirties. It was strange to think I'd be that person coming from headquarters to manage a team that was older than me.

Noelle was a petite woman in her mid-twenties with braces. She had soft brown hair and giggled innocently like a child. She never complained, and I'd find that she'd work tirelessly.

"Ma'am Corna," she said, "welcome to the Philippines."

I laughed. "Why does everyone call me Ma'am?" I asked.

"That is the polite way, Ma'am."

"You really don't have to. Please, I am not that old yet."

"Yes, Ma'am," she said out of habit and giggled.

"Hi, my name is Gio," the final team member said coming up from behind. He reminded me of my twin brother: sweet and incredibly shy. He was short, although handsome. Later someone told me he had just graduated from college, so I was relieved to meet someone my age.

I spoke slowly like I did to the Japanese in TMAP: "I'm looking forward to potentially working together." It wasn't until we actually started working that I realized that Filipinos are some of the best English speakers in Asia.

One White Face

After the three-day business trip, Kimura-san and I returned to Singapore. I was exhausted and had so many personal things to catch up on.

About a week later, I sat at my three–foot-long hopscotch desk completing my first business trip report when Kimura-san placed his hand on my shoulder from behind. It was not his smile but his eyes that suggested good news.

"We'd like to send you with Kom-san to the KDSD training in Japan." There'd been rumors going around the office about a weeklong training from the Kaizen Development Support Department (KDSD) in Toyota's headquarters in Japan. I had tried not to get my hopes up since I was so new, so when Kimura-san revealed the news, I had to keep from jumping out of my seat.

"Wow, thank you. That is wonderful," I said.

"Kom-san will book time in your schedule to share the details," he said. He neatly stacked his papers and zipped up his pencil case ready for his next meeting.

When I left Japan in 2006, I never imagined returning again, much less for a job. I picked up the small, baby blue stuffed dog animal on my desk, a token my mom had shipped me in one of her care packages. I held it, thinking of the past two months of work and how so much opportunity had presented itself. I thought about what it might be like to be able to predict the future – if I had known in 2006 that I'd be working for Toyota in 2007 – would I have believed it? Would I have made the same decisions?

My final business trip with Kimura-san brought us home to Singapore just in time for Thanksgiving, although it wasn't a holiday from work. A new friend I'd met at a dragon boat practice had invited me to his Thanksgiving dinner. Viktor sounded completely American with his "y'alls" and reference to people as "guys." Of Filipino ancestry, he had big lips, dark skin, and jet-black hair, but had grown up in Oklahoma with a Russian name (one his father liked from a novel). Katie had randomly met Viktor separately, and we'd all hung out a couple of times. By coincidence, he not only lived in River Place, but also on the same floor as me when I first moved from home.

The night didn't really feel like Thanksgiving, eating turkey while overlooking palm trees. The gathering of nationalities included a few Americans, Singaporeans, Norwegians, Australians, and Brits.

As I chatted with Viktor and Katie, I told them how Kimura-san had just informed me of another business trip to the Philippines.

"You are leaving again?" Viktor said. He carved another slice from the turkey that he'd purchased from the expatriate grocery.

"Hil, I mean, it's a great opportunity, but you've been traveling a lot," Katie said. "I'm ready to go out again, but you won't be around!"

49

"I know. All I've done this week is catch up on bills, laundry, and a million other things," I said.

"They are really investing a lot in you, though," Viktor said. "You just have to stick it out."

Upon arrival back to the Manila Shangri-La, the hotel staff greeted Kimura-san and me by name. This was my first long business trip, lasting two weeks.

On our first day, Kimura-san said, "I have something for you." He handed me a box with the Swatch brand printed across the top. He'd asked me the time once in Taiwan and found out my watch was broken.

"Until you replace your old watch, please make sure to always wear this," he said. I was embarrassed at first, but realized that he wasn't trying to scold me. He just wanted to help.

After days upon days of sitting next to salespeople to observe their operations, it was finally time to return home to Singapore. Carlos drove us to the airport and I stared out the window hunched over, exhausted from the trip. Suddenly, we passed a lake full of filthy debris and surrounded by houses made of spare metal pieces and plastic tarps. I hadn't seen it on the way in because the flight arrived at nighttime. I only saw it at a glance but was shocked at my first sighting of slums. I knew poverty existed in the Philippines but had not seen it first-hand until then. Although in the same region, the life of the poor contrasted so drastically from the business travelers with our five star restaurants, drivers and airport lounges.

Chapter 10
"Y.M.C.A."

"It's hot here." My eldest sister Elise said as we boarded the taxi. I'd just picked her up from the Singapore airport.

"It's 1:00 a.m.!" I laughed.

"I can't wait for tomorrow then," she said. She'd escaped Ohio's December weather.

Elise was my first visitor in Singapore and had come for three weeks. In due time, I came to value her trip more as I realized how rarely visitors traveled halfway across the world to see you.

We unloaded her things in my apartment and began getting ready for bed, talking about our plans for Christmas. We'd be spending Christmas Day with Katie and her parents, brother, and boyfriend, who were all flying in town for the week. I was jealous she got to spend the holiday with her entire family, but was thankful that Elise would be there at least.

"What's up with your wall?" Elise asked. I looked up at my train map and thought of Peter. I'd been so busy with work that I hadn't thought much of him lately. I'd also trained myself not to because our situation was unfeasible.

"A friend. He had the idea to do it," I said, avoiding eye contact with her.

"He? What kind of friend is this?"

Growing up, Elise and I weren't exactly close, separated by almost five years. However, we didn't fight. Pictures of us as children show her holding me like her baby. We had never really talked about boys much, although she did know John.

"His name is Peter," I said. Then I continued to tell her all about my fall for the nineteen–year-old that was different from any other man I'd ever met.

"We hung out almost every day before I started working. He took me to his house and showed me all his artwork. We stayed up all night listening to music."

"Hilary, he is in college — in England!"

"I know!" I said.

"Well, it's a good idea. I noticed mom's note on the wall. I wish she could have come with me."

"I know, me too. Soon enough. I earn so many miles now traveling for work. I think I might be able to fly her here eventually, depending on how things go with Toyota."

"She would love it."

I turned over in bed, thinking about if I could actually live up to my promise — and how much the experience would mean to enable my mom's return to Asia.

Neither Elise nor I remember falling asleep that night. I woke up for work the next morning nudging a strange body in my bed, but smiled when I remembered it was my sister.

That week, we drank champagne, sang karaoke, and danced at techno clubs. We hiked a tropical forest and dined with expats at posh restaurants.

Sato-san invited us to his home for an early Christmas dinner with his family, along with Kimura-san's family, whom I had never met. I was anxious for my bosses to meet my sister, since each had become so important to me. Before going up to Sato-san's apartment, I took Elise by the River Place pool.

"It was right there," I said pointing at the place where I had met Ren.

"That is wild. What if you hadn't gone for a swim that day?" Elise said.

What if I hadn't? What if I hadn't spoken in Japanese to Ren? What if I'd just thought about it?

Sato-san opened the door with a huge smile on his face. "Oh, you know the Japanese well, Hilary-san!" he exclaimed when he saw the bottle of eggnog I had brought him as a gift to the host.

Elise was quiet and just gave a big smile when she met both families. She was normally shy but even more so when she was unsure exactly how to act.

"Just be yourself. They are totally normal human beings. Don't worry," I'd told her before we arrived.

"Wow!" Sato-san said, looking at Elise and me. "You look so much alike!" Keiko-san nodded in agreement. The children were chasing each other around the room.

"Come, meet Ren!" I said to Elise.

I lifted the little boy that had started it all. He was already getting heavier. Sato-san had invited me over to dinner a couple of times to play with Ren and practice English with him. "Ren-ne, this is my sister. Can you say 'Elise'?" He rolled his head back.

"Okay, fine," I said putting him back down on the floor. "Sato-san, he's developing your attitude."

We sat at a long table in the middle of the living room for aperitif cocktails and then ate a gourmet meal of fresh sashimi.

"Do you know how to use chopsticks, Elise?" I said. I hadn't even thought about it.

Her hands were fumbling the long sticks. She looked up and said, "I mean, I can try." Everyone laughed. Sato-san stood up and went to help her. I watched him in adoration. He'd become more than just a boss.

"So, Elise, tell us a story about Hilary." Kimura-san said.

"Really," I butted in, lifting a bottle of wine, "There's nothing to say. Have another drink."

"Yeah, tell us a story," Sato-san pressed. The wives giggled.

"What do you want to know?" Elise asked.

"What was Hilary like in high school?" Kimura-san said.

I put down the bottle and covered my eyes with one hand. "Are you serious?"

"Nothing bad," Elise began. "She was the Goody Two-shoes in the family."

"A what?" Sato-san's eyes scrunched as if he was in pain.

"Oh sorry, that means she did everything right," she explained.

Sato-san laughed. "No way."

Kimura-san just smiled.

"Well, she was president of her class."

"Ehh!" A reaction screeched from all four Japanese adults in the room.

"And she was homecoming queen," Elise added.

"What?" Kimura-san said. "You didn't tell us that, Hilary."

"It's not going to be the first way I introduce myself," I said.

Everyone laughed again. "Silly Corna family," Sato-san said.

As Keiko-san cleaned up dinner and the kids played on the rug, Sato-san approached me. "Hilary-san," he said, "Toyota will be very hard. I know you don't have family here."

I thought of my mom and looked down.

"May I be like a guardian for you?" he asked.

My face went blank and I dropped my hands to my side.

"Yes," I said. "Thank you, Sato-san." I bowed slightly. I'd never expected him to reach out so much to begin with, and the word *guardian* struck home so strongly. I associated the word with *parent*, and I felt comforted that he cared so much. He knew the many obstacles that lie ahead of me, about which I was completely naive.

We ended the night full and drunk on wine, taking a picture just before our departure. I can still see the picture, ingrained in my mind: two Japanese families sitting on a couch with two American sisters — one strange but intriguing version of a family Christmas.

The next week was Toyota's Dinner & Dance — the annual Christmas party. Everyone called it "D&D" for short. At first, my sister wasn't allowed to attend because the invitation included spouses only.

"That is outrageous," I said to the planning committee, explaining to them that my sister was visiting from my home country. It wasn't until Kimura-san approached the committee that they decided to make an exception for my unique circumstance. I was honored at Kimura-san's willingness to stand up for me.

The D&D wasn't just any Christmas party; it was an Asian Christmas party. Every party had a theme, and that year's theme was "high school."

"How cliché," my sister said as we got ready.

Along with the theme, the committee told us that everyone dresses up and plays pre-party games. "I can't imagine anyone is going to dress up," I said to Elise, totally unaware of the extent of the theme.

Elise and I showed up to the party and discovered we were the only two people *not* wearing costumes. We stopped at the entrance of the hotel ballroom, caught in disbelief at what we saw. All of the bosses, rowdy from intoxication, had started the party early. Dressed in schoolboy white collared shirts, suspenders, and round glasses, they pranced around the room greeting the Toyota team members. All the young women wore short pleated skirts, knee socks, and their hair in pigtails. Everyone was running around the room from table to table with drinks in hand before the festivities began. It was like a mix between the Hong Kong Disneyland and a magazine that a mother would hate to see in her son's desk.

"What is going on?" Elise asked.

"I don't have any idea," I said. I couldn't stop staring.

A couple of colleagues from my department came running up to us. "You didn't dress up!" they yelled.

"I didn't know they were serious!"

"Ha ha, silly Corna-san."

"Why does everyone keep calling us silly?" Elise asked.

"I don't know," I replied again.

The emcee took the stage. "Alright, TMAP!" he yelled, "Are you ready for 2009 D&D?" The crowd of mixed cultures exploded in a roar.

"There's an emcee?" Elise asked again.

I laughed. "Seriously, I don't have any answers to your questions right now. I've never experienced this before."

We found our table number for RDSD and took a seat between Kom-san and Kimura-san. Kom leaned in and said in schoolboy awkwardness, "Hi there." His eyes strayed from making contact with Elise's.

"Oh! Kom-san, meet my sister, Elise," I said. "What is going on?" I asked. Knowing that he was Thai and also a local hire like me, I hoped he could provide some clarity.

"Right. I guess you never see this."

"Nope," I shook my head.

"The emcee will run the whole event. He says a few jokes, plays some games with the crowd. We'll have dinner just before the talent show begins," he explained.

"The what? Talent show?" I said. Elise's eyes got big.

"Yes, haven't you seen everyone practicing in the office after work?"

"No . . ." I said. I assumed it was because I'd been traveling so much.

"They compete for prizes. And then after the talent show, there is a lucky draw," he continued.

My sister sat up quickly. "Free stuff? Awesome." The servers started moving through the ballroom filling teacups with Chinese tea and refilling beers and wine. Some people were drinking both.

The emcee began telling jokes and inviting people on stage to participate in games. Chinese noodles and stir-fried kale in oyster sauce steamed on the table's lazy Susan.

"Have you ever had shark's fin soup?" Kom asked my sister just as it was being served.

She turned her head to me with a concerned look. "Is that a joke?" she said.

"No, it's a delicacy in Chinese culture but I've never had it," I said.

The soup was thick like a clam chowder but opaque and light brown. There were little glimpses of sliced carrot, but other than that it was hard to see anything that looked like shark's fin.

"It's in there. Try a bite. So nice," Kom said.

Elise dug in first, but when she picked up the spoon, it revealed what looked like slivers of bone marrow.

"This is it?" she asked and looked back at me for confirmation. "Here goes nothing."

She kept a straight face as she swallowed the foreign specialty. "It doesn't taste like much."

"Ehh!" Kom rumbled like a Japanese would.

Just as we were finishing dinner, the talent show began. To this day, my sister and I laugh to tears about one act in particular. One of the big bosses who managed an entire department stood on stage in a swan costume that covered just his waist. From his front side, a long white neck stuck out two feet with black eyes and a beak at the end. He shook his pelvic bone left and right, forward and backward, dancing to a techno beat.

Seated with my back to the stage, I awkwardly kept peering over my shoulder, then looking at Elise in awe. I had no words to explain what she was seeing. Instead, I just kept repeating, "I don't know." Meanwhile, the entire crowd roared in laughter.

The party really began after the talent show. Families with children departed for home while bosses drank their responsibilities away. The emcee called the staff to the dance floor. Elise and I soon followed at the convincing of my colleagues. Suddenly, we were all singing along to "Y.M.C.A."

Initially, I was anxious about Elise attending the D&D with me, especially after the protocol issue. I was beginning to understand Asian's ways, their idioms and etiquette. Elise's exposure wasn't much more than what I'd told her. However, I was impressed with how she handled each situation and her adventurous approach. I proudly watched as she ate shark's fin and danced with my colleagues. Something bigger than all of us what happening—the crossing of cultures.

Shortly after the D&D, Elise and I celebrated Christmas together. The occasion is recognized as a public holiday in Singapore, so I had a couple of days off work. As my first Christmas away from home, having my sister there was tremendous relief. Coming from a big family, our holidays usually involved numerous kids running around, everyone eating all day, and grandparents harassing us about when we were going to get married. This year was much different.

On Christmas Day, my sister and I sat on the balcony of my friend's apartment on the fiftieth floor, looking out over Chinatown. Viktor and Katie were both there with their families as well. Viktor joked about how Elise and my mannerisms perfectly replicated each other, while I teased him for being just like his father. Seeing friends around their family explained so much about them.

The sun was so hot we had to stay in the shade with our mimosas. The Christmas feast was made of foreign ingredients with an Asian flare. We ate green bean casserole with green beans grown in Malaysia, a roast raised in Australia, and potatoes harvested in Thailand.

"Maybe it would have felt more like Christmas if we had gone to church," I said to Katie.

"Or it wasn't ninety degrees outside," she responded.

Elise's flight was at 6:00 a.m. on New Year's Day. It was about 3:00 a.m. when I said good-bye to her from a cab on Sentosa Island. We'd celebrated 2008's arrival at a beach party just a ten-minute drive from my apartment. She was returning there to fetch her things and go to the airport. The lie was that I wanted to stay out longer. The selfish truth was that I didn't want to say good-bye from home. I wouldn't be able to handle the emotions and would probably end up visiting 7 Eleven for an ice cream cone.

"Taxi, she is going to the airport," I said as Elise got inside and shut the door, still in her bathing suit and dress.

At the last minute, I leaned over Elise's taxi door. "I'm sorry if I didn't tell you thank you enough."

"Thank you for what?" she asked from inside.

"For supporting my crazy idea of moving to Asia; for being the first to buy a ticket and visit me; for being open to experiencing new things with me."

"Oh, right, of course. You know I love you. Be safe!"

"I love you too."

When I arrived home, I found a note that Elise had left on a Singapore postcard:

> Hilary,
> I couldn't find any paper. Thank you for being such a great hostess and putting up with my moodiness and sloppiness. I had a great time with you and I love Singapore and your friends. I hope you come home to stay soon and if not, I would love to return for another week or so. Good luck in your job and tell your bosses thank you and goodbye. I know you will be successful in whatever you choose to do. I just hope it brings you back to the U.S. soon. God bless America! I love you dearly! xoxo
> Love, Elise

I posted it to my wall and laid in bed staring at until I feel asleep. I didn't wake up until the afternoon of January 1, 2008.

Chapter 11
Young, You Young.

The office opened again on the fourth of January, and suddenly management was back to planning the 2008 goals and activities at full steam. My mind focused solely on preparing for the training in Japan that was only a week away.

American pop music blared from my computer as I hung my freshly ironed suits on my armoire. Borrowed socks and closed-toe shoes from Katie lay paired up on the floor, with their matching outfits hanging above them on the bed. On the floor, my suitcase lay unzipped with gifts for my host family inside.

"Geez, what are you doing in here?" Margaret said, peeking into my room.

I wasn't used to packing for cold weather and this trip meant too much to be unprepared.

"Hey, what in the world are all those drumming noises outside?" I asked Margaret.

She laughed. "Right, I guess you wouldn't know. I hate those things. They signify the beginning of Chinese New Year. You'll see new markets and shops set up on the street too," she explained.

"Oh, well where are they coming from? I feel like I hear them in different places."

"You are funny. They're usually boys from the local neighborhoods that drive around on the back of a truck with the drums. Next time you hear it, look down. They're probably passing our street."

I nodded and turned back to my suitcase. Holding my ticket and imagining my return to Japan was still inconceivable to me. I couldn't get my head around it. This training was a rare opportunity to see headquarters, more deeply understand the way company works, and learn more about the scope of my job in Toyota. I felt a little nervous about how I'd perform among so many kaizen leaders, but I kept reminding myself that the company had hired me to learn, and just like that first department meeting, they didn't expect me to understand everything.

For this trip, I made sure to pack an additional box of business cards. During one of the dealership visits in Manila, I'd run out of cards and had to apologize to the owner. Upon return to TMAP, I received a small box on my desk with a leather business card holder inside; a note from the owner read: "So that you may never forget your business cards again." I vowed to not relive that mistake in Japan.

Although I felt thankful and excited for the training, something about seeing my host family again surpassed the other enthusiasm. I'd asked Kimura-san for approval to leave a few days earlier in order to visit them, and, due to our friendship and the good working relationship we'd built through the Philippines project, he agreed.

I was anxious to tell my host family about what I was doing now. I wanted them to be proud of me; they were the ones who had first instilled an appreciation for their culture in me. Now I'd made it part of my life, instead of letting the study abroad experience drift away like a dream. Most of all, I wanted to thank them. They had treated me like their own. Unfortunately, my Japanese had weakened over the past year. I was not sure I'd be able to communicate any of this to them.

After work on Friday, my flight took off, bound for Osaka. Kom-san had left earlier that week. I flew into the Osaka International Airport and found my way back to my old home in Katano, a small neighborhood near the university I attended, Kansai Gaidai.

I had turned away the offer of my *otoosan*, my host dad, to pick me up from the airport. If I'd found my way multiple times before, I could do it again. The drive was also over a two hours long and I didn't want to burden him.

And so I found myself lost in the middle of Osaka's train hub at 5:00 p.m. on a Friday. I was embarrassed and, as usual, too stubborn to reveal my faltering Japanese to the locals. Instead, I asked for help in English from whatever white person I could find. I felt ashamed that after almost four years of studying the language and then working for a famous Japanese automaker, I couldn't even navigate the Japanese train stations.

When I finally located the correct track, I boarded an express train from the city center of Osaka to Hirakata, the town where I had studied at Kansai Gaidai University. As I walked through the Hirakata train stop to my local line, a mixture of nostalgia and eeriness overcame me. I saw the old staircase I used to always run up in hopes of catching the train home. I smelled baking sugar from the same bakery that hunched between two staircases. The store faced a 7-Eleven, the most reliable shop in Japan and known for having every basic necessity. The tiny bathroom with squatting toilets that had once grossed me out and made me laugh out loud. Now, a year and a half later, my hands were ice cold like they had been so often during my daily eighty-minute commute to and from school. I was standing on the same platform, on my way back home. I was so far from the life I had lived in Japan only a couple of years prior. It was hard to comprehend how much had changed since then.

I wasn't exactly sure how my host family would receive me. They had housed study-abroad students for over ten years, so I could've just been another visitor. However, I felt like we were blood related, sharing an unexplainable kind of love and appreciation for each other.

Walking down the stairs of the Kitano train station, I found my otoosan waiting for me in his Toyota Innova. I remembered so many nights when he'd come home late from the office, exhausted and overworked. No matter what, he always smiled in response to my smile. Sometimes, if he was tired, it looked forced, but not today. His smile seemed to create a bright aura around him.

We hopped in the minivan and drove a mile down the road to my old home. My *okaasan* — host mom — waited at the door for us. I could smell the food cooking behind her in the kitchen.

The house represented an average size Japanese home, though it was compact by American standards. They didn't have a yard to play with their children in, just a front door complemented by a couple feet of sidewalk. The home often felt gloomy inside because they were always attentive to their use of electricity, even with guests, turning lights off if no one was in a room. Affixed to the wall of each room, an individual heater warmed wretchedly cold spaces.

We quickly removed our shoes at the front door, put them in the cabinet, and moved to the kitchen. The kitchen and dining room were combined, roughly the size of a large SUV. As she finished cooking, Okaasan would pass the food on a three-foot long counter top between the tiny oven and the kitchen table. At the end of the table, a 12" TV propped on a nightstand always remained on during dinner.

Each family member had a regular seat that appeared assigned. My host dad sat facing the TV directly. I sat next to him and across from my host mom.

Still with a big smile across his face, Otoosan walked with lead feet in his slippers. He squeezed his way over from the refrigerator to his seat and smacked down a Chu-Hi in front of me. He had always kept extra Chu-Hi, a lemon flavored alcoholic drink, on hand for me when I studied there, but I had refused the offer more often than accepted it. This time, I was eager to share the drink with him.

My okaasan made gyuu-don, a beef and rice dish, with handmade spring rolls and spicy tofu. My mouth watered, as eager for her food as for the Chu-Hi. She had about ten dishes she made regularly. When she was too busy or tired to cook, she would make gyoza dumplings and apologize repeatedly. I insisted her not to because they were still scrumptious. We only ate sushi at home a few times. This meal was usually saved for special occasions like my arrival or their daughter's graduation.

My host mom would devote hours preparing the food. She took special care to place each plate, set of chopsticks, teacup in their correct setting — even making sure the images on the dishware faced us. She wore a pink headband to hold back her hair and groaned in exhaustion after she finally served the food and sat down the food and her preparation mesmerized me. I began taking photos of our meals before we ate. This made her giggle, but to me, her work was simply beautiful.

Hilary Corna

At the end of the dinner and a few Chu-His, Otoosan asked me about John. During John's visit to Japan, my host family had invited him for dinner.

"Oh, no more," I said in broken Japanese.

He tapped my Chu-Hi "Kampai!" and in broken English responded, "Young, you young."

I stayed the night in my old bedroom where I had lived for six months. Everything remained in the same place. An old piano sat quietly nudged against the wall. A makeshift fabric armoire that used to house my college attire stood in the corner. Across from the dresser, my twin-size bed propped just a foot off the ground. I laughed when I saw the same skinny mattress I had spent so many nights on studying for school and dreaming of life after college.

On Saturday, my otoosan and I gambled at the Hirakata horse race track, met Kom-san for soba noodles in Kyoto, and shopped in the Osaka mall, Shinsaibashi. Having never had a father figure in my life, I don't feel a gap because there's nothing to compare my situation to. My otoosan was one of the first men in my life to show me differently.

Sato-san and Kimura-san had also taken up similar roles. Returning to Japan made me reflect on Sato-san's comment about being my guardian. He was treating me like a daughter as my otoosan did. Meanwhile, Kimura-san took me under his wing and taught me business. As time went on, our relationship grew even stronger.

The next Sunday morning, I journeyed by the shinkansen, a Japanese bullet train, to Nagoya to check in for the Toyota training.

Saying good-bye to my host family for a second time evoked hard-hitting emotions. I had never thought I would see them again and was now faced with the same challenging sentiment. I wanted to say so much. I wanted to thank them over and over again for their graciousness, their humility, and their sincerity in wanting to take care of me. I wanted to thank my otoosan for being a father to me, for looking after me and giving me whatever I needed; and my okaasan, for her hard work, love, and selflessness. Their actions had triggered my desire to not only see more of Asia but also to learn more about the world and my place in it. Although further from home, life with my host family had helped me come closer to understanding myself. I'd begun to see myself not as a city, state, or country citizen, but as a global citizen.

But I was unable to say any of this, so I just repeated "totemo arigatou gozaimasu," thank you very much, over and over along with multiple deep bows and several wiped tears. I tried to be Japanese about the situation and hold back my emotion, but it was difficult. The way we are taught in the West is the more you show your emotion physically, the more meaningful the relationship. On the other hand, the Japanese don't need public displays of emotion. They place a high level of value on privacy as a core element of relationships. Their appreciation is mutually understood between the two parties.

Kom-san and I met at the Kyoto station and traveled from there to Nagoya. I couldn't hide my watery eyes and pink cheeks, but Kom just smiled without saying anything, a perfect example of his adaptation to the Japanese demeanor. Although neither of us was Japanese and we weren't from the same country, we'd had similar experiences studying the language and culture. Kom resonated with my sincere love for Japan and my host family. I didn't need to say anything. He just understood.

Nagoya greeted us in the late afternoon with a blue sky. The shinkansen stopped at a station under the Marriott where we were staying, so within minutes we had checked in and settled into our tiny rooms. These were by far the smallest hotel rooms I had ever stayed in. The room was even smaller than my host family's kitchen. Even the complimentary toothbrush was half the size of an American one, and the tube of toothpaste was smaller than my pinky. However, a giant window engulfed the entire wall, offering a gorgeous view of the urban sprawl and mountainside of Nagoya. The Marriott was one of the tallest buildings in the city. The second tallest was the Toyota building just next door.

The first day of training started off early at 8:00 a.m. To get to the Toyota building, we followed an underground path from the hotel. I wish I had had more time to explore that path and its endless maze of food stalls and shops already open in time for the morning rush. The smells of fresh-baked goods reminded me of my daily commute to school in Hirakata. Every train station in Japan had two things: a bakery and a floral shop.

The glass elevators that rode up the outside of Toyota's headquarters bestowed another majestic view of the city, but this time at daybreak. Nagoya applies strict infrastructure rules on the height of buildings so almost all buildings except the Marriott and Toyota were the same height. It was almost harmonious, how flat the skyline was. The mountains encircling the city also struck me, overpowering the cement structures with their beauty.

After so much anticipation, I had finally arrived to the birthplace of all the company's know-how. The wall bore the company's name in bold white letters on a shiny black placard: Toyota Motor Corporation. Goosebumps covered my body, both from nerves and an electrifying excitement. According to a Japanese friend, they call this "chicken skin."

The objective of the training program was to gain "high-quality kaizen knowledge." The quality of activities varied across countries. That week, kaizen leaders from around the world, from Panama to Bahrain to Italy to Thailand, joined in Japan. They were mostly men, but for the first time in a while, I was not the only white face. I immediately bonded with three kaizen leaders from Toyota Motor Italy — via our loud voices and overzealous mannerisms. I quietly thanked some unknown force for bringing me there, especially given my lack of experience and age.

I wouldn't know until much later that there were many faces in the crowd I would conduct business with in the future. One of them was Yamamoto-san, who would become my third and last general manager before I left the company. Another was Yoshida-san, who had been recruited by our executive vice president, Nakamura-san, from his job as a butcher. Yoshida-san told me the story of how Nakamura-san had considered three people for his kaizen leader position: a marine, a businessman, and a butcher. He had hired Yoshida-san in the end because he was the most accurate and detail-oriented, understanding all the different facets of the cow and how the smallest mistake in a cut can change the flavor. It was an inside joke though that the only reason Nakamura-san hired him was because his favorite food was steak.

Yoshida-san facilitated one of the presentations. He happened to be close friends with Kom-san after working with him in a dealership in Thailand famous for initiating advance kaizen activities. Kom-san and I sat in the very front row of the room. Just before his presentation, Yoshida-san admitted his nervousness because of his poor English. His subject was "Maru-Maru Clean", the process of cleaning used cars to make them like new again.

He began his explanation, saying, "Using the machine, it cleans the car seats by removing the elements of smell."

Kom-san and I both started giggling uncontrollably, causing everyone in the room to look to the front. "Smell has elements?" We later teased him. The joke would continue when Yoshida-san became my manager the next year in TMAP, and would strengthen our friendship.

One day as part of our training we visited a rural dealership that had been conducting kaizen for close to ten years. The principal of the dealership gave a speech to the group at the end. Throughout the speech, he spoke of how none of the success they'd achieved through kaizen was because of him, but rather because of his team members: "I regret that in the past I did not have enough power to push this kaizen organization to continue. In Japanese companies, it is uncommon for people to give bad news to top management. I tried to get rid of this custom. Be patient and praise your staff in order to create an environment in which *gemba* leads kaizen by itself."

For the rest of my time with Toyota, I always carried a copy of this speech with me. I frequently passed it along to colleagues when they faced obstacles in kaizen.

On our final night in Nagoya, Kom-san and I went out with some of the other kaizen leaders to a local shopping area. It was practically our only night out because all the others had been filled with work events. I was thrilled when I came across a tiny dishware shop full of delicate bowls, plates, and cups. Nagoya is famous for its china, but other than the teacup and rice bowl my host family had given me when I left in 2006, I didn't own any pieces — as a study-abroad student, I hadn't been able to afford it. We came across a short-ceilinged shop with china stacked in piles to the top. I carefully maneuvered through them looking for a print I liked.

The owner of the shop, a five-foot-tall Okaasan, immediately welcomed me and asked what I was looking for. She couldn't have been younger than sixty years old, but was absolutely beautiful with jet-black hair, smooth skin, and a modest smile.

A strong feeling of home came over me as I walked through the store. I thought of my okaasan just a train ride away and all of her elegant dishes, which made me think of my mother and grandmother, wishing they could be there to share the moment with me.

Just as they came to mind, I found the perfect set of four small bowls and plates, white with blue flowers gracefully painted across them. Upon exiting, I asked the Okaasan if I could take a picture of her. I wanted to remember that moment, the place, and my feelings. She cordially accepted.

Kom-san and I finished our shopping and returned to the hotel. After checking out, I began my journey to Krabi, Thailand, where I was meeting Katie for her birthday weekend. In transit to the airport, I watched as individualistic Japanese teenagers and stylish young professionals headed out with friends to celebrate the end of the week. Graceful women waited quietly for the train while men opened doors for them. Both gave thanks. Secretly envious of them, I wanted to stay.

The country had taught me about respect, modesty, and how to be a lady, three things I felt my home country often lacked. I felt so deeply grateful. Boarding the plane, I bade farewell to the country I admired so much.

The overnight flight was not as bad as I had expected, although I arrived that Saturday morning in the same work clothes I had worn the day before.

I couldn't wait to see Katie and celebrate her birthday. I'd gotten her a tea mug from the same shop I bought my china. It was so strange to think that I was traveling from Japan, and she from Singapore, to meet on a tiny island in Thailand just for the weekend. I was beginning to get a taste of this transient lifestyle that would ultimately change my life.

Thirty something hours later, Katie and I returned home with beat-red tans and bursting headaches, but with rare memories that would deepen our friendship forever. We'd sung happy birthday to Katie multiple times throughout the night with strangers from nearly every continent in the world. We'd danced in a beach club full of John Lennon posters with a local

Thai DJ. We'd sat on miniscule plots of sand in the middle of the South China Sea taking in the beauty, speechless.

As we departed from the island, I was jumping into the long-tail boat with all of my luggage when Katie screeched and pointed behind me. "Hilary! Your passport!"

In juggling all of my things, I'd dropped my passport in the middle of the transparent ocean water.

"You have got to be kidding me," I said under my breath as I leaped into the water after it.

"You are one rare soul, Miss. Corna," Katie said.

"PA, what would I do without you?" I said back. She'd jokingly given herself the title of my PA, Personal Assistant, because she'd done nearly all of the research and planning for our trips.

I opened up my passport under the hot Thai sun and laid it on the boat to let it dry. The ink from a few of the stamps had bled to the sides of the page. For the next 250,000 airline miles I'd fly, I would be reminded every time I went through immigration of that moment — when my best friend had saved me from getting stuck in Thailand.

Chapter 12
Keep Communicate

During the first few months of 2008, my life became unexpectedly consumed with my job. Several of my business trips lasted two weeks, sometimes three. I was receiving welcome gift baskets in my hotel room upon arrival. The valets at the Shangri-La in Manila began to greet me by my first name. The three hostesses at the entrance of Dots breakfast buffet cheerfully addressed me every morning, "Ma'am Hilary, right this way." The chefs smirked and began to make jokes that the Shangri-La was my second home. The fruit guy revealed his crush on me. One waiter, Rommel, became my favorite. Rommel knew I liked my coffee after breakfast and would bring it to me in a to-go cup for the ride to the dealership, Toyota Makati TMI.

"Oh, so you get special treatment?" Kimura-san asked the first time he saw it.

"No, I asked for it. And then he just continued to bring it." I smiled.

I was caught up in the attention and enjoyed it for a while, but the novelty soon wore off.

Work at the office picked up pace, natural for the beginning of the year. Kimura-san had been working on the 2008 plan of activity for our department, Retail Development Support, and had big plans now for Kom and me since we had completed the kaizen training.

The business trips were becoming tiresome, however. My personal life got left behind and my relationships began to suffer.

Finding out that I missed an event, I say to my friends, "Hey, I was here. Why didn't you invite me?"

"I assumed you were out of town. Your schedule is just so hard to keep track of!" they'd respond.

I began to realize that if this was the career I wanted, a traveling one, I'd have to make more of an effort to reach out to friends and sustain relationships when I was in town. It was my responsibility, not theirs.

In March, I was able to get back in time from a business trip to have my whole weekend — since we usually had to work in the dealerships on Saturdays. I met Katie on Friday after work at a mall called Bugis, just walking distance from my office. Neither of us wanted to drink or party. We just wanted to get out. We met for dinner and afterwards roamed the shops when my phone rang. It was Kimura-san.

I stopped. I held my phone for a second, debating whether or not I should pick up.

"Why is he calling you on a Friday night?" Katie asked.

"Ugh, I don't know!" I said, annoyed. "But it must be important. Otherwise, he wouldn't bother me."

I answered the phone with a little bit of aggravation.

"Hello?"

"Hi, Hilary, I'm sorry to disrupt your Friday," Kimura-san began.

"No problem. Is there something wrong?" I was afraid we'd forgotten something for a business trip, or that our schedules had changed last minute, which was becoming normal.

"Well, no, but I need your help. I'm working on my proposal for the India strategy, and I could really use your input," he explained.

It was evident to the team in charge of India that they were lacking some overall vision or strategy, but they were all too consumed with their daily jobs to address the problem and develop a solution. As the second biggest market for Toyota, India represented the future of the company. For example, the company had over 40% market share in the Philippines and sold just over 40,000 cars per year. Meanwhile, we were already selling over 100,000 cars in India and only had 2.5% market share. It was vital for the company and its employees, including myself, that we were successful in India.

It was also pretty cool to think that I could work on the strategy of Toyota in India.

"Kimura-san, it's almost 10:00 p.m.," I said. I'm sure he heard the aggravation in my voice.

"Yes, I know. I'm sorry. It's okay if you can't come," he said.

I felt like I was the boss now.

"No, I'll come. I'm just down the road anyways." I wasn't doing anything that night and this was a small favor to ask after everything Kimura-san had done for me.

"Are you crazy, Hilary?" Katie asked.

"I know. I know, but I have to."

I arrived at the office where I found all the lights off except the one panel above our department. There was another worker there with his headphones on, obviously working on some big monthly supply and demand report for the following Monday. Kimura-san was standing at a white board covered with thought bubbles, arrows, circled words and at the top, one question, "WHY?" I could tell he had hit a wall.

"Thank you for coming, Hilary. I really appreciate it." He stood up and shook my hand.

"It's okay, Kimura-san. Just don't think this is a regular thing." I said it in a joking tone but also hoped to insinuate some truth.

Communicating and maintaining my Western values on balancing work and life to Kimura-san and the other bosses was one of the biggest challenges I faced at Toyota. I didn't believe in over-working just to gain prestige over other employees, or create a false perception of hard working, like many of the staff did.

Kimura-san laughed, "No, I don't."

I worked late if there was something urgent, if I was behind and needed to finish, or if I simply wanted to make something even better. I viewed my work style inefficient if I wasn't completing my job in the allotted eight to five.

Kimura-san and I worked on the white board, with a pitch-black Singaporean sky in the background, until 3:00 a.m. We left the office that Saturday morning with a strong proposal for the new direction of the Indian headquarters.

The slogan: "Quality Revolution."

My heart would later swell when I saw the tagline printed across all of India's paraphernalia.

I worked hard in my early days with Toyota, with very little formal training and resources, but accomplished and learned a tremendous amount by throwing myself into my job. However, as a result, I lost time from my personal life. I've never been tempted to spend my life working for success or money if it meant sacrificing relationships. However, what I would realize much later was that in my quest to be self-reliant—as to not worry the people I loved—I had separated myself from them even more. Consequently, it was becoming easier to just be alone.

Then, when the Philippines project had finally slowed down and I had learned to stabilize my lifestyle, routines as simple as laundry and cleaning,

Katie told me that she was leaving her assignment early to return to the United States.

Katie had faced a lot of challenges with the job at Duke University and NUS. Her long-distance relationship hadn't helped either. She'd had her fun in Singapore and was ready to go home, which I understood. It was three months earlier than she was supposed to leave, though, and I was selfishly upset about her departure. Her specific leaving date wasn't yet decided, but all I knew was that I had only a month or two more to enjoy being with my best friend.

Katie and I had planned a trip that March to Bangkok, so I was excited to have some time with her, although it would be our last adventure together.

Since I'd been to Bangkok the year before, I managed our navigation from the airport to the hotel. After checking in and unpacking, Katie screamed. I jumped while in the bathroom taking a shower.

"Jesus, what's wrong?" I said, racing out in a towel.

"There's a cockroach!" she said. She was standing up on the bed just like I'd stood on my chair in the Tanjong Pagar apartment when I had first seen one.

"Oh, disgusting," I said. I grabbed another towel and threw it on the insect, then smashed it with a shoe.

"Gross. Hil, what kind of place did you book us?" Katie said. It was the only thing I had had to arrange for the whole trip. Katie had done everything else.

"Sorry, Katie. They're normal though. It's just the region."

We spent one very long night out with local Thai friends that was kick-started with a Marilyn Monroe-themed transvestite show and ended with burritos at a Mexican restaurant at 4:00 a.m. As we tried to hail a cab to return to the hotel, a short Thai man approached us, holding a rope tied to the neck of a baby elephant no taller than me.

"Food for baby elephant," he said. He held plastic bags full of fruit. "Only twenty baht." This was less than a dollar.

"Katie, how terrible, we have to buy it food!"

"No, Hilary, this guy is just doing this for money. This is horrible. This elephant should not be in the street."

"So let's feed it! Katie, give me your purse." I'd run out of cash.

She gave me local bills and I bought all of the food the man had with him. Katie turned away as I fed the elephant.

The next morning after we got food and recovered from our headaches, we reminisced about the night before.

"I can't believe you gave all my money to that elephant!" Katie said rolling her eyes but with a laugh.

"That was horrible. It was only a few dollars or so anyway."

"Geez, what a ridiculous night."

On our last day, we went to the famous Grand Palace in Bangkok. After walking the grounds for several hours, we came across a sign at the exit that read, "Palm Reader."

I ran over to it. "Katie, I have always wanted to do this."

"Are you serious? Hil, it's just a money ploy."

"It's only five bucks."

I sat down at the palm reader's small card table against a white stucco wall outside of the palace. The man appeared to be shorter than me. His skinny arms bore dark wrinkles with a few scattered white hairs. He had long hair tied back in a ponytail and round glasses. In front of him, a yellow card with drawings and Thai writing rested on the table.

His face was stripped of expression and he didn't look me in the eyes, just at my hands as he held them. I hunched over with my chin tilted down and eyes looking up at him, smiling. Katie stood behind me. Several minutes passed in silence.

I flinched when he first spoke. "You, hard work, but." He stopped and closed his eyes in search of words. I leaned closer.

"Alone. You alone." I breathed in through my nose.

"When baby, you alone first time. Someone. Someone gone." Without control, tears filled my eyes. I didn't know how he could know about my father.

He said a few more things, but I could not understand the broken English. But then, it was the next thing he said about John that made me believe him and made him worth the five dollars.

"A man," he began, "love you — he love you." Katie put her hand on my shoulder but I couldn't look up.

The palm reader shook his head and looked up at me for the first time. "You leave him?"

My head dropped to my chest and tears made their way down both of my cheeks.

"Keep communicate," he said.

"Communicate?" I asked.

He nodded. "Stay talking. He always love you." Tears dropped from my chin to the surface of the card table.

It took several minutes to compose myself when he finished. "Khab kun ka," I said as I paid him. I thanked him and exited the palace.

"What does that mean?" I asked Katie.

"Nothing, Hil. It means nothing. It's just weird."

"This is not coincidence."

"I don't know what it is, but it's not something to get worked up about."

"Communicate? I've been trying to leave him alone. We lead two separate lives now. It's time to move on." I stopped in the middle of the street

"Exactly," Katie said.

"But then why would he say communicate?"

"Maybe he just means to remain friends."

"No, there's something more to this. How could he have known about my father too?"

"Hil, there's a car coming, let's get out of the street." We walked to a bench on the sidewalk.

"Katie, don't leave me."

She gave me hug, "I'm here, babe."

"I need to sit back down." I leaned over with my elbows on my knees and my head in my hands. "What does this mean? What does this mean?"

Katie rubbed my back. "Let's go get some ice cream."

Chapter 13
Safety First

Flying back to Singapore, I couldn't stop thinking about the palm reader's comment and what I'd given up for my life abroad. The next three, one-week-long business trips made me miss a number of events back in Singapore, including the big St. Patty's Day celebrations with my fellow expatriates. Furthermore, I lost a lot of time to spend with Katie during her final days in the country. It wasn't that the St. Patty's Day event was particularly special—I was just becoming increasingly annoyed at missing out on so much during my business trips.

In the back of my mind, I kept trying to reassure myself that my job was worth it and to talk myself out of bad thoughts. I had an incredible opportunity with Toyota still in front of me, but for some reason, I still felt incomplete.

I'd thought coming home for the weekends would be better than staying in Manila, but it actually made me more drained. By the time I made it home to Singapore, I didn't want to see or talk to anyone. Sometimes I'd even just go to the River Place pool alone to have some quiet time and catch a tan.

While I was in Manila that April, Katie confirmed her last day at work. Due to our schedules, we only had two weeks left together. She moved her things out of her apartment and stayed with me for a few days before leaving. That final time was so precious. Every day, I woke up to the reminder that I was losing my best friend.

Katie left for a vacation to Vietnam when I left for Manila again. At this point, I was nearing my tenth business trip, and my passport was filling with Filipino stamps.

It was election time in the Philippines, and there had been some recent uproar in the Filipino political arena against the current president. There was so much tension in the community that some staff at the dealership couldn't report to work because roads were closed. An eerie quiet drifted throughout the office that trip.

Only a few days passed before the predicted government protests began to break out. The door of the obeya room—where the kaizen team met regularly—swung open, crashing against the wall so loudly I thought there'd been an accident with customer vehicles in the body and paint workshop. Kichida-san, a kaizen expert and advisor to TMP that we worked with, entered and began frantic discourse in Japanese toward Kimura-san.

"Hilary, let's go," Kimura-san instructed in the most polite of ways.

"Go where? We have a meeting this afternoon with Anna," I responded.

The calm, non-discernable expression that typically rested on Kimura-san's face had changed dramatically. He stood up swiftly, yet still maintained the natural smooth and efficient movement the Japanese emulate no matter what the circumstance. Packing his computer and complementary cords, he neglected to wrap them with the Velcro that he always used to ensure their compactness within his bags.

The only thing I could think was perhaps Mr. Christian, the executive vice president of Toyota Philippines, had called for an emergency meeting. But still, Kimura-san would have never responded that way.

"The protests have spread out. There is word of guns, and they are starting fires on Makati Avenue. We need to get our things from Shangri-La and head for the airport. We are leaving tonight."

Protests are normal and frequent in Asia. They rarely though, if ever, required us to suspend our business trips. Rather, we would just return to the hotel and wait. It felt as though Kichida-san and Kimura-san were acting like my two brothers, James and Dan, playing a prank on me because everyone knows how gullible I am. But they were my Japanese bosses and playing a prank about protests was the last thing they would dare do.

I stuffed my Lenovo laptop that Toyota had assigned me into its home: the laptop bag gifted to me by Katie's father when I received the job offer from Toyota. I stacked all my papers usually kept in perfect order and shoved them into their plastic envelopes.

Everything happened so fast that there was no time to acknowledge the terrifying feeling I had inside. The only thing I could think about was that this was exactly what my mom was afraid of and had so often warned me about. I'd always defended Asia for being safe and said that things were exaggerated on television and in the movies. I didn't know how I'd defend this.

Kichida-san led us down from the third story of the dealership to the service workshop on the first floor, via the new car showroom. I squealed and dropped my bag to the oil-greased floor as I heard people shouting in the distance. Kichida-san graciously picked the bag up and tossed it in the trunk of the shiny navy blue Camry that provided our daily commute from the hotel to the Toyota Makati dealership.

The streets were blocked with hundreds of Filipinos, both men and women, with signs. Trash bins rampaged with fire and people chanted repeatedly against the recent election nomination. My intestines fell deep in my abdomen as I tried my best to stop repeating "Oh my God."

I kept asking myself why I was here. In striving to succeed, I'd found my life threatened as I worked for a Japanese company in a corrupt third world country.

Why can't you just be normal, Hilary? I screamed to myself. Why do you always have to be different?

The decision to target seemingly impossible goals had major implications I hadn't even considered, including my physical safety.

We drove down the highway to the airport. As we reached safety out of the city, I promised myself not to tell my mother about what'd occurred, at least not until much later. I couldn't terrify her. Even after leaving Singapore, I never did tell her.

"Singapore Airlines economy class is full," Kimura-san said as we drove up to the airport. "You will have to fly business class with me. Complete the form when we get back and I'll get approval from Nakamura-san."

"Business class? But the cost is triple the normal price," I said. Although afraid for my life, I was also afraid of getting scolded for the additional cost. The company's standard policy limited business class to only managers and above. I'd never heard of an entry-level employee getting approved to fly business.

"Safety first, Hilary," Kimura-san replied as if reading straight from a Toyota handbook.

We checked in and sat unharmed in the airport lounge. With my legs crossed, I tapped my hanging shoe to the heel of my foot repeatedly.

Returning to perfect Singapore made the whole incident seem like a bad dream. I immediately called Sato-san to tell him what had happened. He'd just returned from a two-week business trip to Rome where he was starting a project with Toyota Motor Italy.

"Oh, Hilary-chan, I am so glad you are safe," he said

71

"I've never felt so threatened before in my life."

"You are courageous. Don't worry, you are okay now. At least you got to fly business class!" He made me laugh.

When I reported to the office the next day, two things were waiting for me. On my desk a shoebox-sized care package waited for me from my mom, this time full of Valentine's Day streamers—two months late—St. Patty's Day socks, and Easter candy. Since her children had become adults, Mom had started her own tradition of not giving Christmas gifts, but giving holiday socks instead. It had transcended every holiday now.

As I was unloading all the gifts, Kimura-san approached me and handed me a white envelope. I stood up, unsure of what was inside. He bore a smile.

"Thank you for all of your hard work, Hilary Corna. This is your annual bonus."

In the midst of all my travel, I'd completely forgotten about the bonus. I took a small breath, wanting to say something but not sure how to appropriately respond.

"Congratulations," he said, placing the envelope in my hands.

"Thank you," I responded quietly as he turned around and sat back at his desk.

It was a little awkward as it was so open in the office; I felt like everyone was watching me. I looked around, but no one seemed to be paying attention. In due time, I saw this happen to them all as well. The bosses always handed over the bonuses by hand.

I didn't know whether to open the envelope or wait until I was alone. I slipped it into my pocket and walked to the restroom. As soon as the heavy mahogany door shut, I frantically opened the envelope at the same time thinking of all the things I could spend the money on. However, I hadn't talked to anyone about how much money to expect. When I saw the amount of the check, I fell back against the door and slid to the floor. The check was over twice as much as my monthly salary.

It was my first time to ever receive a bonus from a real job. Maybe the rare, life-threatening situation had been worth it.

During Katie's final days in Singapore, I helped her take care of last-minute tasks like closing accounts and shopping for souvenirs. She had so many bags that we had to weigh them with her kilogram scale to make sure she wouldn't go over the airline's allotted weight. She left me with several things that couldn't fit. One was her scale—which I never used. I always hated converting the number from kilograms to pounds. She also left me with a little coin dish in the shape of a Mexican sombrero. I kept it on my desk along with my mom's gifts as a constant reminder of my friend.

We went for a pizza dinner on her last night -- ironic, considering it was the last time she'd have access to so many options of Asian food. We sat before the Singaporean skyline trying to find words to carry on a conversation other than small talk, but there wasn't much to say. She was leaving.

Her flight left early in the morning, typical of international flights to the United States, so we woke up about 3:00 a.m. We were both deliriously tired and unable to handle the emotion. The cab driver helped Katie load her three stuffed bags into the trunk and backseat and took a seat at the wheel.

With her book bag on her back and her arms full of two carry-on bags and a purse, she hugged me as tight as she could.

"Goodbye, PA! I love you!" I said

"I love you, too!" She said back.

I'll never forget her waving from the back of the Toyota cab as I stood alone in the dark, quiet street. My first best friend abroad was leaving me. She was going off to follow her own endeavors. It was my responsibility as a friend to support her, although I didn't want her to leave.

As I trudged back to my apartment and crawled into bed, I thought about John and all the other people in my life I had selfishly left to pursue my dreams. I had hurt them, and they hadn't wanted to see me go, but I'd done it because I knew it was right for me. They still love me. As I do Katie.

Yet, I felt like she was moving on to bigger and better things by returning to the States to get her master's degree. Meanwhile, I was stuck in Singapore.

Years later, I got used to this process of bidding farewell, and rather than being scared of it, I learned to be thankful for the time I had with friends. At that moment, I'd made the mistake of comparing my path to Katie's because I was unsure of what my path looked like. And that scared me.

My decision to live abroad had affected more than just my career. I was realizing that there were consequences of moving so far away from home -- consequences I could have never predicted. I'd gained friends around the world, memorable experiences, and a prominent career. I'd lost convenience, security, best friends, and my overall support system, including family, and the man who loved me. Whether it was all worth it or not, I still wasn't sure.

Chapter 14
Enough About Singapore

The neon pink poster board read "Welcome Home Hilary!" in all capital letters. My siblings were holding it at the bottom of the escalator at baggage claim in the Columbus, Ohio international airport. My mom and her dog Moose attacked me with hugs and kisses. I felt loved. My other sister Ariana and her fiancé Josh were living in Georgia at the time and would arrive that weekend.

Questions ran through my mind. What is my name? Where am I? What day is it? I felt delirious, barely able to respond to all of their inquiries about my journey. I was regretting taking the additional fourth flight that had saved me a mere US$200. From my door in Singapore to my door in Columbus, I had traveled for forty hours.

My eyes felt like I had been watching TV for two days straight — which I practically had with the movies on the plane. My knees ached from being bent for so long, and my entire body hurt from inactivity. I had no appetite whatsoever. The airlines give you so much food that you walk off the plane despising the act of eating.

When we arrived home, I immediately unloaded my suitcase in the front room. I was so anxious to give my family their gifts, which took up almost all of my luggage space. My brothers got polo shirts from the Philippines that cost me five dollars instead of seventy dollars. My sisters and mom got pashmina scarves from Singapore that cost me only one dollar per piece. I'd also brought a dress from a Korean boutique for Ariana to wear at her wedding shower.

"It's late, Hilary," Elise said. "Can we do this tomorrow? People have to work in the morning."

My mom walked upstairs to bed and everyone left. I sat alone with my luggage on the floor of the dark living room with just the hall light on upstairs. I began to refold everything I'd pulled out, disappointingly. I didn't want to pack again. I wanted to let everything go. At least, I thought, at least I was home.

Ariana and her fiancé Josh arrived the next day. Katie was in Cleveland visiting her boyfriend, so she came down just for the day. I waited for her with Elise, Ariana, and Josh at a popular Irish pub in our neighborhood. When she arrived, I pushed my steel chair back and raced over to hug her.

"PA! Where have you been?" I laughed.

We hugged and she laid her head on my shoulder. "I've missed you, Hilary."

"Me too, Katie."

Elise came up from behind. "Last time I saw you, we were celebrating Christmas in ninety-degree weather!"

Katie laughed. "Hi, Elise! Yes, nothing about that day felt like Christmas."

We were sitting at an outdoor table. It was hot out, but nothing like Singapore. The place was bustling full of happy-hour patrons.

"Remember when we saw the elephant in Bangkok?" Katie reminisced. We were sitting close to each other at the corner of the table. "And you made me buy all of the bags of food the owner was selling to feed it!"

My head fell back as I laughed. "It was sad!"

Ariana and Josh randomly chimed in but were busy talking about the wedding appointments they had for the week.

"I think I still have a headache from Krabi," Katie said.

I raised my eyebrows. "Need I remind you of the shots you were taking from random friends that night?"

"Oh, and the man that had prettier hair than me!"

"He only let you up on stage," I said.

"That was the life. We were so lucky. You are so lucky! Life in Singapore is so easy." Katie sat back in her chair.

"All right, enough about Singapore," Ariana interrupted from across the table. Her tone of voice implied a joke but it felt literal. I rolled my eyes and Katie just stared to the side.

"That was their life, Ariana," Elise butted in. "You don't know. You've never been."

I crossed my arms. Josh didn't say anything.

Elise continued, "Going out was so much different abroad — those crazy people in costume at New Year's and your ridiculous D&D!"

"You went to the D&D?" Katie asked.

"Yes! It was insane."

"It's just Asia," I said quietly.

"That dinner with Sato-san and what's the other one's name?"

Katie cut in, "Kimura-san? Did you meet them too?"

"Yes. That was the most amazing dinner ever. Sato-san is so sweet," Elise said.

I caught myself in a stare thinking of them both back in Singapore.

After dinner, I walked Katie out to her car, not knowing that it'd be the last time I would see her for three years.

"Don't worry about your sister. I've gotten similar responses. It's hard for people to relate who haven't been," she said.

"Sure, but you don't have to be so rude about it. There's so much I want to share."

"Find the people that want to hear it then," she said.

"Love you, Katie."

"Love you too, Hil."

It was bizarre to see Katie in Columbus, Ohio and have her meet my entire family. Our life in Singapore was so isolated and so separate from everyone else that it was difficult to fuse our stories with others'. I knew her as Katie in Singapore, not Katie in the U.S.

That night, I could only sleep for three hours in total. I was like a zombie. Singapore's time zone was twelve hours ahead, so I imagined what I would have been doing, which was probably attending afternoon meetings. I was much happier being home.

That weekend was Ariana's wedding shower — the main reason for coming home during the summer — and would be the first time I saw my extended family since my graduation party a year earlier. I was enthused to tell everyone about my journeys, my work, and the people I'd met.

"Thanks, Hil, I really like it," Ariana said about the dress I'd bought and hand-carried from Asia for her. She looked stunning. Ariana walked into my aunt's house where the shower was being held, and I followed behind.

"Ariana! Congratulations! Come in!" My Aunt yelled.

"Hilary?" My aunts and cousins stood in the entryway together. "Hilary is here!" My cousin, Gianna, said. I grinned. "Welcome to America," she said jokingly as she gave me a big hug. We grew up best friends because we were the same age. She'd always had a sarcastic sense of humor, though.

"So are you like so excited for American food? You must be," she said, answering her own question. We were sitting at the table as Ariana accepted gifts in the living room.

"Well, not really," I said. I twirled my baby blue paper cup in my hands.

"Whatever, I mean, what do you eat there? Like, noodles or rice all the time? I bet you can't get good Italian food there."

"You can find good Italian food, it's just expensive. And no, there are many other options."

"Whatever happened to that guy you were dating then?"

My eyes darted up. "John was his name."

"Yeah, do you guys still talk?"

"Not really. He is dating someone else now."

The games were beginning, so we moved into the living room. Suddenly, we were wrapping each other in toilet paper like wedding dresses and walking down fake church aisles. I watched from the side, only participating when asked.

My favorite aunt who had always been very career-oriented and supported all my endeavors growing up came and sat next to me in the corner of the room.

"So how do you like it in Singapore? Is it hard to live there?" she asked.

Speaking quickly I said, "Oh, I love it. It's safe, clean, efficient — and warm! It's not hard at all to live there."

"That's wonderful, Hilary. That makes me happy to hear. And what about your job? What exactly do you do, anyway?"

My job was so out of the ordinary that it was hard to explain. "My job is incredible. I could have never been able to do the same thing here in the States. I basically run a team to improve the operations of a dealership. Then we share the best practices within the country to other dealerships and then within the region to other countries."

"Wow, that's fascinating. What is your favorite part?"

I sat up straight and touched my finger to my lips. "I've never been asked that question."

"That's okay, you don't have to answer."

"No, it's a good question," I said. I paused and watched for a moment as my family cleaned up toilet paper from the floor. "It's the people. I work with everyone from the frontline staff who speaks no English to top management that have extensively traveled the world. I learn something from each one of them."

I gazed in the distance as I remembered Francis, Gio, Christian-san, and others from Manila. It was strange how far and almost fictional they seemed.

Other than my aunt's brief conversation, everyone else's questions at the shower imitated my cousin's.

"I hear you go to jail for chewing gum," they'd say.

"No, that is not true," I'd respond.

When I saw someone for the first time, the conversation usually went like this:

"Hi, Hilary! How is Singapore?"

"It's wonderful."

"Do you like it?"

"Yes, I love it—" but before I could finish, they'd cut me off.

"So, when are you coming home?" This question depicted the common thread of the conversation. It seemed everyone just wanted to know when it was going to end. I realized much later that they asked the question not out of disinterest, but because they struggled to relate to me, just as I did to them.

The whole day revolved around my sister, as it should have. She gleamed with a rock on her finger, a plethora of gifts, and a fiancé who was on his way to pick up the new household goods. When we were children, Ariana had forced me to play house with her while I wanted to do other things. As a nanny and teacher, she had always loved children, and her values revolved around raising a family. I felt in the wrong for not desiring this kind of lifestyle. However, I was slowly realizing that simply, my desires in life differed.

At the end of the day, I couldn't let go of my guilt over not enjoying the occasion more. It would take a long time to understand why. There was something about going through the motions of those kinds of events that bothered me. It wasn't that I was not happy for my sister getting married, but I didn't like the predictability of the occasion. From the games to the gifts to the cake to the thank yous, everything seemed so trivial—a boring and forgettable couple of hours.

Meanwhile, my life abroad surprised me daily, thus, created memorable moments. Between listening to seventy-year-old Singaporean taxi drivers talk about war to walking past Bangladesh workers sleeping in tents to smelling medicinal mushrooms during a visit to my Chinese doctor, my senses frequently underwent stimulation. As a result, my way of thinking and living improved, and I grew.

I wish I could have realized, though, at Ariana's shower that there is a time and place to share my growth from living internationally. That day was not about me, it was about my sister. As a sister, I should have put aside my own desires for a shower of love and supported hers.

After a week of wedding planning, Ariana and Josh returned to Georgia. My Mom and I drove up to Chicago for the weekend to visit my best friend in college, Ava.

"I just saw you a few weeks ago!" I said to Ava jokingly when we arrived.

"Not soon enough," she said.

"I need to borrow clothes from you. I have nothing to wear tonight," I said. We were meeting John for dinner. I had been in touch with him only a couple of times by email since he'd begun dating his new girlfriend earlier in the year. I didn't know what to expect of our interaction. The last time we'd seen each other, he kissed me and pleaded that I not leave him.

When I walked into the sushi restaurant I saw nothing around me, only John. My heart fluttered like it always did when I saw him, and I all but felt air between the floor and my feet. He hugged me so tightly against his tall warm body. It was a sincere, I-miss-you hug that I would never forget.

"It's so good to see you," he said, looking down on me with a smile. He was over six feet tall, so I always looked up at him.

I squeezed his forearms. "Likewise. It's wonderful to see you after so long." It'd been over a year.

For a moment, we locked eyes and I almost forgot we were standing with Ava and my mom.

"Hi, John," my mom said. She had met him several times during our relationship.

He gave her a big hug too and said, "So what do you think about your crazy daughter?"

"She is doing her thing right now, that's what I keep telling myself," Mom said. I hugged my purse. Bringing them together, along with Ava, made my aura glow like a star's light. They were three of the most important people in my life.

Sleek furniture and modern decor filled the trendy Japanese restaurant. Dressed in chic clothes, a bustling crowd of gossiping young professionals overwhelmed the calm interior design.

"This is one my favorite new places," John said. Japanese food was always one of his favorites. He had adored our dinner in Japan with my homestay family.

"Yeah, it's nice," I said, peering over the white faces. There were no Asians there, so I was curious about the quality of the food.

We ordered a bottle of white wine and a few appetizers.

"This is for you, Hil," John said. He raised his chilled wine glass. "If anyone could do it, it'd be you."

Ava laughed. "It's so true."

"She knew what she wanted," my mom said, raising her chin, "and she went after it."

I held my head down but glanced up to see John's reaction. Without saying it directly, Mom had pointed out that I'd exchange John for my accomplishment, as if it was him that I didn't want, him I didn't go after. His light blue eyes revealed nothing.

"That she did," he said with a smile. He was a man. He had probably gotten over me. I didn't know that entirely for sure, though, and my heart kept telling me that he just knew how to hide emotions.

We talked about everything from my work to a trip Ava took earlier in the year to visit me for my birthday.

"It was incredible," Ava said, breaking her chopsticks open. She was a pro at using them now.

John looked over at me and put his hand on my arm. "You have no idea how much I would love to come." His touch gained the attention of my entire body.

"It's not the money or time. I have that. It's just that," he paused and shook his head, "I can't. It just wouldn't be right." I understood; he was referring to his girlfriend.

John was adventurous and loved to travel. It was one thing we had a lot in common. Although he was an accountant and had gone through school and life traditionally, he liked planning ahead for things to look forward to. He was open to anything. It was one thing I found so attractive about him.

My mom had a mouthful of sushi when she butted in, "You'll get there if you're meant to, John." I rolled my eyes. Thanks, Mom. For a moment, I pictured the palm reader in Bangkok. He'd said to just keep communication. That's all I was doing for now.

"This is delicious," Ava said, obviously changing the subject.

"Yes, it's good. But why must they put so many sauces on the sushi?" I asked.

John grabbed a piece from the platter and held it up. "That's what makes them so tasty."

"You've just had the good stuff—you can't compare," Ava said to me. It was true. From my sushi lunches with Sato-san to entertainment dinners on business trips, I'd had some of the freshest sushi and sashimi on the globe. I was learning to tell the difference and was not sure if I could ever go back to grocery store sushi. I never did.

"What? Do they not have these in Asia?" my mom asked, still chomping down.

I laughed. "No. Cream cheese? And all these sauces? Sushi in Asia is very simple. That's the idea. You appreciate the taste of the fish."

"Well, I think it's scrumptious," John said.

I didn't want to come across as rude; I just wanted to share and educate them on the differences. This would be a constant challenge, identifying those people back home who wanted to learn more and those who only took my sharing as a lecture.

After dinner, we walked outside. It was much cooler at night than in Singapore, even if it was summer. I couldn't stop fidgeting.

"Well, I hope it's not another year and a half until we see each other again," John said.

"Yeah, me too. I'm happy everything is going well for you." The comment felt stilted, but I didn't know what else to say.

"You also. Keep kicking ass, Hilary—it's what I always loved about you."

I dropped my chin to my chest and closed my eyes.

"Give me a hug," he said.

I felt just as comfortable with him as the first day I met him. I still loved him. That never changed, although I wished it would.

"Let me know later if you go out," he said. We walked in different directions to our cars. As John walked down the street and under the train tracks, I peered back, but he wasn't looking. He had hands in his khaki pants pockets and his head down. A loud train rushed across the tracks above him. Even if I had yelled back, he wouldn't have been able to hear me.

My mom returned home to get some sleep since we were planning to leave in the morning. Ava and I stayed out.

"Should I text him?" I asked Ava.

"No, I don't think it's a good idea, Hilary," she said. She was always the responsible one.

He ended up texting me at 2:00 a.m., "Are you guys still out? Let's meet up!" He wrote. We had just finished our drinks. "Please Ava, I have to talk to him," I said. She shook her head. She didn't think it was good idea. I sent a text back asking where he was.

We showed up to find he and his friends fairly intoxicated.

John and I ended up leaning against the side of the building on a quiet street, both crying.

"Why did you leave me?" he asked. "I know you're happy where you are, but you tore my heart apart." He was sitting against the building, staring at the ground. I was pacing the sidewalk.

"I know. I'm sorry, John." I stopped and grabbed his hands. "I miss you and think of you all the time."

He stood up and pushed my hands away. "Why would you say that? That makes it worse, Hilary."

I knew what I was saying would hurt him more. He didn't have to tell me. I just wanted him to know the truth, even though it wasn't easy to understand. The whole situation had never been easy to understand. Everything that defined who we were as a couple had been complicated. Between our five-year age difference, our long-distance relationship, and staying together while I was studying abroad in Japan—nothing had ever been simple. But I still loved him.

I desperately wanted to kiss him. I wanted to tell him to wait for me. I wanted to tell him to break up with his girlfriend. All of my wants were unfair and selfish, however. He was vulnerable that night, and I was entirely guilty for making him that way.

My mom and I drove back to Columbus early the next day.

"How was last night? Did you have fun?" she asked from the driver's seat. I was curled in a ball, reclined in the passenger seat. My head was throbbing.

"Yeah, we had fun," I replied. She would have been angry if I had told her I saw John again, much less had the conversation we did.

"How do you feel about returning to Singapore?" My flight flew out the very next day.

"I'm ready to go home," I said.

"Please don't call it home."

I looked over my shoulder at her, but she was staring ahead at the road. "Sorry, Mom," I responded in a soft childlike tone.

A few minutes of silence passed.

"John loves you. You know that?" Mom said. I closed my tired eyelids and remembered his innocent smile and his passionate hug at dinner.

"Yes, I know," I said with a glimpse of aggravation in my voice. I turned back over and held my forehead, rubbing my temples.

"I'm just saying."

"Mom, we are living different lives now."

"Love doesn't disappear, Hilary."

The view of the drive from Chicago to Columbus is flat and straight, but full of country homes and beautiful landscapes. In those homes, people have families whom they care for and love. I knew John loved me. I'd always known. When you love someone, no matter the situation, that love doesn't go away. Even if I wanted it to disappear, it couldn't.

Had I make a mistake by giving up John for my career? I could be back living in a home with him and live near my best friend. I could have a perfectly normal life in a trendy city with a circle of friends, a steady job, and a man who loves me. I liked my life in Singapore, but something always seemed so empty when I came home from a trip.

"Mom!" I yelled. "I really don't want to talk about this." The truth is, she was right, but I didn't have a solution.

Year II.
July 2008 — June 2009

Chapter 15
There Is No Secret

I'd never been happier to see my apartment building than when I returned to Singapore after my two-day-long journey from the United States. It was night, and all I wanted to do was climb in bed and forget about the fact that I had to report to work the next morning. As I stood at the front door and frantically searched for keys in my purse, I heard a noise behind me. I turned around to see the grandmother that lived across from us. For no reason besides curiosity, I decided to finally greet her after months of only exchanging nods.

"Hello," I said.

A huge smile spread across her face from cheek to cheek. She glanced to either side down the hallway, as if she was checking to make sure I was speaking to her.

"Hello," she responded in a strong Chinese accent. I smiled in return and happy to be back in Asia.

When I opened the door, I found Margaret watching TV in the dark. This was common of her.

"Wow, I was wondering where you were," she said. "I didn't know when you were coming back. I thought Toyota sent you on another business trip already."

"I leave at the end of this week," I said. I took off my flip-flops and left my bag at the door. "I'll move this tomorrow. I'm exhausted."

"Leave it," Margaret agreed. "You need to go see the Chinese doctor."

In Singapore, you have the choice of seeing a Western-style doctor or a Chinese doctor. The Chinese doctors include massages as treatments covered by insurance, so I'd recently found one right under our apartment.

"I know, but I won't have time. Peter's going to be here tomorrow, and then I need to prepare for Manila."

"Peter?" Margaret knew the overall story and had met him when he helped me move into the apartment.

I joined her on the couch, which rarely happened, and propped my feet up. I was never an avid TV watcher because I was so busy with other things. Margaret was watching American Idol, one of her favorite shows.

"Yes, Peter," I said. Just saying his name rejuvenated me. "He's on summer break from school and has been in town visiting his parents, but I was in the States, of course. Tomorrow's the only day we have to hang out before he leaves."

"Leaves for what?"

"New Zealand," I pouted. "He's spending the summer there to learn how to be a ski instructor."

"Nice life."

"Yeah, but I wish he'd stay!"

"Hil, what is he now, twenty years old?"

"Yes, and I'm only twenty-three!" I said, already prepared for her next comment.

"He's still in college."

I laughed. "Fine, ruin my fun. I'm going to bed."

My room was extra clean because the maid had come that morning. "Ah, thank you, Marielle," I said, to no one in particular. I remembered the time my mom found out I had a maid. We were on the phone when the maid arrived one day. I ended our conversation saying, "Gotta run — maid is here!" My mom yelled back, "You're what?" Having someone clean up after me was certainly not a lesson she taught me.

I unloaded my purse, found the boarding passes for my first trip home, and taped them to the wall under my one-way ticket to Singapore. I turned off the light and my blue star night-light sent a glow up the wall. It was nice to be able to look out from my bed and see Chinatown and the Singapore skyline. The wind cooled the hot summer air and blew it lightly over my tired face.

It'd been almost a year since I'd seen Peter; I wondered if he had changed at all and if we would still get along as well as we had when we first met. We had maintained communication through e-mail, but nothing in-depth. I almost hoped the chemistry had dissipated so I wouldn't have to say good-bye to it again.

When I arrived the next day at the Singapore River, where Peter and I were to meet, my body almost collapsed from under me. Peter was sitting on the steps of the bank with a bottle of wine and two small plastic cups, his thick black hair flowing in the breeze. I took a deep breath to recompose myself and tapped him on the shoulder from behind.

"My Billy, darling!" he said. Short for my nickname, Hil Bil, he naturally made his own version over the past year.

"Hi, Peter," I said. He hugged me so tight that I couldn't stop smiling.

"'Tis so good to see you, my dear. You are as beautiful as ever," he said. I blushed and didn't tell him that I'd changed my outfit three times getting ready.

We sat by the river for the entire evening, talking about everything from his school to his parents, from my work to my troubled trip home. The bottle of wine sat between the two of us.

"Your feelings are all natural," he said when I told him about how uncomfortable I'd felt at Ariana's shower. "Don't worry."

Although I was honest, I didn't reveal everything. Hearing about his life in England made me jealous, and I still wanted to seem happy with friends and work abroad.

"I'm trying not to worry. My life is pretty good. I mean, I do work a lot, but I've also been able to see some pretty amazing places."

"Yes, you spend more time in my home country than I do," he said, laughing. He was referring to the Philippines where his mother was from.

"No wonder I like you so much," I said. "I adore the Filipinos. They are so loving and have such a fun culture. No matter what's going on in the office, they're always cheery."

"They are lovely," he agreed.

I told him about how the Shangri-La staff knew me better than some of my friends, about how I'd partied with celebrities at the new car launch party in Cebu.

"They must love having you around," he said. "You're such a different face to them."

"It's strange. I am, yet it's as if they've accepted me as their own. I barely even notice anymore."

We got up from our spot by the river to buy another bottle of wine. Our first was empty. By the time we returned, the sun had set, and the sidewalks flooded with bodies.

"You've garnered their respect," Peter said. "I wonder how."

I looked out over the river. It was so still that it almost perfectly reflected the city's skyline.

"I don't know. I'm just myself," I responded.

He leaned forward and rested his hand on my knee. "And it is precisely that for which they respect you."

His touch suddenly reminded me of our first night together, getting rained on under the stars. Nothing had changed since then. The unexplainable infatuation still endured the time and distance between us.

I moved our second bottle of wine and shifted closer to his side. "So, tell me more about you. What's it like at school?"

"Oh, it's brilliant. You saw the photo of my wall?"

"Yes, it's covering your whole room."

"Yes, ma'am, and getting bigger," he said proudly. I could've watched his lips move with that British accent all night. "I have so much fun. I sometimes go to class, but otherwise draw and film my interests at my own leisure. We go to the shore of the bay and drink beers over campfires. I love it."

"As you should," I said.

"Tell me, Billy, what of your love life?"

"Love life?" I pulled back from my admiring. This was a dilemma. I didn't know whether to tell him the truth, that it was lackluster, or that I was dating, in hopes of making him desirous.

"Yes, because I must tell you. I am sort of dating someone right now."

I pulled back even more, letting his hand fall off my knee.

"Oh, you are?"

"Yes, but it is very early on. I am just getting to know her," he said a bit defensively.

"You don't need to say anything, Peter."

"But I do, my Hilary. Seeing you again makes it so different. You do something to me that I cannot articulate," he said. I dropped my chin and closed my eyes, but he continued. "I feel completely out of control by the way you make me feel." He paused in a choke sort of silence.

"I'm not seeing anyone," I said. "You were such a fortunate encounter. I've never met anyone since like you, but I haven't been looking, either."

With his soft hands, he took my chin and pulled it up. My eyes revealed drunkenness from three glasses of wine, but I'll never forget the look of affection in his face. Before I knew it, we were kissing on the bank, and we didn't stop the whole taxi ride home.

It was hard to focus the next morning at work. I'd said good-bye to Peter again and didn't know when I would see him, although he claimed he'd be back at the end of summer after the ski training.

Dialogue with Peter was different. I didn't notice or care what was going on around me. Days could pass and it wouldn't matter. He understood my life and could relate to it, unlike many of my friends back home. I just wished he could be a part of it more consistently.

A storm of change came unsuspectingly at work when I returned from the States that June. The executive vice president who had hired me, Nakamura-san, was leaving TMAP. He had served his allotted time of five years. Nakamura-san had strongly supported the Philippines project, and because of his relationship with Sato-san, my success in the company had always been well looked after. Each boss also had a different management style, and it took time and mistakes to understand his expectations. I had finally reached that point with Nakamura-san, and the two of us had become friends; we were able to joke and talk about things outside of the office. This was a rare type of relationship at Toyota, and it was all about to change.

The new EVP, Hamada-san, had dark features, including jet-black hair, and stood just a few inches taller than me. He always dressed in classy

navy pinstripe suits, wore stylish designer glasses, and sometimes even
threw in a splash of color with a purple tie.

A stark contrast separated my former from my new boss. Nakamura-
san was fairly transparent, loud, and spoke in English a lot. Hamada-san
was quiet but always seemed aware of his surroundings. We didn't know if
he'd be as transparent as Nakamura-san. He evoked intimidation at first,
which could be expected of any new boss, but he always smiled, shook
everyone's hand, asked questions, and listened. It is the Japanese way to
spend time understanding the condition of the regional office before
rushing to judge or make any rash changes. We observed his demeanor
and facial expressions to gauge his reactions but were rarely able to
evaluate him.

Hamada-san took Nakamura-san's desk that faced our department: the
RDSD. Because of the open-air concept, we could always see whom the
EVP was meeting with. He could also monitor us in this way so we had to
pay close attention to our discussion's details, voice level, and
professionalism.

I wanted to make a good impression as I had with Nakamura-san, but
this time, I had to take a different approach. Hamada-san wasn't hiring a
new staff member; he was getting to know an existing one. The
expectations would be very different.

I'd gotten in the habit of coming to the office by 7:00 a.m.; two hours
earlier than everyone else, to manage the menial aspects of my job, like
expense reporting. Since I was still catching up from my long visit home, I
had dedicated one such morning to clearing e-mail. The lights were all off,
except for one panel above the EVP's desk. I did not expect to see Hamada-
san sitting there. He didn't even look up when I entered the office, but my
heart instantly started thumping in my chest and I paused. My desk was
only a few feet away from him. What would I say? The GM hadn't formally
introduced me to him yet, and introducing me would undermine Kimura-
san's authority.

I walked slowly and inaudibly toward my desk, holding my breath.
When Hamada-san looked up to acknowledge my presence, I bowed
slightly and greeted him good morning in Japanese.

"Ohayou Gozaimasu," he responded with a smile. I took my seat and
disguised my big exhale with the starting noises of my computer. As I
examined Hamada-san more closely from the corner of my eye, I realized
why he had come to the office two hours early. He was studying an old,
printed English dictionary. It made me smile to myself, and I figured that
even the big bosses faced barriers. This not only reduced some of the
intimidation I felt around him, but also showed me a side of the bosses I
could relate to. I too had started out at Toyota feeling out of place, like a
minority, and had struggled to earn the trust of my colleagues. Now, I'd

almost forgotten that I was the only Caucasian. Hamada-san not only had to earn the trust of his employees, but also of the region. I felt a strong sense of responsibility to help him, and I decided to start by acclimating him to the Philippines project as swiftly and efficiently as possible. Within Hamada-san's first week, he met with all the departments to learn about their responsibilities. When RDSD's meeting came, Kimura-san delegated me to speak on behalf of the Philippines. After my brief introduction on the activity of our dealership, TMI, Hamada-san stood up and drew on the white board:

| Result | ⟷ | HR development |
| Zeka | ⟷ | Ikusei |

In Japanese, *zeka* meant result and *ikusei* meant HR development. He quickly understood the challenges we were facing. We weren't able to make much concrete progress due to the distributor's lack of direction and understanding of kaizen. In very broken English, Hamada-san said, "Please strengthen value and respect between distributor, TMAP, and TMC." I nodded in agreement, but lacked any real motivation. He continued by saying, "Progress one step forward over one year."

I sighed and later vented to Viktor, "I cannot imagine working another year at TMI. The problem is deeply rooted with top management and out of my control."

"That is part of the learning experience, Hilary. You have no idea now how valuable this is."

Even in my frustration, I knew Viktor was right. It felt like a lifetime, but identifying the problem in nine months was, in actuality, very quick. That lesson would be priceless.

Hamada-san was scheduled to visit our *gemba,* our place of work, so Kimura-san, Kom-san, and I had two weeks to prepare the dealership. Deepesh, a new company transfer from India, was assigned to the project but primarily just for observing, so he didn't carry much responsibility.

Shinken Shoubu, Kimura-san wrote on the board. "Do or Die."

"TMI has responsibility being Toyota dealer," Kimura-san commented. "But what does this mean? Do we need to investigate more and clarify what it is to be Toyota dealer?"

I sat with my arms crossed.

"Shoganai," Kom-san said. This was a common Japanese phrase that meant there was nothing we could do about it today. Deepesh sat next to him in a daze.

Sato-san took me to lunch that week for sushi at the Ritz Carlton—a treat I'd grown to look forward to—in order to hear about my trip home.

"It was tough," I began. "There was so much about my life I wanted to share, and it felt like no one cared."

"You have grown fast," he said. "While, they still live the same."

I nodded in agreement. I'd have to learn that my family's choices were okay, and how to filter the discussion for who cared and who didn't, instead of forcing what I'd learned onto everyone.

"My friends are another subject. Two more of my American friends returned to the U.S. in the past few months, and now all I have is Viktor."

"Viktor is good man! How is he?" Sato-san asked. A lady in a kimono delicately positioned plates of sushi, tempura, and chopsticks in front of us. Her movements reminded me of the way my host mother in Japan would arrange the plates for dinner.

"Good, but he's busy traveling, like me," I continued. "I just feel like I'm starting all over in both my personal life and career. I've been so anxious to show good results at TMI, but now Kimura-san is talking about the purpose of being a dealer owner!"

After carefully pouring soy sauce for us both, Sato-san set down the bottle and looked up at me. "Kimura-san is right, but TMAP cannot overcome Philippines management issue. Anxiety, I fear."

"I know! But then what am I to do? And now with Hamada-san here, I don't know what he'll want to do with the project."

"He is positive and energetic," Sato-san said. "I think he will be good for TMAP."

"Yeah. I like him too. But, do you think he understands?" I asked.

"Who does?" he responded, shrugging. "Please, enjoy your sushi."

I picked up the plastic chopsticks and ate my delectable pieces of sashimi.

More changes occurred in TMAP with the new year, including a new team member to RDSD, Yoshida-san, whom I'd met during the kaizen training in Japan. Having completed his exchange term with the Toyota Motor Corporation (TMC), he returned to TMAP, his home office. Since he didn't have a project to start, and Kom-san was preoccupied with the India project, Kimura-san asked Yoshida-san to take Kom-san's role at TMI.

That July, we held a welcome lunch for Yoshida-san, and I spent a few days sharing the status of the project with him. During one of our breaks at the foot of the building, Yoshida-san said something that would stick with me forever. "You should consider to smoke," he said. Startled, I turned my head from watching passers-by on the street. "It is good chance to speak with management."

I was speechless for a moment, so he continued explaining that smoking is actually a tool for communication. It was the one chance that the lower staff and higher-up managers could converse in an informal way.

"Are you serious?" I said, gathering myself to avoid being disrespectful. I continued in a polite yet unyielding tone, "I would never sacrifice my health for the sake of my job." I remembered the smoking rooms inside Toyota's Japan headquarters. Yoshida-san must have used them often. Although we didn't have such rooms in Singapore, there was a smoking area at the bottom of the office building. I always assumed Yoshida-san was there if I couldn't find him.

But I was truly dumbfounded by his comment and couldn't help but wonder what other kinds of sacrifices people made to succeed in Toyota.

For the next week, Yoshida-san attended the meetings with Hamada-san to understand the TMI activity and would join the next business trip the following Monday. There was a lot to catch up on.

Our driver, Carlos, picked Kimura-san and I up on our first day in Manila and drove us to TMI. Deepesh and Kom were in a separate car behind us. Carlos' comment that morning cast a light on my entire week, and a significant memory of my time abroad. He'd mentioned that his wife was pregnant with their fourth child, and it was going to be a girl. They had been debating on a name for some time.

"Ma'am Hilary?" Carlos said, looking in the rearview mirror at me.

I was busy organizing my things. "Hai, Carlos-san?" Even though neither of us was Japanese, we sometimes spoke conversationally in the language. This was common of Toyota employees.

"I really like the name Hilary. Would it be okay if I name my new girl with your name?"

Kimura-san looked over at me with a smile. I stopped what I was doing and looked up at him in the mirror. "Hilary?" I asked, surprised by his request.

"Yes, I liked it before, but even more now I know you."

"Of course I don't mind! Are you sure?"

"Oh, thank you, Ma'am Hilary! My wife will be very happy."

Without even realizing it, I brought my right hand to my heart.

"Thank *you*, Carlos-san. It is a privilege."

The week continued in full force before Hamada-san's visit. I expected help from Yoshida-san, given the extensive training he'd just completed in Japan, but was taken aback by his actions. He sat impassive every day during all of our meetings, not saying a word.

He later told me, "Hilary, I was new and did not understand everything so I could not interrupt your work." I realized that it wasn't fair to expect him to instruct us, since he'd only recently joined the nine-month-old project. I thought back to my first meeting with the company where I made that insignificant comment about where the kaizen conference, not realizing until later that I had no place or knowledge to have made it.

When Hamada-san arrived, we went through the standard gemba observation of a top management visit. Someone on the team received a call that he was near, and all the dealer, distributor, and TMAP staff congregated at the entrance of the dealership. As Hamada-san entered, the distributor's top management followed behind him, making nervous faces to the team checking that everything was ready He bowed, we bowed — everyone bowed — and the observation began.

The dealer staff member explained the sales process — vehicle presentation, insurance registration, finance registration, and so on. We then walked over to the workshop to explain the service process. Once complete, we walked upstairs via the office, where the kind Filipinos greeted Hadaka-san in unison, like a choir, "Morning, Sir."

We entered the body-and-paint workshop and walked all the way back to our cockroach-filled obeya room. The Obeya means "big room" in Japanese but has a similar concept as a "war room". The space contains highly visual charts and graphs depicting the timing, progress, milestones and countermeasures for any project.

The Japanese higher-ups never said exactly what was going through their minds. This wasn't their style. It still surprised me, though, that when we took our seats, Hamada-san began to tell a story. I listened like a school kid sitting on the floor by my teacher.

"The former Toyota presidents always said that there is no secret to Toyota," he began. "We welcome competitors to visit our production plants. Reason why?" Everyone was quiet. "There is no secret. It depends on management style. Even though they wish to copy, let them. It is not easy."

I grinned with pride for the success and integrity of the company. Furthermore, my smile derived from the empowerment I felt for finally having a glimpse of what this truly meant.

He continued, "In TMC, good managers are teachers, maybe sometimes strict, but good teachers, not controllers."

Hamada-san's former boss was Yamada-san, one of the founders of the famous Toyota Production System. "Whenever I fail, he would always ask, 'Okay, what will you do?' without giving instruction or idea. Very good one for chance to learn."

I looked to Kimura-san and remembered all the times he had asked me that very same question, which usually left me even more confused and frustrated. I originally thought that it was his job as a boss to advise me.

Hamada-san continued to explain, "This management style is what makes the 'secret' of Toyota today versus other competitors. The challenge is from now on. I've seen dealers start kaizen but cannot sustain because the style of management isn't there. Must encourage staff to strengthen over one year, then ten years. The length and result of kaizen step is not important, but more that gemba people step small, together, and continuously."

It was exactly what I wanted TMI to hear. I was shocked that, within an hour's time, the executive vice president understood the dealership's situation and persisted they establish the right direction. As a result, we arranged for the Philippines staff to visit Thailand and see their dealerships so they could see what successful kaizen dealers look and act like. We called such dealers *Pika Pika* dealers, which means "shining" in Japanese. I was just excited to have something new to work on.

Chapter 16
Of Course, Darling

No one refers to seasons in Singapore because the weather never changes. That said, the summer was a busy one for me. After the Philippines milestone, I had the incredible opportunity to attend the 2008 Summer Olympics in Beijing—the result of being a Coca Cola Scholar back in high school. At one point during a table tennis match, I found myself cheering for Singapore, Japan, America, and Italy at the same time, unsure to whom I was most loyal. I also returned to Manila to plan for our Thailand observation.

Between work, travel, managing personal tasks, and catching up on sleep, it took nearly two months to activate my social skills again. I spent most of my time with Viktor and his friends because they usually had plans that I could join without much initiative. I always admired how well Viktor cared for his friends, despite his travel schedule that often trumped mine.

Out one night, Viktor, his friends that I didn't know very well, and I were discussing the subject of expatriates one night in a dark bar with lounge chairs and soothing lounge music playing behind us.

The three Asian cities that tend to have the most expatriates are Tokyo, Hong Kong, and Singapore. Expatriates generally favor one city over another. For example, they either love the dirty hustle and bustle of Hong Kong or the balance of nightlife with safety and cleanliness in Singapore. I obviously preferred the latter. Tokyo, however, has its own loyal entourage, which I got a glimpse of during my study abroad experience.

Expatriates are typically male—so over conversation led to the subject of Caucasian men dating Asian women.

"As a woman, living in such a world, I think it's awful," I said to Viktor's friend from Hong Kong. "Every day, I see men my age walking down the street with young Asian women who, in all likelihood, they will not marry."

"True, they probably won't," he said, sitting back in the couch as I rambled on about my opinion.

"They're just living their fantasy," I said.

Viktor butted in, laughing, "Some guy's dream come true." Viktor wasn't even attracted to Asians, although he was one himself.

"Exactly," I said, though slightly offended. "It's not funny. It's gross. Then those that do marry concern me even more because it makes me think they're just running away from something. What happens to these people if or when they move home? In Asia, the men get treated by Asian women like they sit on a golden platter, and then they have to go back to reality."

"Have you ever wondered if maybe that's what the men are supposed to do?" Viktor's friend chimed in.

"Supposed to do?"

"Like, perhaps that's what they need to do to get to their next step. We can't define what anyone else's path should be. Maybe some white guy's soul mate really is Asian? Or what if he was really sad before he came to Asia, and by having an Asian girlfriend, he's gained happiness in his life again?"

I sat back in my chair and crossed my arms. I'd never thought of it like that before.

"Anyways," he said, "we're all here for a reason. You too. Some people could judge you for your decision to not date an Asian, but why? It's your path."

Viktor joked, "I'm Asian. Hilary, you could date me so people don't judge you." I laughed, turning around and smacking his arm.

His friend continued, "And yes, these guys will come home someday and probably not be the same. But haven't we always had those people in the world? Example: explorers."

"Interesting," I said.

"You're an explorer too. They don't have to be bad."

His analogy made sense to me. Sure, it wasn't the most enjoyable thing to watch male expatriates chase Asian women, but it was their own doing and really none of my business. Getting wrapped up in their problems distracted me from my own problem that I didn't have my own boyfriend. I thought I was certain that I didn't want to date abroad, but the desire to share my journey with someone was beginning to overwhelm me. It would usually hit me when I sat alone, in front of some beautiful sight, like the Taiwanese landscape or when I heard something funny, like my Filipino colleagues calling me Mrs. Clinton. All of my unaccompanied experiences felt less significant.

The following week, Sato-san requested a few of his closest colleagues to listen to his presentation on the activity in Italy. He was seeking our input first before presenting to Hamada-san. I was flattered to be a part of the group.

Five of us sat around a table in the Corolla conference room, anxious to hear what Sato-san would share. He usually had tremendous success, achieving results in less than the time allocated for the project, but as with all kaizen projects, he faced several of the same issues we were struggling with in the Philippines.

"Many of the top management criticized my position and authority," he said. It was his first time studying the Italian car market. I felt the same way about the Philippines. The management had no reason to trust me, so I'd have to show them by example to earn their trust.

Sato-san had also had difficulty empowering the sales staff to reveal problems and propose countermeasures.

"Competition is very strong in Italy," he said. I chuckled, thinking of my Italian family members who make a game of criticizing each other. "And they didn't want to disclose their sales tricks to others," he continued.

I was realizing slowly that kaizen had almost nothing to do with the tool or solution, but how you nurtured people to create an environment cohesive to change — an environment that empowered them to develop the answer on their own.

As much as I had appreciated Kimura-san's encouragement and backing for the past year, I wished that I could have worked with someone like Sato-san who had experience with kaizen and could guide me better. Kimura-san sometimes apologized for this directly, but it wasn't his fault. It was just difficult that we were both starting the process from scratch and learning together.

September third marked my first anniversary serving Toyota, and I was wondering what I wanted next out of my career and life. Usually, my dealership attire I wore at gemba consisted of Hush Puppies flats, black slacks, and a button-up shirt. I didn't wear any make-up either. But that day I dressed especially formally for the special occasion.

The air felt thick in my throat and heavy on my skin as I walked from the office to the restaurant to meet Sato-san. When I looked up, dark clouds patrolled the sky, soliciting rain soon.

British-inspired architecture painted in bold summer colors lined the streets. The canary yellow, baby blue, and peach-painted buildings always reminded me of New Orleans, where I had visited once for Mardi Gras.

I zoned out as I imagined the leaves changing color in Columbus and began reflecting on all I had experienced in the past 365 days. The world's largest car manufacturer, Toyota, had claimed the first year of my career. I was only twenty-three years old, and I had already seen so much. My life was beautiful. I was so far into my daydream that I almost knocked over an auntie enjoying tea on the side of the bustling street. I apologized to the old woman and continued walking.

My mind wandered again with thoughts of John. In the time since I'd left, he and I had only spoken once. He initiated a chat with me randomly online a few weeks prior. I had mentioned my anniversary with the company to him. It made me feel he was still a part of my life, talking about such a personal thing.

"You've accomplished more than most people in their whole career," he replied. As I walked down the quiet side streets of Singapore, I kept thinking of the palm reader and wondering if I was doing the wrong thing by maintaining communication with John hoping that he'd wait for me.

Sato-san and I met at a new French restaurant. It was an early dinner, and I was the first to arrive. Dark on the inside, the restaurant's style evoked New York posh and edge. I ordered myself a lychee martini, a specialty of Singapore.

Sato-san had just returned from his monthly visit to Rome. His purple embroidered initials stood out on his crisp white shirt pocket. For an operations man, people jokingly deemed his style as a bit eccentric.

"Ciao, Ilaria!" he exclaimed as he entered the restaurant.

People often confused Sato-san for being Italian, not Japanese. His dark features could pull off both. Sato-san revealed his secret, however, when sipping wine. Within seconds, his bright-red face exposed his nationality. The Japanese are the only culture in the world that has a missing enzyme in their DNA that causes the blood to rush to their face when they drink. It's not harmful—just makes them look like tomatoes.

He hugged me, instantly easing the tension I felt. He always made me feel safe. He was not just a mentor, but had become like a father, encouraging and believing in me. "Congratulations! I am so proud of you. One year you have been with Toyota. Are you happy?" He often asked me this question.

"I am. Thank you so much." I don't have a problem finding words except when I'm with Sato-san, someone to whom I feel so deeply indebted. I can never find the words that adequately show my appreciation. So I just say thank you a lot.

We spoke of the Philippines project and all the challenges we had been facing with Toyota Makati.

"You will not able to change the mind of Genie-san," he said, speaking of the president of TMI. "This is beyond your job."

I knew he was right, but was too mulish to admit that I had failed. "I have to come up with a way. She trusts me now and asks for my opinion."

"This is step one," he nodded. "But the project already is almost one year old. Hilary needs a new project. I'm concerned Hilary is tired."

"I am tired," I admitted.

From behind, the waiter opened a bottle of champagne and began pouring it into my glass. "Let's not dwell. Let's celebrate!" Sato-san said. He smiled, quickly changing the tempo. "Cheers, to swimming in a pool!" he reminisced.

I laughed out loud, although on the verge of wanting to cry. I lifted my glass and answered, "To swimming in a pool."

Our dinner concluded over three hours later. We were the first and the last guests in the restaurant. Our conversations often extended such periods. The cab took me home first, despite being out of the way from Sato-san's condominium. As usual, Sato-san paid for everything.

"I know you don't make much money," he would always say.

And I would reply, "Thank you."

Our friendship meant so much more than just nice dinners. He had lived up to his promise to be my guardian. He looked after me both in and out of the office, there for me if I ever needed anything.

Viktor was another man in my life who had become an important mentor and friend, and his advice was usually exactly what I needed to hear: "Just keep doing what you do. It's gotten you this far," he would say.

We communicated with the Philippines team, by e-mail and phone to keep progress of their activity. Management had expressed more interest and attention, and the team expressed incredible excitement for the Bangkok trip. The visit would be a major milestone for the team.

For two days in Thailand, the Philippines team connected with the local Thai teams. They shared success stories and discussed improvement points. After observing the dealership operations for a day, the Filipino team shook hands with the Thais. The Filipinos were so forward and friendly, much like Americans. Although quiet at first, I watched the Thai team slowly open up and laugh at the frequent Filipino jokes.

When we assembled in the meeting room, the Thai dealer owner advised the team, "When you can do kaizen the right way, once, then it is endless." They all shook their heads as they listened to the owner speak. I grinned at Yoshida-san who was there with me. "We had much opposition. What was achieved was deemed as unachievable," the dealer owner continued.

The team's sincere intent to study and learn from the Thais' achievements made me proud. At the end of the trip, the team met for a few hours to digest the trip and share their reactions.

I was shocked when I heard Genie-san speak. "My God, I'm thankful."

"The role of management is key — patience and humility," another team member said. "This is an eye-opener but will require a paradigm shift."

A third added, "If you think your people can't do kaizen, then it's you that doesn't understand."

The overall reaction was unanimously positive.

We broke into smaller groups and discussed the best way to proceed. Now, it was the task of mine and the Filipino team to summarize the trip and try to share it concisely with the EVP of TMAP, Christian-san. We flew straight to Manila instead of returning to Singapore in order to ensure the team took prompt action.

Unfortunately, when we reported to Christian-san, he didn't convey the same enthusiasm as the team members that attended the trip. Typical of top management, he communicated concern that the kaizen activity was slow and can't be expanded rapidly. I felt that he totally lost sight of the purpose.

Just a few days later in Singapore, we shared the report with Hamada-san, and he also expressed his discontent in the project. "The will is very weak. The distributor top management intention is not there. Kaizen is only a way. It's not a project."

I tried to hold my mouth shut. Hadaka-san's first visit had been much more positive. After feeling like the Thailand trip was a success, I felt discouraged and out of ideas.

When I received Peter's message on Facebook that he was coming back to Singapore, my whole body trembled in excitement. I longed to be near him again, and I longed for a distraction from work.

"Oh, Peter's in town? See you next month," Viktor said, jokingly.

Peter and I spent hours lying together and talking about life, love, challenges, and our crazy pursuits. Our conversations never ended. We had a tradition of going for dim sum at his favorite place, where we'd feed each other dumplings and play footsy under the table.

"You're wearing my bracelet!" I suddenly exclaimed one night as we lingered at the restaurant over hot tea. I'd bought the bracelet from a market in Manila and sent it to him in London. It reminded me of his hippy style.

"Of course, darling. It is a daily reminder of you."

My eyes glowed with adoration, but was it really fair for us to have daily reminders of each other, to be living this fantasy time together? I didn't know what would happen between us, but I wanted to enjoy what time I did have with Peter without worrying about whether or not it could ever be more than this.

After dinner, he took me to his favorite art store a few floors down from the food court. He took my hand and guided me to a section of notebooks.

"You must write down your memories, Hilary," he told me.

"Huh?"

"I want you to have a notebook," he said as he scoured the aisle of options.

"I don't write, Peter. I've never really used a journal."

"I'll help you start."

I smiled. "Every time I try, I stop. It takes too much time."

"This one! It's perfect," he said. He handed me a black notebook about the size of my palm.

"It's tiny," I said.

"That's what's so great about this," he explained. "You don't need to write a novel. You can easily keep it with you wherever you go, and when you get inspired, you write a short note down so that you remember. You can even draw if you want."

"All right. We'll see."

When he left the country, he accidentally took the notebook, forgetting that he was holding it for me in his bag, but I had made a promise to him that I would write. I went back and bought another.

This good-bye to Peter wasn't as difficult as the ones in the past because I wasn't sure if I even wanted to see him again. I'd grown used to the process. The whole scenario felt emotionally dangerous, and I didn't know how to feel, so after he left I just ignored it—or at least tried to.

Chapter 17
You Are America

The world was struggling. Economies were failing, and some of the largest companies in the world were crumbling overnight. Toyota discontinued all business-class privileges on flights, forcing management to fly economy class again with their staff. The only person able to fly business class was the president and his board members, which was generally for safety.

No one could keep track of the chaos. It was frightening. Every morning, I would wake up to headlines announcing the devastating world economy. But I was able to escape it all by hiding in my little seemingly impenetrable Singaporean bubble where I drank champagne with friends and went on frequent vacations.

I was doing all the necessary planning before another big trip home, including souvenir shopping, laundry, catching up with friends, and going for my first dentist appointment abroad, which made me feel even more like Singapore was becoming my home.

"Wow!" the dentist exclaimed.

"What's wrong?" I asked.

"Nothing! Your gums are so pink!"

I responded through gritty polishing toothpaste, "Thank you?"

"This means you have a very healthy mouth. Like puppies do. I do not see healthy teeth like this often. In Singapore, we do not promote it well. Fried and dried meats, chili sauce, none of it is good. Cannot."

That weekend, I traveled to Malaysia with friends from TMAP for a colleague's wedding—one of the few times I ever saw my coworkers outside of the office. It was the first Asian wedding I'd ever attended, the marriage of a Japanese woman and Chinese man. This was a relatively rare match. She had grown up in Thailand and spoke Thai, while her Chinese fiancé had been born in Malaysia. The dynamic of their relationship fascinated me, how they were able to make it work even across multiple cultures.

I felt a bit uncomfortable at first, as the only attendee who wasn't Asian, but I relaxed when everyone welcomed me with cheers. The wedding replicated the extravagance of Toyota's Dinner & Dance party with an emcee, elaborate decorations, and a cake that was taller than me. The bride even had three dresses that she changed into throughout the night. She was gorgeous in every one.

I was exhausted the next Monday morning after the five-hour bus ride from Malaysia. I had to be alert, though, because a big week waited for me. Kichida-san, one of our Japanese advisors, was coming from Manila to meet with Yoshida-san, Kimura-san, and myself to discuss the Philippines project and how to proceed with it.

"Activity forced on dealer, so distributor now has no responsibility," Kichida-san explained. "Now is a good time, however. The before operation was very chaotic. Now, standard that is in progress."

Yoshida-san commented on the need to set a clear target for the Filipino team. He continued, "To do, we must be there long-term to build trust in our word about clear target."

I gasped, unable to imagine spending more time at TMI. However, I contained my selfish thought and said instead, "I agree. There is an opportunity." The manager, Francis, had told me that the dealership's general manager, Gio-san, had begun asking more questions and visiting the people in kaizen projects to observe their status.

I pulled my chair forward. "The dealership is beginning to see the need, but they now need the support system."

During our next business trip, Kimura-san and I developed an action plan with the TMI team, thinking this would help inspire them to fulfill it. What happened instead was that they had no idea where to start and got caught up in trying to do too many things at once. Gio-san suddenly took over all decision-making and began to take action, like we had told him. One of those actions was canceling the process that we had implemented to help ensure on-time invoicing for new car deliveries. I was in the obeya room when I found out.

"He *what?*" I screamed in shock.

"He thinks it is extra work for the invoicing staff," Anna responded.

"Extra work? Her job is easier now! He doesn't even know how to do the process. How does he know it is extra work?" I didn't expect Anna to respond.

She looked to the ground, "The staff must follow. It is their boss."

Gio, Francis, and I were in the middle of a meeting with some other staff. Unfortunately, I couldn't hold in my emotions.

I pushed my chair back and stood up. "This is ridiculous. If he doesn't need my help, then I'm leaving. He can obviously handle it on his own. Does he think I like coming here?" I began pacing the room. "Every month, I travel to *your* country to help *your* people and give up my entire personal life. Every month! And then he's just going to go do this?"

Anna added, "He hasn't even tried to understand."

I was already in tears at this point. I couldn't hold them back. The project had too much work behind it, and he had finally gone too far. Improving the invoicing process had been our one success, and he was going to take it from us, and from me.

What I didn't realize at the time was that this project was not mine and should never have been mine. My project was cultivating the people so they could improve the process on their own. Though the situation was not ideal, Gio-san was taking a huge leap forward, which I could have taken as a success. Instead, I blindly took it as an insult.

"Anna, let's go to Starbucks."

She laughed. "Hilary, I can't just go to Starbucks. I'm working. I'll get in trouble."

"You are with me. It's fine. Anyways, it's obvious that Gio-san doesn't need us anymore, so we can leave," I said as I gathered my bags.

"Um, okay." It was obvious she was nervous about the whole situation but trusted me and followed me out the door.

I bought her a Starbucks frappuccino and we sat down on some red couches. Without saying anything, Anna shared a story with me. "Hilary, kaizen has changed my life," she said. "Before, I was bored at TMI. I would go out every night and come in late the next day. I slept in the obeya room and just browsed the Internet. I was almost going to quit. Since you and Kimura-san have come, everything changed. My entire perspective on life has changed. Even my family has noticed that I am different! Like the other day, my friend and I were shopping and I wanted to buy something and I sat there for ten minutes observing it and thinking if I really need and how I would use it. Finally, I put it back while my friend kept encouraging me to buy it. I am more analytical now than I have ever been before. I am more aware of problems and come up with creative solutions to them."

The entire time she spoke, I leaned forward with my elbows on my knees, my hands over my mouth, catching the tears as they fell down my cheek. I began to release a year's worth of tears. Anna had no idea that her words would change my entire life. I felt appreciated, that my work was acknowledged. I had been aching for this within Toyota. But verbal acknowledgement is not a component of the company culture.

Everything suddenly seemed worth it. Every business expense, every flight, every frustration, every breakthrough, and every failure was worth it, because Anna's life had improved, both personally and professionally.

I realized that my reaction in TMI that day had been entirely selfish and unprofessional. My irresponsibility directly resulted in Gio-san's action. Guiding him should have been my job, and I had failed. I hadn't given him the resources or tools he needed. Now, I see that it wasn't so much a failure as a hiccup we needed to breathe through.

"It was the best we were capable," Kimura-san said back in the office. "It wasn't any one person's fault." He was always a positive thinker, but he was also right. The first kaizen project we ever conducted was almost certain to fail, but Anna's story made me feel like it was a success.

During my time overseas, the 2008 US presidential election absorbed the attention of everyone back home as well as in Asia. In the early part of the year, my exposure to the campaigning was limited to hotel and airport TV reports and foreign newspaper articles. As Election Day drew closer, I strained to keep track of it all — the scandals, the ploys, the debates, and the wardrobes. Everyone in Singapore was discussing the candidates, and many were watching the debates. A lot of them knew more than most Americans.

One day in November, I was sitting in the office pantry with Yoshida-san and Kom-san for a morning tea break. They'd both heard about my outburst in the Philippines but never mentioned it to me directly. In the company's culture, it wasn't appropriate to identify people's mistakes. If someone dropped papers on the ground, no one looked — much less helped — in order to save face.

They did, however, ask about the trip overall. "I hear TMI is doing their own kaizen now!" Kom-san said. "That is great. Please, come to India next. We need help."

"They are trying," Yoshida-san confirmed.

"Yes, they are doing great. Gio and Anna are working together now without instruction. They are finally taking ownership."

"Good progress," Kom-san said. In his words, I noticed that he never attributed the success to my doing, but I was becoming okay with it. I was learning the value of humility.

Kom-san's tone rose in excitement when he asked, "Don't you leave soon for your sister's wedding?"

"Yes, at the end of the month. I feel like I just got over jet lag and I'm already going back," I said.

"Oh! Is that the girl whose picture is on your desk?" Yoshida-san asked.

"Yes, that's my sister's teaching photo."

He slammed his black work shoes to the floor and covered his eyes with his hands. "Whoops! I thought that was Hilary-chan before you put on weight!"

I looked at him in shock and then laughed when I remember that English was Yoshida-san's second language. He wasn't always the most tactful.

"I haven't gained that much weight!" I said, giggling. It felt good to not care for a moment, to breathe, to laugh.

"Hey! Isn't today America's election?" The headlines had been plastered all over the coffee shop downstairs.

"Yes. I haven't been able to pay attention because I've been in a meeting all morning, but we should know results by tonight."

"*Maa*, I hope good results," Yoshida-san said. "Whatever happens in America affects us. If you guys shop less, we sell less."

I nodded and looked out a tall window over the vast, blue Marina Bay imagining America far away from us.

Kom-san said, "You are so lucky to be able to vote. What an honor to have a contribution to the future of the world."

The teapot began to boil, so I stood up to get my cup. "Interesting. I've never thought about it like that."

"Of course," Kom-san chuckled. "You are America."

"Unfortunately, not everyone understands it like that, that they actually impact the world," I said, pausing for a moment at the counter.

The world was changing, and we were all a part of it, regardless of our race, nationality, or gender. There was almost no nation unaffected by America's decision.

I returned to the Prius conference room to meet with Kimura-san and an advisor from Japan. A couple of hours later, after concluding the meeting, we bowed in thanks. "Arigatou Gozaimasu," we said repeatedly over the conference table.

Just as we were departing the cold, gray-walled room, I heard the Japanese man yell, "Hilary-san!"

I stopped abruptly and looked back in confusion.

"Wakaranai," Kimura-san said, also confused.

The man stood up from his chair and looked me straight in the eye. "It's Obama. Your country has black president first."

"Wow," I said, unable to comprehend the significance of the moment. My arm was too weak from the shock to keep the door open. I moved my back against it.

"It's on my phone," he said eagerly.

Hilary Corna

"Wow, thank you," I said. I stepped away from the door, bowed again and exited the room. Kimura-san followed behind me.

"This is big news," he said.

"Yes, this is. Please excuse me. I need to go check the news online."

"What about lunch?"

"I'll be fine, thank you." I ran in the opposite direction toward my desk.

Everyone had already left for lunch, so the office was quiet. It was just past midnight back home. I frantically read articles to understand the results and the reaction of the country. All I could think about was how I wished I could be sharing the moment with my fellow Americans. Despite the distance, I could feel their spirit and pride. I wanted to announce to Singapore that I was, indeed, American.

Chapter 18
Sorry, Mom

My four siblings, my mom and her dog were waiting for me at the bottom of the baggage claim. My brother held a poster board he'd made to welcome me back for my two-week visit. Every detail made me feel at home: seeing airport travelers who were bigger in size than me, hearing English, instead of Singlish, on the news, my mom's dog licking me on the cheek. At home, I no longer felt alone.

Brisk air across my chest physically reminded me of November in Ohio. Thanksgiving had always been one of the most celebrated holidays in my family, and we usually held it at the local Italian club. My grandma and grandpa accepted greetings from everyone as they entered, but stayed in their seats at the table. My underage cousins ran to the bar for drinks. Everyone returned to the buffet repeatedly and ate excessively. The night eventually ended with my uncles singing Journey on a karaoke box.

"It is so good to have you home again so soon," my aunt said, hugging me when I entered.

"Yes, all because of Ariana's wedding," I laughed. "Definitely don't expect twice in one year again. It's a long trip."

I did the standard round of hellos and took my seat at our table with a plate of antipasto and multiple bottles of red wine in the middle.

"Hilary, why aren't you drinking?" my cousin Gianna demanded, standing over me with another bottle.

"I'm so dehydrated from the flight. I just need water," I said, smiling.

"Oh, come on. Here, just a little." She poured some wine into the glass in front of me, but I didn't touch it.

"Go get food. It's ready," she said.

"I'll wait for everyone else to go. I'm in no rush."

She looked over at the buffet table and back at me again, but avoided my eyes. "Okay. So Singapore is good?" she asked.

"Yes, it's great. I mean, it's hard. There are a lot of things changing now because of the financial crisis, but we'll push through."

"Yeah, yeah, I'm sure. Cool. Well, tell me more later. I'm going to get me some stuffing!" And she walked away.

The holidays just weren't the same. I felt separated from my relatives even when I was with them. The questions they asked about my life abroad were close to verbatim from my first trip home: How is it? Do you like it? When are you coming home? It was as if the world was ending because I wasn't in Columbus, Ohio. In reality, not much had changed. My cousin Gianna was still in school, my Aunt Maria was still teaching, and Grandpa still went to church every Sunday. Meanwhile, I was desperate to find someone to talk to who could understand my experience. As a result, I called Katie.

"Hi-ra-ri!" she said when she answered the phone. This was the way the Japanese way pronounced my name, and we often joked about it.

"Ka-tie!"

"How are you, my love?"

I told her about Thanksgiving.

"That's normal, Hil," she assured me. "Don't worry. I sometimes feel the same way too, even though I wasn't even there as long as you. They love you and are doing the best they know."

"Yeah, you're right," I said, still unsettled.

"Americans are so fat! It was one of the first things I noticed!"

I threw my head back in laughter. "Yes! It was ridiculous on the flight. No one could fit in the aisles. Now I understand why seats are so much smaller in Singapore." I once saw a ride in Japan with a sign posted that read: "If Japanese, six people can board. If American, three people can board."

"What else have you noticed?" she asked.

"Now, this was weird. The other day, I saw someone drop her purse at the store, and everything fell out onto the floor. I hesitated to help her. I tried to not even look at her at first. This is so Japanese! I guess because I didn't want her to lose face?"

Katie laughed. "You're brainwashed!"

"I know!"

We spoke a little longer before she had to go, reminiscing about Krabi and our easy life in Singapore. Laughing with her and talking about the privileged life of the expatriate made me relax and not worry so much.

While home, I reached out to John to talk, since the time zones didn't require us to arrange a detailed schedule. I was lying on the old white couch in my mom's living room while she cleaned for the out of town guests. Outside a November gray sky kept the afternoon dark. I nuzzled underneath my blanket. It was the first time John and I had heard each other's voices since Chicago. Waiting moments before his call, I fidgeted with the phone. If I could trust anyone to be inquisitive, it'd be him.

"Hey, Hilary," he began with his deep but soft voice. Instantly, nostalgia took over and I imagined myself lying in my college bed during our endless long-distance phone conversations.

"I saw your pictures from Hong Kong and that Asian wedding. They were so cool," he said. "Didn't you feel weird at the wedding? You were mixed in with a bunch of Asians."

I laughed, "Yeah, that's what my life is like every day now. Other than my American friend Viktor, I rarely see white people. And Viktor is of Asian descent too!"

"Wow, I'd miss talking about American stuff. Isn't that hard?

"Sometimes," I said. "But most of the time, it's fun. It kind of gives me an excuse to not do things perfectly — and to make mistakes."

"How do you mean? I would think they'd expect the American to do things right."

"Sure, but they understand that I am still learning their culture. They don't expect me to know everything." I told him the story of my first department meeting where I had made that comment and my boss had indirectly scolded me.

"That makes sense," John said.

"It's intriguing, because what happens is that it creates an environment where I feel safe to constantly try and try, whether I fail or not. In the end, I usually do things better and faster than I ever expected." I was sitting up with excitement now.

"It really sounds like you are learning a lot, Hilary."

"I am."

"And what's this about you being on *The Today Show* during the Beijing Olympics? First of all, that is incredible you could attend the Olympics."

"Yes, it was incredible. How'd you know? Did you see my Facebook photos?"

"Yep."

"Right, well *The Today Show* was there, but no one in Asia knows what it is or who the hosts are. Also, it's not Chinese culture to want to be on TV. So the crowd was almost empty!"

"Strange, I've never thought about that before."

"Totally. I didn't either until I saw it. My friend dared me, so I got up on his shoulders to get in the background, right behind Meredith Vieira, with the Bird's Nest behind me."

John was laughing on the other end of the line.

"I called my mom and told her to turn on *The Today Show*. She just started screaming."

He laughed, "Oh, your mom. I can imagine. So how'd you get the photo?"

"Would you believe she had the common sense to grab her camera and take a picture?"

"That is awesome."

"Yeah, a smart move by mom."

Our laughter slowly subsided.

"So what about your personal life, Hil? Have you been . . ." he paused. "Are you seeing anyone?"

I broke out in an anxious giggle. "Seeing anyone? Have you seen what my schedule is like?"

"I was just asking."

"John, I hope you know that was never something I even wanted out of my life in Singapore." I did think of Peter, though, but the dynamic of that relationship just seemed so unsustainable.

"Well, please know I'd be there in a heartbeat to visit if not for my situation." I knew he was referring to his girlfriend.

"And I'd equally be excited to show you around," I said. I didn't like talking about her, so I never asked how she was. "I should probably go help my mom now."

"Send my best to Ariana and have fun. I guess I'll just talk to you when I talk to you."

I held the phone in my hand for a moment after I hung up. It was weird to see John's name as a contact. I loved that he understood what I was going through and that he cared. I still thought of him often and had this fantasy, although far from fair, of him waiting for me to come home. Had I made a mistake giving up John's love for Asia? Like a mother's piece of advice that lingers in the back of your mind, this question lingered in mine. Yet still, I couldn't wholeheartedly answer it.

"Hilary! What are you doing on the couch?" my mom yelled as she walked up the stairs. "Do you have any idea how much we have to do? The bachelorette party, rehearsal dinner, and wedding are all this week!"

I was still looking at my phone. "Sorry, Mom."

She came over and stood in front of me. "Who were you on the phone with just now? It wasn't John, was it?" I rubbed my eyes, giving her the answer. She sighed. "Really? I'm telling you, you need to cut off communication with him and let him move on with his life."

"I know, but Mom, you don't understand. There's no reason we shouldn't be friends," I started to explain, but frustration instantly overwhelmed. I sighed. "Never mind. I'll feel better when I get home. I don't have to deal with the situation in Asia."

Hilary Corna

"Don't call Singapore home. Please, Hilary."

I looked up at her standing with a broom in one hand, a coffee in the other. "Sorry, Mom."

Events packed the remainder of the two weeks fully. I attended my five-year high school reunion but stood in the corner as others played pool, struggling to carry on a conversation with my old friends. As the maid of honor, Elise planned a bachelorette party for Ariana. As a bridesmaid, and sister, I should have helped but blamed the time zones and business trips for my lack of involvement. Instead, I got to just partake in the festivities.

Ariana's wedding was flawless. As she graced the chapel aisle, my chest filled with an overwhelming amount of joy. Behind the joy, I sensed that my siblings were moving on without me. Elise had graduated from college and was starting her career in the army. James fell head over heels for his new girlfriend while finishing up his final year in college. Ariana was in love.

When I got on my flight back to Singapore, I received a text from my mom that said, "On way to get a Christmas tree with Dan. Will miss you this Christmas Hilary but know that my goal driven daughter has her plan to follow. It is important that our goals can be met."

I leaned my head back against the headrest. My mom's encouragement always helped me keep my goals in sight, but I wondered how long I might stay in Singapore. There was still so much more I wanted to see and to learn, but what I really wanted was someone to share it with.

Chapter 19
A Student Again

America was changing and so was Toyota. A couple of weeks after I returned from home, they took away our green tea.

"Where is the green tea?" I asked our tea lady.

"Ah! No more. Green tea is gone. Only for guests. You know this one box cost SG$8. Same size box of Chinese tea is SG$1!"

I stood there shocked as she walked out of the pantry, wondering how the company could think that cutting a green tea expense would really help their bottom line.

I immediately returned to my desk and e-mailed Viktor: "They freaking took away the green tea! What the heck?! Do they really think that's going to help?!"

His reply was simple: "You work for a Japanese company."

Soon after, HR had informed us of a new policy for limiting office supplies, only ordering based on need, which required us to print, complete, and submit a paper form. They only processed the order forms once a month, so I would have to borrow supplies from others when I ran out.

I didn't know it at the time, but December 8–10 would be my last days in the Philippines. The purpose of our final business trip of 2008 was to follow up on TMI's activity and help to the team plan for 2009. Although brief, the trip was busy.

After the incident with Gio-san, I tried to be extra courteous and official to make up for my lack of professionalism. Kimura-san hosted the management while I paid more attention to Anna and Gio. We encouraged them to continue kaizen and keep communication. We'd have to wait until the new year to receive direction from Hamada-san.

The daily volatility of the financial markets was making every company reevaluate their priorities, including Toyota. Hamada-san had brought new ideas to the company, and it was our responsibility as loyal staff to trust his guidance and decisions.

One decision was to move our kaizen activity from the sales division to the service division. This was a significant act by management because it completely restructured the kaizen leaders' roles and responsibilities. It was only because of Kimura-san that I found out the reason for this change: a push from the Japan headquarters, Toyota Motor Corporation (TMC). Their organization was structured this way, and they wanted ours to replicate it for the purpose of streamlining all the offices.

We were informed that RDSD would be disabled almost overnight and its projects reallocated to other departments.

"These massive changes in the company are almost once in a lifetime," Kimura-san told me. "You are lucky to be seeing the process as the company goes through it."

Fortunately, I was on Hamada-san's good side. He liked the work I did in Toyota Makati, my perspective and respect for the Japanese style. He didn't want me to move to the service division, but in Toyota, you are associated with either service or sales. It is rare to move, but if you do, it is almost impossible to move back because you become an expert in that area, thus moving up in the leadership and organization. More importantly, you lose your *senpai*. A senpai is usually your boss or someone older than you who act as a guardian or mentor. They're not assigned, but form organically. Sato-san and Kimura-san were both senpais to me.

When you switch to a different division, your senpai has a harder time supporting you, and you risk flattening your career growth within the company. I was the perfect example of this phenomenon. Kimura-san had looked after me for the past fifteen months. He made sure I got the recognition I deserved in terms of reporting opportunities and promotions. His position would remain in the sales division. He wanted me to work under him in his new position, handling operations for Indonesia and

Vietnam, but the top management wouldn't agree to it; they were under the impression that Kimura-san favored me.

I was adamant to stay with kaizen, even if that meant not having Kimura-san as a boss. I was also looking for a new project where I could start over fresh and apply what I had learned in the Philippines from the beginning. The Philippines project had become disheveled from mistakes, obstacles, and the changing environment. On top of it all, the real problem had never been resolved: top management at TMI did not feel the urgency to improve.

Within only one year, I felt like I had learned so much, yet still learned so little. I was only beginning to see the real meaning of kaizen. I remembered Anna and Gio. They were the ones that mattered. They were the reason I wanted to continue working in kaizen.

Every time I reported back to headquarters in Singapore, I would see the entry-level staff plugging away at their jobs. These people generally reported to the office, sat at their desks all day preparing reports with forecasted figures, and verbalized these reports to their bosses; the next month, they did it all over again. Their bosses were tough, too, fitting more of the Japanese boss stereotype than any of the kaizen bosses. They dealt with more urgent deadlines than the kaizen teams.

In addition to the de-motivating deadlines, I couldn't imagine staring at those gray table inserts every day. Or running between meetings just to be assigned another paper to output, constantly being put in your place by top management—it didn't surprise me that our office struggled with a low retention rate. The jobs did not energize people compared to conducting kaizen in dealerships.

Kaizen was dynamic and enlivening. Every dealership brought new problems and new circumstances, not allowing cut-and-paste solutions but inspiring creative ones. Every project was different—the way the dealership looked, the personalities of the staff, the culture in that particular region. It wasn't just about how many cars the salespeople were selling but *how* they were selling them. Kaizen wasn't just a game of numbers.

Despite the announcement that RDSD would be disbanded, a few of us knew where we'd be relocated. Unlike Western companies, Toyota does not fire during reorganization but works to find each person a new role.

I'd often told Kimura-san of my desire to continue studying kaizen, but he informed me that Hamada-san wanted me to stay in the sales division. "I don't want to lose good talent," he told Kimura-san. There was still some negotiating to do.

Kimura-san initiated multiple discussions with Suzuki-san, the GM of the Philippines area operation. He found out that Suzuki-san wanted me on his team to help apply kaizen to their supply and demand operation in the Philippines — improving the matching of car model and specification production with the right amount demanded by the market. Aware of the challenges and the persistent obstacle of top management, Kimura-san did not recommend that I take the assignment. Unfortunately, the authority did not fall in his lap but required a collective decision by all management.

The staff is not usually involved in this process, but I actively chose to be a part of it. Americans, especially young ones, are more apt than Asians to voice their concerns or opinions about their future in a company.

Weeks passed. Every time I saw the bosses in the office, I struggled to read their mannerisms, but they acted normal, revealing nothing of the matter. I had to consciously stop shaking my leg.

I had three options: I could join the Philippines supply and demand kaizen team. Under Kimura-san, I could apply kaizen to the Indonesia and Vietnam area operations. Lastly, I could switch to the service division on the thirteenth floor and continue to conduct kaizen. Top management wanted me to do the first, Kimura-san wanted me to do the second, and I wanted to do the third.

When Kimura-san returned from the meeting with Hayashi-san, he sent me a text message to meet him downstairs for coffee. This would become our standard way to keep in touch, because once my department manager changed, there really was no reason for me to communicate with Kimura-san anymore.

"I'm afraid they will not take care of you. You know this, right?" he said. "You will have to look after yourself, and I'm not sure doing so, you will get you very far."

I understood what he was saying, but nothing seemed more unattractive than leaving kaizen. I wanted to learn more about kaizen. I wanted to understand why my Japanese advisors could do it so easily when even the smartest of technical experts within the company and around the world struggled with the concept. I wanted to understand why my teachers asked me, "How do you do it? How do you earn the trust of gemba?" I didn't know how I was successful at it. I needed to study more, but it would be much more difficult without the support of my senpai and the big bosses giving me opportunity to do so. Kimura-san was trying to tell me this in his own words.

Later that week, I was sitting at my desk responding to some e-mails from Francis and Gio when I heard a voice behind me. "Hirari-san, please come with me." It was Hayashi-san, the senior vice president. I jumped out of my seat before he finished saying my name.

"Hai," I responded frantically. It was quite unusual for an SVP to approach a staff member at her desk. All communication between these two levels of employees happened primarily in the meeting rooms.

We took a seat in the Wish conference room because it was the only one open. Wish was a sedan Toyota model made just for Asia.

We sat next to each other, also strange for the difference in organization level. Usually, we would sit across the table, but Hayashi-san seemed friendly and approachable.

"Tell me what you would like to do, Hirari," he asked me. I deflated in relief.

"Thank you for taking the time to ask me, Hayashi-san." I told him I was interested in continuing to learn kaizen. His crossed legs and arms showed me that it was not what he wanted to hear.

"*Maa*, okay." He nodded with eyes half closed, thinking.

After multiple attempts at convincing me to stay in the sales division, Hayashi-san sat back and rubbed his eyes. I wasn't getting my point across. Hinting and beating around the bush works if you have a common language, but it wasn't working here.

"I do not want to work in area operations," I began. "And to tell you the truth, I would have to leave the company if the top management forced me to work in area operations." I sat up with a strong back, even though this was a very risky thing to say.

His facial expression didn't change. Neither did his body language. He sat there motionless. "*Maa*, I understand," he said. "Please, just reconsider and let me know."

"Of course," I said, bowing my head. "Thank you, Hayashi-san."

He stood from his chair. I followed. He bowed and left the room. I bowed as he exited. Then I fell back into my chair, hands over my eyes in disbelief. Such an approach by top management was unheard of in Toyota. I knew, though, it was a good sign. They would never put forth so much effort for a staff member they didn't want to keep.

I followed up with Hayashi-san the next day with a brief e-mail informing him of my unchanged decision but thanking him for his humble interest in my future with the company.

When I told Kimura-san about my meeting with Hayashi-san, he raised his eyebrows and smirked. He hadn't known top management planned to approach me, but their action illustrated the value they placed on me. He shared with me that through the communication, he could sense the decision neared an end, and that the fate of my career was really up to the top management. "We've done all we could," he said.

A few days later, Kimura-san came to my desk.

"Coffee?" he asked.

"Sure!" I said. It was mid-afternoon, and I needed a jolt.

We exited the elevators and then Centennial Tower. As soon as the sun hit our faces, he looked at me with a smile.

"It's confirmed."

I stopped. "Confirmed? What's confirmed?"

"The management just informed me that you've been confirmed to conduct kaizen in the service division. Tanaka-san will be your new boss as of January first."

"Oh, thank you, Kimura-san!" I reached out to give him a hug.

Tanaka-san was the kind of Japanese boss that made you smile. His expressions were as animated as a manga cartoon. Like Kimura-san, he was often described as "not your typical Japanese." You could identify him from far away because of his distinguished laugh echoing through the open-air office. With most of his assignment overseas, other managers referred to Tanaka-san as a traveling Toyota manager. His worked primarily with the service area of the dealership operations, which covers the main workshop procedures for handling the customer and the vehicle. He had no experience in sales kaizen, but he was willing to take on the challenge.

Before HR confirmed that I would work under Tanaka-san, I had to ask him directly for permission to join the Dealer Operations Kaizen Department, the DOKD.

Rubbing sweaty palms together, I asked myself multiple times if I was making a mistake. The decision would change my entire working environment, and I wasn't sure yet if it was for the better.

I put off making the call for nearly an entire day. After lunch and a last-minute word of advice from Viktor, I knew what I needed to do. I walked to the pantry near the nineteenth-floor meeting rooms, where no one would interrupt my call.

"*Konnichiwa*, Tanaka-san. You can talk, now, okay?" I began, leaning against the wall.

"Oh! Hirari-chan! *Konnichiwa!*" He exclaimed. "*Hai, douzo.*" He allowed me to go ahead.

"Yes, thank you," I proceeded nervously. "As you know, top management wants me to stay in the sales area. I am grateful for their concern, but this is not of interest to me." I moved over to a chair and sat down. "From my experience in the Philippines, I feel I have only begun to understand kaizen. I want to learn more. If you will allow, I would like to move to DOKD and work with you to study more." I ended and then took a deep, silent breath.

"What does Hamada-san want for you?" Tanaka-san asked in a more serious than usual tone. Although he already knew, his question came out of respect and protocol.

"He would like me to work on Philippines supply and demand kaizen with Suzuki-san, but I already informed him that it was not what I wanted."

"You have a strong intention to stay with kaizen," he confirmed, his voice low.

"Yes, I do."

"What about Kimura-san? Does he know?"

"Yes, and he supports my decision to stay with kaizen."

Suddenly, Tanaka-san was his normal, cheery self again. "Well, good! I would like to have you on the team!" He was practically yelling. I jumped up and threw my arms out like I was in a Broadway show. But before I could get any farther into my celebration, he said, "You know it is a hard time for Toyota right now. If you join me, I want you to stay at least four years."

I nearly choked, and my arms fell. "Four years?"

"Yes, four years. You will be a student again in DOKD. You will spend time studying first."

"I understand. Yes, I want to stay and learn."

"Okay, please inform Kimura-san of the final decision. He will inform top management."

Within seconds, I had made the decision and, like America and Toyota, began to ride my own wave of change.

Chapter 20
Carmen Sandiego

It was that time year again, time for the company's annual Dinner & Dance. The Singapore streets blinked with neon-colored Christmas lights, shaped into life-sized animals and Chinese cartoon characters. Singapore loves Christmas. The country gets all the same holiday paraphernalia as the United States, except for real Christmas trees. I missed the smell of pine, and its absence made it feel less like Christmas.

During the season, the majority of Americans families in Singapore would either travel home to the States or somewhere else for a beach holiday. There were very few single and young Americans that remained in Singapore, so Viktor and I went to a Christmas party together. Instead of snow, there was a downpour of rain, and everyone agreed when I commented, "The rain sets the mood better than if it had been sunny and humid!"

The following weekend was the D&D. I served on the planning committee that year, excited to make up for my lack of participation the year before. The theme chosen: Eastern Triads versus Western Mafia. For the party, employees could choose between dressing up like an Eastern Triad (an Indian mobster, Japanese *yakuza*, etc.) or a Western Mafia member (Al Capone-esque).

Singaporeans absolutely love to dress in costume, and their creativity always shocked me. The group that worked on the India project dressed as the Indian mafia with floor-length black getups, dark sunglasses, and a red line down their foreheads. Some even wore stockings over their head. Most of the ladies wore ultra-sexy black dresses, as if they were the pimptresses of the mafia men.

As usual, everything was tame until the talent show began. Chinese, Singaporean, Japanese, and Indian dancers all dressed in belly-dancing outfits lined the stage. Among them was Hayashi-san, wearing pale blue Indian pants that were scrunched at the ankles, belly-dancing bells around his waist, a sequined purple bra, and a women's wig of curly blonde hair reaching down to his waist.

I wish my sister had been there to see it.

I kept asking everyone just to make sure, "*That* is Hayashi-san?" They confirmed it with a nod and a straight face. It reminded me of the extreme shock I'd felt the year before when I saw the manager in his swan costume.

The planning committee had our own costume. We dressed as Singaporean cops who were maintaining the two crowds of triads and mafia. It made me feel like I was participating in a mild way.

The funniest part about Hayashi-san's performance was that, when he finished, he returned to sit at his table, still dressed in a belly-dancing outfit while the rest of top management wore black suits. He sat between the EVP of the service division—my new boss come January—and my old boss, Hamada-san. They sat calmly, ate, and conversed as usual.

The party ended a great success, and I took pride in partaking with the local staff in the planning, but looked forward to even more. Viktor and I were leaving the next morning for a Christmas trip to Malaysia.

For our first dinner, Viktor and I ate noodles at a Malaysian outdoor food market that smelled of fish and chili oil. We met a pleasant Irish couple and struck up conversation about generational travel. "You're young and are entitled to travel," the wife said to us across the round yellow plastic table. "We are old, and some think we are not entitled."

It was something I had not thought about before: the perspective of travel of the generations before me. It made me appreciate my own generation, for its flexibility, and my mother, for supporting me in all the crazy endeavors I had attempted, including travel.

"If we were all the same, the world would be a boring place," her husband added.

A good portion of our Malaysia trip included trying new foods. The country was home to one of my favorite lunch dishes called yong tau fu, a soup of steamed vegetables. The best foods can be enjoyed at hidden local shops. I struggled not to stare at their cooking conditions, but I decided to just ignore the hand-held ingredients and crusty pots and simply enjoy the best yong tau fu I'd ever tasted.

Viktor and I also treated ourselves to US$10 full-body massages. The Malaysian masseuse gently washed our feet before they guided us with slow steps upstairs. They held the door for us to enter, serene massage rooms with incense burning and classical music playing inside.

After our massage, we strolled into a small, local bar full of Malaysian college students and sat down for a drink. Natural of Viktor, he struck up a conversation with the young adults and before we knew it, we were up on stage singing American music with them. I love performing on stage, so I wasn't shy, but the kids singing with us made me even more comfortable. They were so friendly and so normal. They treated us like friends instead of foreigners. We sang, laughed in shock at how many American songs they knew, and goofed off during songs that we had no hope of being able to sing. We screamed together for one of my all-time favorites, "What's Up?" by 4 Non Blondes. I had a hard time giving up the microphone to leave, but we had a six-hour drive from Malacca to Penang the next morning and needed to get some sleep.

The next morning, we loaded up Viktor's Lexus and continued our journey passing flourishing green jungles and sweet pineapple farms along the way. The limestone cliff sides of Southeast Asia never ceased to leave me in awe of their beauty and power. The tips of the limestone reflected light from the sun, while the stone's crevices hid their true depths.

After our six-hour drive, we arrived at our Holiday Inn, which welcomed us for Christmas with nonalcoholic champagne. We made it just in time to see the sun set on the beach and ran to take pictures to show our families in mock of their cold weather.

The next day, we basked in the Malaysian sun until we couldn't take the heat any longer. Later, we explored the island of Penang on a rented motorbike. I had never ridden one, but Viktor had promised to show me how. I relished the feeling of fresh air across my face, and the sight of long, lush greens hanging over my head, while driving through the depths of the green jungle and mountainside. You could smell the life in the humidity. I let go of all my thoughts and concerns from the year and just felt the air, reminding me of my Jeep — the one I had sold to make all this happen. If I ever felt overwhelmed in high school, I'd take the top off of the Jeep and drive. There was no other feeling like it.

It was Christmas Eve. Viktor and I went to dinner at a restaurant in an old colonial house that had belonged to a British general. The home was stunning; it stood tall and white with intricate, regal architecture. We were taken aback by the "Let's Party" gift pack given to us as we sat down. It was filled with noise poppers and a party hat, as if we were celebrating New Year's instead of Christmas. After dinner, we decided we should try a night on the town in Penang and ended up in a bar called "Slippery Señoritas," packed full of local partiers. There was a band on stage dressed in red and black, and seconds before the clock struck midnight, they broke out in a countdown.

"What is this? New Year's?" I screamed over the music to Viktor. We just laughed and counted along with them.

The next morning at Christmas breakfast, we watched as a crowd of people bustled to the beach and realized that Santa was with them, playing games with the children. He was far from round, and his skin was dark, but it did lighten my heart and make me think of my family back home. I wanted to be with them, but since I couldn't, I tried to make the best of the situation by enjoying the hot weather and Viktor's company. I knew he was facing the same struggle; we didn't say it directly, but I know it helped us both to share the holiday with someone.

On Christmas afternoon, we spent three hours at the spa. Not growing up with much, I was still getting used to having money to treat myself, relishing in accomplishments, and tried to convince myself that I deserved it.

On Christmas night, Viktor and I went for yet another mouthwatering seafood dinner. We ordered juicy scallops and lobster that melted in our mouths. We ate steamed white fish served with the head, eyes, and tail. Everything was fresh, only hours from the fishing boat and sea.

We played Uno at the beach bar and, a few drinks later, we found ourselves making snow angels in the warm Malaysian sand and dancing under a tiki-bar roof.

On the drive home, I stared out the car window at the vast, green landscape. In wanderlust, a memory came to mind. As a child, I had always loved the show *Where in the World Is Carmen Sandiego?* I'd watch as the antagonists scanned their maps looking for Carmen, and I cheered for her, hoping she would not get caught.

I was beginning to understand why I was always on Carmen's side. Traveling had always fascinated me—the new places, people, and cultures. But I had my own map to navigate. I was an adventurer, curious by nature, and I sought to improve myself by learning about what other people do and think. Maybe I had, in fact, been a global citizen since birth, just like Carmen.

Chapter 21
He was Asking About You

"Congratulations on your promotion to Senior Executive Officer, Hilary," Tanaka-san said.

Hilary Corna

The company holds a ceremony annually for the group of promoted team members. It was across the street at the convention center — short, brief, and traditional. There was no coffee, and no food. We sat in chairs as a HR staff called our name to walk across a small stage and accept a certificate from our EVP, Hamada-san. Then we reported back to work.

Only two significant changes took place. One, my title now had "Senior" in it instead of just "Executive Officer," which seemed silly to me as I had only worked for the company for sixteen months. Two, my pay increased, minimally, by about SG$200 or US$150.

Yet my promotion created a little controversy because some colleagues didn't believe I was worthy of it yet. A lot of debate occurred in the company about how to balance the rate of promotion with incentives for employees to decrease their attrition rate. Toyota was one of the lowest-paying multinational corporations in Singapore, and the automotive industry is not as attractive as finance. Young Singaporean professionals are very judgmental about careers, possessions, and status quo, making Toyota an unfavorable place to work.

No one said anything, but I could sense some tension in the office after my promotion. I was now at the same level as a forty-year-old team member, as well as someone who had served two more years than me. I sensed some of my coworkers thought I was favored since I was Caucasian, so it was hard to feel proud of the promotion. I knew I had worked hard at TMI, but I felt guilty.

Despite my strong objective to stay with kaizen, I was apprehensive about the new organization change. I reported to the first official workday of the year, but this time to the thirteenth floor instead of the nineteenth. Tanaka-san introduced me formally to Yabuuchi-san, the EVP of the service division, second in command under the President.

He also introduced me to my new department members, Alan and Alvin. Alan was a Chinese Malaysian who commuted across the border of Malaysia and Singapore each morning. He was tall for an Asian and wore stylish rectangular glasses. Alvin was a handsome Indonesian who had migrated to Singapore with his wife only a few years prior. They were both friendly but didn't say much.

The first couple of months in my new position were very slow. DOKD met with the management to discuss the direction of each department and activity. They call this a *hoshin*, or annual plan. Until the *hoshin* is completed, it's difficult to move forward with anything, and since our department was new, it required a substantial amount of input from all parties involved from pricing to technical support to marketing. The financial crisis had run a circle around the company and was challenging us in ways we'd never expected.

118

The new seating arrangement in this department made me even more uncomfortable. In RDSD, I sat furthest from Kimura-san and faced the door. He couldn't access me easily, and I could see people walking in the entrance. Now, in DOKD, my back was to the door, and I sat right next to my boss. I had to be even more attentive of the work I was doing on my computer, to how loudly I laughed. One day Alvin sent me an email commenting on a colleague who sat across from me that was hung over. After laughing out loud, my friend shushed me as Yabuuchi-san had just returned to his desk.

Even more so, the seating divided Alan and Alvin from the former sales members—Oak and me. Each pair of staff sat on one side of the hopscotch line with our backs to each other. As a result, we would rarely speak. This was especially challenging in the beginning as we didn't know anything about each other.

During a meeting a few weeks into the New Year, Tanaka-san, Yoshida-san, and I sat discussing the year's projects. I used the opportunity to recommend an idea to them.

"Tanaka-san, maybe it would be good to do something together as a department—like a barbeque or something."

"Maa," he sighed. "Let's discuss."

His evident disinterest annoyed me because I could sense confusion and even some misunderstandings happening between the staff, but the problem was very simple—no one really knew each other. Yet, everyone wanted to.

The process to get the *hoshin* approved took around six weeks. Managers made drafts, shared them among other departments seeking input and revisions, and then Tanaka-san approved at his level. After two to three more revisions, the hoshin was submitted to Yabuuchi-san for final approval. He was never satisfied with it on the first round. This was always very frustrating because he'd change only minor words—from *should* to *could*, for example. I didn't understand the need for such details in a planning paper.

In the meantime, the staff had to fill time before we knew what our projects would be for the year. In a half-day meeting, I shared with Alan and Alvin our work in the Philippines, which I was still following up on with Kimura-san, despite the organization change.

When an American study abroad group visited Singapore later that month, I was thrilled to host them and interact with Americans again. The students were on a three-week program called "Doing Business in the Pacific Rim" and would visit offices and take production tours in Singapore, Australia, and Vietnam—a lot to see and understand in such a short time.

Kimura-san reached out to corporate planning on my behalf to inquire about the students visiting Toyota. Unfortunately, there was not enough time to for Toyota to prepare.

As a result, I helped the students make contacts with other corporations and businesses where I had connections. I spoke to Viktor about the possibility of them visiting his office.

I stood tall and proud as I greeted the hot, disheveled undergrad students in the lobby.

"You really have adapted," one professor commented, impressed by my respectful bow.

"Sorry! It's just become second nature," I said. "Please, follow me."

I ushered the students upstairs to the 40th floor to meet the president and vice president of the company's Asian headquarters, who ended up dedicating their entire Monday morning to the group of twenty students.

Kimura-san had graciously approved me to spend the morning with the students, and Viktor had reserved their finest boardroom with the newest technology, and even ordered a spread of croissants and bagels for the students. Viktor began a presentation on the company, sharing their goals in Asia and future plans. I sat back, listening just like a student, in awe at the challenges the company had ahead. The professors and I were equally blown away with Viktor's knowledge and professionalism.

Unfortunately, I was disappointed in a large number of the students. Many of them arrived at the headquarters in unironed khakis, loafers with no socks, and sunglasses on. The ladies were equally guilty, some of them wearing short low-cut summer dresses. A couple of the students in particular fell asleep in the middle of the presentation, and it wasn't due to jet lag. Apparently, a good portion of them had celebrated their arrival in Asia with a night out.

I was utterly embarrassed and turned my head back to the front of the room, trying to maintain my composure even though I was seconds away from standing up and shaking the ones that were sleeping. That would have been my American side pushing through.

These kids had so much opportunity in front of them to inquire, to learn, to expand their horizons, to network internationally, and they were acting as if they were back in North Carolina. I was furious with their lack of respect, and I was ready to scold them like a mother, but I refrained. Instead, I just planned on mentioning something to the professors. It wasn't my place to say anything, and even if I did, the students would probably get defensive

Viktor did share with me later that he noticed a blatant lack of interest and respect, but there were some students who were very involved and took a lot from the visit, for which I was grateful. Overall, the student's visit was successful, but I wanted it to be the best.

My disappointment continued into the night when I brought some of my colleagues from Toyota to meet the students. Meeting Singaporeans provided them with a rare opportunity to understand local culture from people their age. The students just bombarded them with questions like, "Where's the best place to go out?" and "Is it legal for us to buy beer here?" I neglected to invite the students out with me as planned and instead, I left promptly to meet Alexandre and some of my other French friends, alone.

The rains were terrible that month, pouring down and creating a suffocating humidity. When I arrived to the bar, I chugged half a beer and slammed it on the table in frustration. "I can't believe these kids! I wanted to show off Singapore. I feel like I failed."

"Oh, don't give yourself such a hard time. The students probably took more from it than you think," Alexandre said.

"Definitely, but it just perfectly represents what concerns me so much about American youth. They know so little about Asia."

"It's true. What's the percentage of Americans with passports, anyways?" he asked.

I rolled my eyes. "Something like twenty percent."

His eyes opened. "Outrageous, Hilary. Do they know nothing about today's world economy?" He asked in a sarcastic, yet truthfully concerned tone.

"It's funny you say that. The one class I always wanted to take in either high school or college was Global History, but it either wasn't offered or American History was recommended over it. So I never took either."

"Wow, that's a prerequisite in middle school for us. How old are these kids?" Alexandre asked.

"Like nineteen or twenty," I said with head bowed.

"Well hell, that is pretty young. They're reaching out, Hil, doing something different just like you. Gotta give them that."

"Yeah." I thought of what I had been doing at that age — finishing over two of Japanese studies and preparing for a semester study abroad. But my case was rare.

Still, I couldn't help my concern for my peers. In the past, Americans didn't need to understand Asia. We had economic control. But with the financial crisis, things were changing rapidly, and the West was losing authority of the global economy. I predicted that everyone would suffer if my generation didn't begin to understand Asia more deeply than just sushi and martial arts.

About a week after the students left, President Barack Obama gave his inauguration speech. He accepted his position at 9:00 p.m. in Singapore and 9:00 a.m. on the East Coast of the United States. The skyline lit up the black Singapore sky out my window, with Chinatown's lights below. Even after submitting my small absentee ballot in the mail slot at the Singapore post office, I still felt detached from the events in the West. I wanted to watch the speech with another American, but I could not find anyone so I ended up streaming it live from my computer at home. As the night grew later, I fell asleep. My 7:00 a.m. meeting the next morning consumed my mind.

Soon after the inauguration, I was on my way to Sydney for my first holiday of the year. I was visiting my friend Steve, who was John's old roommate from Chicago. I had known Steve since John and I first met, and I wanted to flaunt my accomplishments, mostly hoping that he'd tell John later.

Steve and I had a blast sun-tanning and people-watching at Bondi and other famous beaches. I learned there is a hole in the ozone layer above Sydney, so we had to be extra cautious of the sun. We visited koalas and kangaroos at the zoo and partied at some of the best clubs I'd ever seen. I had a hard time with the people, however. The ones I met were not very friendly to strangers. It seemed to be a very cliquey kind of public, definitely not a place where I felt comfortable striking up a conversation with someone at the bar.

"You can't just introduce yourself to people here," Steve explained. "You have to get introduced by another. Then, you are welcome to join the discussion."

Although living in Australia is very expensive, the way of life is marvelous. Everyone spends a lot of time outdoors. There are over seventy beaches in Sydney. The view is gorgeous standing from the cliffs overlooking the sand and deep blue waters. There are spectacular restaurants in any neighborhood you choose, and niche styles in boutique shops. There were no commercial chains in sight.

Yet I was almost offended when I saw the portion sizes in Sydney. My sandwich was literally the size of my head. People criticize Americans for eating too much, but in Australia, the portions were significantly larger. I'd bring my leftovers home for Steve and his roommates.

On one of my last nights, Steve and I stayed up late talking, and I wasn't going to pass up the chance to ask Steve about John and me.

"Well, if you weren't in Singapore, would you be with John?" he asked.

"Of course," I responded without hesitation. "Absolutely." But, my response to Steve was purely emotional. I had no real idea what life would have been like had I stayed in Ohio. Honestly, it was childish of me to say anything.

"John and his girlfriend fight all the time, Hilary, and have almost broken up several times. I was talking to John last week, and he was asking about you."

The thought made me tremble. Why is it that a girl can take such a little comment to heart? John and I weren't exactly on speaking terms; his girlfriend apparently didn't want him talking to me. Why did it make me happy to hear that they were having trouble?

The next day, I sat under a tree overlooking Bondi Beach waiting for Steve to pick me up and take me to the airport. The shade cooled my skin; I'd had enough sun in January to last me a while. The beach was packed with tanned tourists from across the world, as always.

I worked to mentally prepare myself for the adjustment back to work. The uncertainty of my new position on the thirteenth floor made me apprehensive to go back. Not only that, but it had been so nice to hang out with other Caucasians. Yes, the portions were large in Sydney, everything was expensive, and some people were haughty, but I had one thing in common with them that I didn't have in Singapore: our race. And along with that race, similar cultures with similar thought processes, belief systems, and humor. I didn't need to speak slowly, in simpler vocabulary, or struggle to read mannerisms and body language. Life was easier.

Now I'd have to adjust back to the Japanese way of working, the Singaporean way of living—a daily effort to adapt. But that was exactly what I loved so much about life abroad—the daily surprises that kept me stimulated, observing, and thinking. I'd developed new taste buds for food, listened to new rhythms of music and danced to it, and smelled new fragrances of flowers and foliage. I'd even learned to walk, speak, and eat like a lady. Living in my comfort zone in the United States certainly proved easier, but in Singapore, I was growing, and growing faster.

Chapter 22
Yes, No, Ice Cream

"Hilary-san!" Tanaka-san got my attention quickly as he moved from his desk to the side table of our office.

"Hai," I said and immediately stood.

"We would like to send you to India with the TMC kaizen team. Is this okay with you?" he asked, as if I had a choice.

"Of course," I said calmly, although the new assignment made me want to hug him.

"Okay. Maeda-san will tell you more." And just like that, I was involved in the India implementation of e-CRB, Evolutionary Customer Relationship Building.

I sent out an e-mail that afternoon to my family.

> It was announced today that I will for sure be the
> support from Asian headquarters to Japan headquarters
> for India Sales Kaizen operation. A lot of people are
> concerned of the cultural challenges (e.g. working with

Japanese bosses who speak minimal English and are much more strict than even the Japanese bosses here. And being in India.)
   You know what I say? WATCH ME!

Over the past month, I had been traveling to a town called Johor Bahru in Malaysia just over the border from Singapore. Tanaka-san and Yoshida-san wanted me to work on a project until the India assignment came up. February 2009 marked my first business trip for e-CRB to Bangalore, India. Our business routine in India differed from in the Philippines. A driver, Gistto, picked us up every morning from the hotel and took us on our ten mile, but one-hour commute to the dealership. Traffic never wanted to be on our side and there was no hotel closer to the dealership.

   Gistto arrived at the hotel early every morning. A fresh dot of red color called a *bindi* marked the space between his temples, indicating that he had already prayed at the temple that morning before work. There was a small statue of Ganesh at the front of the Innovo. He is one of the most well-known and worshiped deities in the Hindu religion, widely revered as the Remover of Obstacles. Gistto bought white flowers every day to hang like a circular rosary above the Ganesh statue. Out of all of the drivers, he was my favorite. He was polite, always available, and drove safely.

   I'll never forget the day Gistto called in sick, and we had a different driver who ended up running over my colleague's toe and rear-ending a bicyclist.

   The Indians have a saying: "When a Westerner baby learns to drive, the baby says, 'Vroom Vroooooom!' When an Indian baby learns to drive, the baby says, 'Beep! Beep! Beep! Beep!'" In India, people beep their horns going left and right, forward and backward, moving or not moving. I wondered if there was some secret horn language that only they knew. I held my stomach from carsickness before I finally adapted to the speeding and swerving.

   My new dealership, Nandi Toyota, was located on a rural side of Bangalore, in Kerala. I entered the obeya room, overwhelmed to find almost twenty people scattered around. The three huge fans placed in the corners of the room didn't keep people from sweating. There were no windows to the outside, only one that overlooked the service workshop. Different teams had come for three weeks: the technology team from Nagoya, sales and service kaizen operations experts from Nagoya, software support team from Bangkok, and us, the TMAP regional coordinators. I realized immediately that the organization of all of these people was going to be our biggest challenge.

No heads turned as Kom-san and I walked into the obeya room because that would call attention to the obvious: a young white woman had just entered the room. Seeing white people in the city or in rural areas was not common.

However, I was incredibly intimidated by the size of the team, their position, and their breadth of knowledge. In such an important project, the bosses' expectations of me changed, and I wasn't sure I could live up to them.

Since Kom-san was the manager and had been traveling there for a year, he slowly walked me from one corner of the obeya room to the other, introducing me to each team member. One by one, the staff stood up and either shook my hand or bowed, depending on their nationality. They focused their attention on their computers, only taking notice of me when their turn came to be introduced.

"Ohayou Gozaimasu," I said as I greeted the Japanese. To the local Indians, I said, "Namaste," and to the Thais, "Sawadeka."

With a variety of names from Pep to Kumar to Yamaguchi, keeping the names and faces organized in my head was going to be a challenge. The situation reminded me of my first month at TMAP. All the Chinese names had sounded the same.

I worked with the dealership team, which consisted of three local Indians—Mahesh, Deepesh, and Reshma. Mahesh and Deepesh were in service, so I worked more closely with Reshma who was in sales.

Reshma was of average size and height with soft, black hair and round, green eyes. She always wore her hair back and never wore makeup. She was much lighter, a bronze shade, because she protected her skin from the sun daily with a box-shaped navy polyester pantsuit. Reshma was incredibly polite and formal, paid strict attention to authority, and never voiced any complaint.

She wasn't a manager yet, but she had been working for the dealership for seven years and was now the only female involved in the project. Reshma and I became friends almost instantly.

For three weeks, the Indian kaizen team reported the findings of their operation study to visitors from Indonesia, Vietnam, Thailand and Japan. We met daily in a conference room so they could explain every process in the dealership, from filing an insurance application to handling a missed service appointment. The Japanese bosses sometimes shut their eyes, making everyone else think they were sleeping. Kom-san explained to the team that they were actually just focusing and listening.

When the Japanese management and other smokers took their break, Kom-san, Jimmy-san, and I visited a local shop for a fruit juice. There were two small shops outside of the dealership exit. Both were open-air and mere feet away from the dusty highway, making for a loud environment.

Trash covered the dirt ground where the shop's patrons stopped in for refreshment on their walk along the highway. A trash bucket covered in swarming flies sat next to the shop, but tossing trash on the ground still proved easier for locals. I felt a little uncomfortable during my first couple of visits to the shops because of their dirtiness and the other customers, some of whom wore no shoes and carried no belongings with them, but I could control the fear as long as I was aware of my surroundings. In a year and a half, I never had anything stolen.

One of the shops also sold snacks and drinks, including coconut bars, spicy nut mixes, and bottled soda. The storeowner kept a jar of water full of mint leaves to keep flies away. I loved to watch this owner make chai tea. He had a small table that could only hold a skillet and pot. Beneath the stovetop, he protected the little fire from the wind with ripped pieces of aluminum. First, he boiled milk, then added cardamom and other spices. He'd stir the concoction until just right, and then take a ladle and pour half a serving into a sample-size paper cup. The chai tea cost about ten US cents.

The first time I asked for tea, the shop owner could not look me in the eyes. He spoke absolutely no English. The Indian patrons stared pointed from their seats with grins on their faces. He seemed nervous, like a little boy talking to a girl for the first time. I smiled as I waited for the tea, wanting him to know that I welcomed conversation. I felt no prejudice toward his position in India's caste system, and I wanted to give them a positive experience with an American.

Next door, the fruit juice stand stood in bold colors—pink, orange, and green—like a tiki bar. A glass showcase in front burst with local fruit from jackfruit to mosambi, a sweet lime, to podkoam, a blackberry. Watermelon juice remained my favorite. The young workers smiled eagerly when I approached the counter. I may have been the first Caucasian woman they'd ever seen.

Unlike in the Philippines, where we ate lunch out each day, the dealership owner in India provided lunch for the e-CRB team. Sometimes he ordered pizza, but only when people couldn't handle the kick of the local cuisine.

We ate in a meeting room just next to the obeya room. The room only sat eight people, so we'd have to take turns eating, with the local management usually going first. Indians don't eat lunch earlier than 1:00 p.m. or dinner earlier than 8 p.m. As a result, our lunch often arrived at 2:00 p.m.

The room held just one table and a small sink where everyone washed his or her hands before the meal. Most people from Bangalore ate without any utensils, and only one hand. Using the naan bread as a spoon, they cupped the meat and vegetables into their mouths. While their thumb and fingertip held the naan down, their pinky pulled and tore another piece of bread. Their hands remained clean.

A spread of local dishes occupied most of the tabletop, including butter chicken that melted on the tongue, chicken curry that burned the tongue, and naan bread and sliced cucumbers with yogurt for a cool down. In addition, vegetarians, who were almost half of the locals, could eat an assortment of oiled vegetables.

After gaining five pounds during my first trip to Bangalore, I began packing my lunch, along with two-liter bottles of water. The fans did not replace the lack of air-conditioning in the obeya room. The dealership supplied purified water in large vats, but no bottled water, and foreigners were not encouraged to drink the local water because our stomachs didn't have the same lining to manage the contaminants.

As soon as we arrived at the dealership in the mornings, the tea men put my lunch in the refrigerator; it was usually for paying customers, but the management had approved my request to store my lunch in it.

Like most dealerships, Nandi had "tea men" whose only job was to serve drinks to guests. Both men looked skinnier than the leg of a chair in their uniform of black pants, a white shirt, and black vest. They made their rounds promptly at 10:00 a.m. and again at 4:00 p.m. They walked up and down three floors of stairs all day, which explained why they were so skinny.

The first couple of times I spoke with them, they hid behind one other shyly. Their English didn't expand past "Yes," "No," "Coffee," and "Tea."

I wanted to lessen the tension they felt, so I asked Reshma how to say "thank you" in the local dialect. There are over fifty dialects in India, so sometimes even the staff could not understand each other.

When the tea men took my lunch from me the next morning, I brought my hands to my chest as though in prayer and said, "Dannyavad."

Their blank stares turned into huge smiles, and they giggled. The tea men poked each other teasingly and nodded back. "Dannyavad."

Every time lunch was served in the meeting room next door, I asked them for my packed lunch.

"Ice cream?" They'd ask. Their yogurt didn't come in a package like mine so they assumed the container was ice cream.

"Yes, ice cream," I'd respond. A couple times I tried to explain but the conversation did not make it far so I began to simply ask for my ice cream, every day.

The TMAP team was catching an overnight flight back to Singapore, so we arrived at the Bangalore airport around nine p.m. after a long day at the dealership. The security line was split in two, one for males and one for females. I shook my head, wondering if I was hallucinating from exhaustion.

We walked into a small tented area as the security scanned our bags, and a lady dressed in an Indian army uniform guided me to stand on a pedestal. She pulled my arms above my head and waved a scanning wand around me, then patted me down with her white-gloved hands. After she stamped my boarding pass for clearing, I crossed my arms over my chest, greatly disturbed by this intrusion on my personal space. Only after several more visits did I get used to the standard screening for all women traveling through India, but I always had to roll my eyes, look away, and try to think of something else to keep from getting angry. Those were the few seconds of my trips to India that I always detested.

Chapter 23
Health Is the Only Thing You Have

The day after I returned from India, Sato-san held a barbeque at River Place to celebrate Ren's third birthday. Almost two years had passed since I first met the family, and Ren had grown even more handsome. His babyish round cheeks were taking the shape of a boy's, and Keiko dressed him in classy, brand-name clothes. He now stood to my waist.

For his birthday, I got Ren a toy car to add to his collection and a picture of us playing in the pool. I didn't want him to forget our time together when he moved to Italy. He sat on the floor holding the frame in his tiny hands with the wrapping paper ripped up beside him.

"Ren-ne, tell Hilary-san thank you," Keiko-san said to him.

"T'ank you," he said, dragging the syllables. He was still learning *th* because the Japanese language doesn't have the same sound.

"Doitashimashite," I said. You're welcome.

He handed the photo to his mother and picked up the next present. "Oi!" He picked up the car and showed everyone.

"Sugoi-ne!" Sato-san exclaimed. Cool!

Keiko-san laughed. "Ne-another car."

"Sato-san, Ren is getting quite a bit of an attitude for a little boy," I said, smacking Sato-san's arm playfully.

Keiko-san giggled and nodded. "Yes, my wonderful son. We spoil him."

The dinner Keiko-san made was exquisite, but I expected nothing less. Sato-san loved to spend his money on high-quality items, especially food. Keiko-san popped a bottle of Italian Prosecco as soon as we walked in the door, and our glasses were kept full all night. Sato-san had bought Kobe beef straight from Japan and grilled the meat only slightly, leaving a trace of blood like he liked.

For dessert, Sato-san had something special to share. "This is twenty-year-old aged balsamic vinaigrette. We went on a tour of Italy to see different balsamico. I didn't know they could be so different! This one is for dessert." In a small, porcelain Japanese bowl, Keiko-san served us a teacup-sized serving of vanilla bean ice cream with sliced strawberries and balsamic drizzled over the top. Even though the thought of mixing salad dressing and fruit was strange to me, the separate tastes definitely seemed like they belonged together once they hit my tongue.

I was putting my shoes on at the door to leave when Sato-san gave me my own bottle of balsamic vinaigrette as a thank you for coming. This is common of the Japanese, to give thanks after receiving thanks, and even when they are the hosts.

"Sato-san! You didn't have to do that!" I said, and bowed to receive the gift. After all this time, Japanese customs still surprised me.

"I am grateful to have you a part of Ren's life-ne. Thank you for coming," he said. I wanted to hug him, because that's what I'd do back home, but I didn't.

"I am grateful to be a part of Ren's life," I replied.

At my own apartment, Margaret and I were getting to know each other a lot more—mostly because I saw her more often than any of my friends.

"You and your steamed veggies," she joked with me as I cooked dinner one night. I was never much of cook, and she was a phenomenal chef. One of her famous dishes featured fried sardines. "Oopsy! Sorry, Hilary. The house is going to smell like fishies!" she would say. She'd shut the door to the kitchen, but the stench would smell up the apartment anyway.

Margaret loved watching TV. Nearly every Saturday, her and her boyfriend would watch American movies. She loved watching *American Idol* and *The Bachelor* and would fill me in on the status of each show when I came home from a business trip.

That March, we renewed our lease in Tanjong Pagar. My first real-life apartment out of college felt like home. In the building next to us, I'd found my favorite nail technician, a fruit juice seller who always knew I wanted watermelon, a wonderful hair stylist, and a massage therapist and Chinese doctor who welcomed me with a smile. Next door was my bank, grocery story, and post office. I started to see familiar faces instead of strangers. I had established relationships with my neighbors. I didn't want to change that after it had taken so long to build.

I was washing and drying the dishes one day when I realized that signing another lease meant I was staying in Singapore another year. I held the towel in my hand for a moment, thinking. Another year meant I would pass the two-year mark Amanda's mom had told me about. I didn't really know how I felt about that. I knew I didn't want to go home yet, but I hadn't thought about when that time would come.

To celebrate re-signing our lease, Margaret and I held a housewarming party. We planned the party for a night just before my next trip to India, which happened to be right when Peter was coming back to town.

Peter and I met for our dim sum lunch, like we had the last day I saw him. Despite how worried I was about our indefinable relationship, when I saw him walking up the stairs, my body tingled just like the first time. "So lovely to see you again, my dear Billy," he said. I hugged him so tight. It'd been so long that I had almost forgotten how he felt for me.

I showed Peter my notebook that he had made me buy. "It's almost full," I said. His big brown eyes smiled at me. "I write down all the silly quotes from my bosses. I wish I'd started sooner."

"It's good you started at all," he said, taking a bite of his dumpling.

"These are delicious," I said. I swallowed my last scallop and chives.

"Those always were your favorite," he said. Peter grabbed my hands across the table. "I look forward to this lunch every time I come home. Before, it was because of the dumplings, but now it is because of you."

I lowered my head and blushed. I couldn't deny the way I felt for Peter, but I hated how illogical our situation was. Unfortunately, Peter didn't come that day with good news.

"I need to tell you something, Billy," he said. I pulled back, but he kept a hold of my hands. I was ready to smack him if he said something about another woman.

"My family is leaving Singapore. My dad's retiring, and we are all moving back to England." My jaw dropped and I stared at him with an emotionless face. "Billy, I'm so sorry. I can't tell you how badly this makes me feel. Every time I come to Singapore, I look forward to seeing you the most. I adore our time together." I still couldn't say anything. I was losing my mentor—Sato-san—and now my lover. "I'll be back one more time in July for the final move with my parents," he paused. "Tell me how you feel, Hilary."

"I mean, what can I say?"

"The same."

"Of course it's the same for me! Of course I adore our time." My voice rose slightly. "I put down everything else when you come into town. You know this."

"I just want to enjoy the last of our time together," he said. I shut my eyes and exhaled. Peter leaned over and held my chin in his big, soft hands and kissed me. His lips had suddenly become even more captivating. "Let's just be together and not dwell. Let's be grateful you ever stabbed me with a plastic sword."

I had no one to talk to about Peter. I couldn't talk to Viktor because he was a guy. I never talked to my mom about men. Katie had met Peter and knew the story, but we'd been playing phone tag across the time zones. I

needed someone to talk to now. I didn't want to have to schedule a call —
by that time, I probably would have numbed myself to the situation again.
The idea of Peter and I actually building a relationship rarely crossed
my mind. A flight from Europe to Asia cost over a thousand dollars and
took ten hours. When dreaming, yes, I imagined him finishing school and
me moving to Europe and together, watching films and sipping espressos.
But then I remembered he was a child. Peter still studied. He still
wandered. That wasn't what I wanted, or needed.

The only person I had to tell was Margaret. As we prepared for the
party, I told her about Peter's bad news.

"Oh, hippy Peter, the nomad. Well, what did you expect?" she said.

"That's the thing. I was never expecting anything in the beginning. But
it's just all grown organically."

"Honey, it sounds like it might not be in your control . . ." Margaret
said. She rolled her eyes and continued writing out nameplates for the
food. "So you have one more visit with him in July?"

"Yeah. Which is ironic because that's the month that my mom is
coming to visit." After weeks of confirming dates, I had finally booked her
flight with my miles. It still hadn't sunk in that she was coming.

"Are you going to introduce her to him?" she asked.

"Definitely. At least, I'd love to."

My friends from across the world came that night. Natasha from Hong
Kong, a few of Margaret's Filipino friends and her British boyfriend, my
half-French and half-Japanese friend Audrey, Kirk from New Zealand,
Viktor, and of course, my Peter.

After the housewarming party, we went to a popular club — Zouk — for
its monthly glow party where everyone dresses in neon colors. The
nightclub was packed full of people, like always, including random people
dressed like cartoon characters. We danced on stage all night to techno
music. Being out with friends was so refreshing, although I was nervous
about how Viktor would react to Peter since the two of us had gotten so
close and he knew almost the entire story. Viktor said he approved of Peter
by the end of the night, but there was really nothing to approve of, because
what we had was far from a relationship.

After a couple of weeks, I prepared for my next business trip to India,
which was scheduled for twenty days. As I worked on the schedule,
Yoshida-san rolled his chair over quietly. He took a small stuffed dog that
my mom had sent me off my desk and leaned on his armrest, a big smile
across his face.

I peered to the side. "Yes?"

"Hilary-chan."

"That's my name. Don't wear it out."

"I see you becoming a general manager someday," he said, still smiling.

I turned my head in surprise. "Pardon me?"

"You can. You have the qualities of a GM."

"Oh, I don't think so." Kimura-san had always supported my growth in the company, but I had never thought anyone else saw me being successful here.

"But yes. You should think so, Hilary-chan."

"Why do you say that?" We were about to have our annual appraisals, so I knew that there must have been a managerial conversation behind the scenes.

"You are a leader," he said, "and you care about kaizen people."

I hadn't smiled that big at work in a while, but I had to be truthful with him. "Oh, thank you, but I don't want to be a GM. I don't want my life to be consumed by work like theirs are. It's important to me to have a balanced lifestyle between work and family and friends. For the Japanese bosses, everything is just work."

He nodded. "Hai," he began, "do you know the reason they work so much?"

"Because they're trained that way?" We'd spoken before about the issue of balancing your work and personal life.

"*Ma*, so-so," he said. "If they go home, they will be bored. Work is their life—they make it that way. In Japan, we are not taught to pursue our own interests. It is frowned upon." I shook my head in disbelief, and he continued. "Imagine me. I have hard time because I think like you, but I'm Japanese, so it cannot be allowed. They expect me to think like them."

I'd never thought of this perspective.

"Ma, shoganai," he said. He shrugged and moved back to his desk.

"Thank you, Yoshida-san," I said.

"Nani?"

"For the compliment that I could be a GM. Thank you."

He tilted his head in a slight bow.

Before I left for India again, I made plans to have a small, outpatient surgery. I told Yoshida-san in advance that I'd be absent that morning from the office, but I would return in the afternoon.

Unfortunately, I have always had an aversion to blood. My stomach churns whenever I look at bruises, scratches, or drawn blood. The moment they numbed me with a needle that day, I began to cry, and I cried harder when the doctor started to stitch. The nurse rubbed my shoulders and spoke with me, trying to distract me from the surgery, but her efforts did little to make me feel better.

I thought of the first time I had gotten stitches as a child, of my mom holding my hand by my side. I thought of my first experience overnight in a hospital and how John had left his own birthday party to come stay with me. But I was far from my support system now.

I laid there shaking and crying after the surgery ended and the doctor had tied up the seven stitches. The nurse told me I was welcome to stay as long as I needed. My tears made the cotton sheet wet. When I had first moved to Singapore, my mom had asked me who would take care of me if something happened, and I had always responded with, "Oh, don't be silly, Mom, I'll be fine."

When I finally gathered my composure, I sent a text to Yoshida-san to tell him that I did not handle the surgery well and had to take the afternoon off.

"Of course, that is fine," he answered. "Health is your number one concern. It's the only thing you have." The big bosses always said this. "Please let me know if you need anything."

As much as I appreciated his support, I realized my real problem was not with the pain, but with the situation. The closest person I had that day was my boss. This was the lifestyle I had chosen.

Chapter 24
I Need Courage to Leave

The e-CRB project in India was scheduled to go live in mid-April, which would make me miss Sato-san's farewell. We scheduled a lunch to say our good-byes.

I left my desk promptly at noon and headed for the elevators, but the elevator stopped on nearly every floor below mine, and for some reason, this made me anxious. I was still trying to figure out what I wanted to say to Sato-san. I didn't want to rehearse what I had to say, but at the same time, I wanted to make sure I remembered everything and respectfully communicated my feelings in their entirety.

Sato-san had become the closest thing to a father that I had ever had in my life. I wanted to thank him for that. I wanted to tell him how much I'd miss him, but assure him that I'd be okay because of what he taught me. I wanted to tell him how I wished he wouldn't go, but that I was happy he was following his dream. My life would be better if he stayed in Singapore, but his life would be better if he left for Rome.

At the bottom of Centennial Tower, I followed the mass of black-haired heads toward the outdoor escalators and followed the path toward the restaurants that surrounded the fountain. Sato-san was already waiting for me at the entrance of a famous Japanese soba restaurant.

Lunch began just like any other; the two of us chatted about office gossip and he gave me an update of his project in Italy. As we finished our meal — mine hardly touched, as I was too busy talking — we both realized our time was coming to an end.

When we spoke about India, Sato-san said, "You should be patient. Learn. Then you can survive anywhere. You already know kaizen philosophy. Just focus on technique." I could feel tears swelling up, but I held them back. I was listening to him, but I was also thinking of my beginning days at Toyota, when Sato-san always made time to answer my questions no matter how busy he was. He continued slowly and quietly, "Not until I left Toyota did I truly understand courage.. I need courage to marry Keiko, to make Ren, to move to Singapore."

I imagined him leaving his successful dealership to work for himself as a consultant. His courage reminded me of my mother, and as close as I felt to Sato-san, I was beginning to see that there was still so much more to him than what I knew. I saw myself in him, in his desire to courageously take on new challenges in an effort to know his path and follow it, no matter how scary.

I leaned forward and whispered, "How did you know to take those risks?"

"They were what I wanted," he said without hesitation. "Continue to adapt your ways, but don't ever lose your values."

I looked around at the bustling crowd of busy professionals. I wondered if I valued work over other aspects of life. So many people learn about values as children, but get too busy to revisit them as they grow older. For some people, religion, or failure, or a traumatic experience forces them to understand the true meaning of a word like courage. For me, it was living abroad.

Family was one of Sato-san's most important values. Keiko and Ren had opened up to me like my homestay family in Japan, but I worried that Ren would forget me as he grew older. I worried that I would forget Ren. He was my visual reminder of how beautiful life is when you live with courage and agility — like I had been on the first day we met in the River Place pool.

"Don't worry," Sato-san assured me, "we will remind Ren of you with your photo."

I listened closely to his final comment and later repeated it to others.

"In America baseball, the famous players are the ones who throw the strong fast ball, but in Japan, it's the one who can throw a curveball, fastball, etc." I sat confused until he elaborated: "Those that can adapt are seen as more strong."

The check had been paid. I was using every excuse to elongate our time, but Sato-san's actions made it clear that he was ready to leave; he gathered his things, shifted to the side, and folded his hands on the table.

His Japanese customs were kicking in: don't dwell, be thankful, and move on.

"These are my last words: Be Positive. This is the only way to secure your life from difficulties," he said as we stood up from our chairs.

Unfortunately, the only feeling I had was sadness. We left the restaurant and followed the path back up the escalators, stopping before the office building. I choked on my words, unable to speak. I couldn't hold back my tears despite my attempt at maturity and professionalism. I wasn't saying good-bye to a colleague. I was saying good-bye to a friend, a senpai, a father.

"Don't get upset, Hilary-chan," he said. *Chan* was used instead of *san* when speaking to a younger woman, like a daughter.

"I know," I responded. "I know I shouldn't."

"I will miss Hilary-chan."

I said my final good-bye and turned away without looking back. The farewell was harder than I ever expected and much more than I could bear. I practically ran into a public bathroom and collapsed against the wall of a stall, sobbing for thirty minutes. I held my churning stomach and kneeled over the toilet. I couldn't stand. I was gasping for air when the tears subsided, and I began to pray to my father in heaven. I always prayed to him instead of God. I asked him for strength and courage to take on the rest of my life in Singapore without Sato-san.

It was past 2:00 p.m. when I pulled myself from the bathroom. My eyes had swelled and my makeup had rubbed off on the toilet paper now in the trashcan. I felt lighter, somehow.

I was an hour late for a meeting, but tardiness was my last concern. Nothing mattered that day. No one mattered but Sato-san and the fact that I was losing him. What do you do when your guardian leaves you? Sato-san treated me like a daughter. I was indebted to him. He had given me a wonderful opportunity and believed in me. He had given his word to management at Toyota on my behalf. And life was never the same once he left.

Chapter 25
Sunday Night at Nandi

Although no one ever talked about the parameter, there was a gauge Toyota staff used to measure the success of a report: the number of questions asked. The goal? No questions.

When I first started reporting for the Philippines project, I had spent an entire week preparing forty to fifty slides in a PowerPoint presentation. Inevitably, I had spent most of the meeting time reporting rather than receiving advice or discussing next steps.

Now that I was on Tanaka-san's team, I had to create a report on one page.

"Make it easy for me," Tanaka-san said.

I went to Yoshida-san for help and he said, "In one glance, management should be able to see what took place last business trip, the results, and the next step." I took in a big breath of air. Forty slides appeared harder because of the volume, but in actuality, this style was easier because I didn't have to think deeply about what my work meant; I just said everything. Decreasing the report length meant I had to identify the important parts of the report. This task was difficult, but with practice, I was finally able to reduce my preparation time from five days to half a day — from endless slides, to a one-pager. This style saved time and improved efficiency — kaizen at its finest.

"The purpose of your involvement is to study," Tanaka-san told me. But over the past four months, my frustration with the organization and leadership of the India project had steamed to its peak. Only months earlier, I had been running my own project in Manila, and I felt as though I had taken a step backwards; now, I was just a student.

Yoshida-san and Maeda-san were both positive about my job performance during my appraisal, although Maeda-san said he had only worked with me for a few months and couldn't give many comments. Yoshida-san and I, on the other hand, had been working together for over a year now.

"Initiator. Outstanding communicator. Strong. You are all these. I find that you often say exactly what I'm thinking," Yoshida-san commented.

His positive response was a relief to hear, considering the bitter emotion I often felt toward the company for taking over my life. After our conversation, I felt guilty and slightly embarrassed for not working harder to resolve my internal frustrations. My appraisal had actually been better than I was performing.

Nandi's "Go-Live" date was scheduled for April 13, 2009. The teams from Thailand, Japan, Singapore, and India only had about two weeks to understand the current operations as they were and visualize how they were going to change with the new system. More importantly, we had to inform and teach this to the frontline staff. Time was not on our side.

I was back on a plane to India for a three-week stay to help prepare for system implementation and to support operations post-implementation. I did as Yoshida-san said and just listened, but I didn't like what I heard. Chaos described the workflow of the project. At any given point, I had no idea who was doing what, where, when, or even why. I missed Kimura-san's support and empowerment, but convinced myself that there were things that I could learn from these trips.

The e-CRB project was the brainchild of the company's president, Toyoda-san himself, and its origins reached back more than ten years. His dream was to utilize technology to standardize all customer processes after the purchase of a car. Doing so would keep all customers happy so that, when they were ready to purchase another car, they would buy from the same dealership. Thus, you achieved Toyota's ultimate goal: Customers for Life.

The goal was ambitious and admirable, but I felt like it was unrealistic in India. The market was young, and the buyers were usually first-time car owners. Price also determined the behavior of the customer, a principle that didn't exactly promote loyalty to individual automotive brands. Toyota's stance was that they wanted to catch these customers during these early stages and inspire this kind of loyalty. The idea had merit but was incredibly challenging, and I was skeptical, along with many.

TMAP almost always had to report to work on Saturdays. When Sunday came around, our minds and bodies were exhausted, but not just from work. They were exhausted from the commute, the noise, the traffic, and the overall Indian lifestyle. Over a year and a half of traveling to India for Toyota, I left the hotel on Sunday only three times. My social life had plummeted, and my thoughts surrounded what took place in Nandi Toyota. Toyota and its Indian customers had shaped my entire life.

On Saturday, April 11, we were supposed to go for a group dinner, but everyone said they'd rather go back to the hotel. We had spent enough time together during the week.

On Sunday, April 12, I had to leave the hotel, but not by choice. The Go-Live was the next day, but we'd only received the computers from Indian customs on Saturday, so we still needed to set them up. I knew the only thing I could do was smile and try to make the best of the long day ahead.

Like always, Maeda-san, Kom-san, myself, and a couple other team members left the hotel promptly at 8:30 a.m. When we arrived, we found the computers all waiting on a truck outside the dealership. Luckily, we were permitted to wear jeans that day. Carrying the boxes and computers with my Indian, Japanese, and Thai colleagues, I felt like I was a part of their team for the first time, not just an observing white student.

I noticed Maeda-san using pliers to open the boxes.

"Can I help?" I asked.

He looked up and motioned me over with his hand. Maeda-san was tall and skinny and kept a straight face at all times. He was from service, so he always wore cheap, casual clothing since they often got dirty in the workshop. Like my other bosses, he'd worked all over the world but had spent a lot of time in Panama and Italy. He'd only been in our office since

Tanaka-san took over in January, so he'd been busy with management. I felt disconnected from him.

I walked briskly over to him and knelt down on the floor. He took the pliers and held them up. "Watch," he said. He cut a slit in the box and then used the pliers to leverage the box open. Strength was not necessary.

"Ne?" he said, tilting his head and raising his eyebrows, asking me if I was ready.

"Hai," I answered. I attempted to follow his same process, but when I tried to cut a slit with the pliers, I couldn't. I tried to leverage the box open and, in doing so, nicked my finger.

He smacked his knee and smiled. "Safety first," he said, pulling the pliers out of my hand. We placed the computers in their designated spots throughout the dealership, cleaned up, and waited for the electrical contractor... for three hours.

During the team's idle period, we began joking with each other. "This project is apparently so important to Toyota, but we can't even hire contractors that come on time," Kom-san said.

I took advantage of one of these conversations and actually observed an Indian coworker. He was in charge of the IT system for the entire dealership. He was short, round, and had deep brown skin, large beady eyes, and buck teeth. Suddenly, I knew exactly who he reminded me of — the beaver from the Disney movie *Lady and the Tramp*. I began laughing hysterically.

"What's so funny, Mrs. Clinton?" My Indian colleague, Prasanth, asked. They always called me that because of my first name. I welcomed their joke because I realized that it was one of the few ways they could relate to me.

I held my hands over my mouth. "Nothing, nothing!"

"Really? Tell us! We have time!"

I was in tears by that point. I wasn't sure if the comparison I saw was really that funny, or if I was just delirious from the seven-day workweek.

"No, really," I said, pinching my cheeks. "It's really nothing."

Even if I wanted to explain, they probably wouldn't understand the analogy. I wished there was another American there to see the humor in the situation. Laughter was the only way we could get through that difficult Sunday.

In the afternoon, I joined another conversation with Prasanth. "Do all Americans talk so much?" he asked me.

"What?" I asked through my laughter. Everyone around me was nodding. "Well, I have to fill the dead air when you guys are so serious!" I said. They all laughed with me. I did talk a lot, but I'd noticed that my openness often lightened the mood; I used it like a tool to calm high-stress business situations.

The contractors still hadn't arrived, so Kom and I went with some other team members across the street for a coffee. We didn't go often because we had to walk across the highway, which was like an obstacle course of speeding cars, trucks piled high with produce, and old school buses with people hanging off the sides. A muddy, fenced median split the road.

The locals hardly acknowledged the cars nearly running them over. My colleagues and I were less agile, dodging the cars, leaping over the median, and running ahead of cars again to finally reach our destination. The sight would've been comical if it had not been terrifying.

In the coffee shop, the air-conditioning helped cool the sweat that I had broken from our trip across the highway. Joking to Kom-san, I said, "This better be a darn good coffee!" In Bangalore, nearly every drink they make is sweet. Only after many visits and many mistakes, did I determine how to order coffee without milk or sugar. "No sugar!" I'd say with pouty lips, or, "Without sugar. Sugar bad," with crossed arms, all in an attempt to describe what I wanted.

This visit was the first time the coffee shop made my coffee correctly. I exploded in appreciation like I had just seen the light of day for the first time. "Yes! Coffee with no sugar! Thank you so much! This is wonderful!"

The salesman's eyes got big; he could not understand what he did that was so special.

After we enjoyed our successfully prepared coffees, we conquered the obstacle course again and returned to the dealership to find that one of the new improvements made by the dealership had been finished.

"They installed the overhang," Maeda-san said, pointing it out. The cover was meant for service customers to protect them from Bangalore's excessive rain.

"Wait a second," Kom-san interrupted. "What is that?"

Above us, the transparent overhang revealed three rows of dirty tire marks. The plastic had apparently been driven across while lying down somewhere.

"You have got to be kidding me," I said, groaning.

Kom-san pulled out his camera to take a picture. "*Ma,* it's okay. Indian quality-ne."

We walked into the dealership to then find that the contractors had just returned. Three hours had passed. Even though we had enjoyed our jokes and coffee, we were glad to get back to work.

Three men were working in dirty T-shirts, ripped jeans, and ten-cent sandals, and with a bucket of tools that looked like they were from a dumpster. They spoke in the local dialect for quite some time as tall Japanese men in black slacks and ties stared over their shoulders, waiting for them to complete their job. Roughly two more hours passed before the contractors realized they were lacking supplies. They told Prasanth and left to buy the materials. Again, we found ourselves waiting and wondering if we'd ever be able to leave Nandi, but we were all a part of e-CRB and had to wait until the job was done, even if there was nothing we could do to help.

Around 7:00 p.m., I went to the customer lounge to take a nap. As I lay on the cheap, black plastic leather chairs, I imagined the lounge during the day, not full of customers, but their drivers. The customers' drivers were the ones who visited the dealership to get their cars serviced. The Indians themselves who owned Toyotas were too rich and too busy to be seen here.

Every day, I'd watch the drivers enter the dealership, confused about what line to go to. They spoke no English; often their skin was as dark as the leather chairs, and they would stare at me with their intense dark eyes. If I was in a poor mood, I would look down or away as our paths crossed in the workshop reception area. But if I were in a good mood, I would look straight back at them and smile. Some of them continued staring, probably just as confused at seeing a white woman as they were about what line to get into. However, the majority of them smiled in return.

The drivers, all men of course, would sit in that customer lounge all day long and watch TV. I'd watch as they stared in the descent of boredom. The smell of complementary chai tea did nothing to hide the oily body odor that filled the room. The couches were always full, and some drivers had to stand, but they were used to having to wait in whatever environment at whatever length of time for their bosses, the owners of the vehicles. That night, I was in their place, the roles turned as I waited for the contractors.

The lounge was dark, punctuated only by the sharp lights of the reception area on the other side of the window. Night had already fallen, and I had dozed off when the sound of hammers and saws woke me up. I was not sure where Maeda-san and the others were, but I definitely wanted to return to the hotel. The seven-day workweek had exhausted me to the core.

I needed to help them get this done so I could get out of there.

The contractors stepped away from me as I began to clean the lobby floor with a broom and dustpan.

"Please continue," I said. "Do not mind me."

Their faces were blank. I attempted to use some hand gestures to show that they didn't need to move for me and could go back to what they were doing.

Their faces gleamed with smiles and they giggled as I continued to sweep up their mess of sawdust and wood remains.

Roughly thirty minutes later and near the completion of the job, I turned around to find that Maeda-san had returned to the dealership's first floor with Kom-san and Prasanth-san. Maeda-san was taking photos of me helping the Indian contractor pick up the side of a wooden plank that we were trying to hang to hold the computer screens.

"What are you doing?" I laughed.

"No worry!" Maeda-san said with a smile. He pointed to Kom-san. "Keep working!"

Maeda-san wanted evidence to show me helping get the job done, despite the long workday and late night. This was the Toyota way of coaching. He never told me, through the exchange of words, whether I was doing something right or wrong, but he illustrated it through his actions. For example, in the mornings, if he didn't greet me, "Ohayou Gozaimasu," I knew something was wrong. Teaching this way avoided lecturing and promoted a sense of mutual trust.

During the next business trip report to Tanaka-san, Maeda-san pulled out his camera. Without any judgment, but a huge grin across his face, he pointed to the photos. "This is Hilary," he said, "day before Go-Live. 9:00 p.m. Sunday night at Nandi." I sat up straight with my hands in my lap, a smile tugging at my lips. I was trying to be modest. I didn't realize I had become so much like them.

Chapter 26
Khawy Seu Hilary

Soon after I returned from Nandi, I headed out on a weeklong trip with Viktor to Laos. There, I turned twenty-four and discovered true beauty: the simple life.

The French had colonized Laos in the late 19th century, evident in the brightly colored buildings and the baguettes available at every shop. We arrived in Vientiane, the capital city, which is separated from Thailand only by a river. At that time, some called Laos "the Untouched Asia" as it had only been open to tourism for a decade or so.

Within just a few hours of being there, I noticed how kind Laotians were. The tourist-trade workers in other countries often grimaced at the sight of foreigners with money, or tried to drive hard bargains. In Laos, women at temple gates smiled as they accepted our entrance fee, merchants at the market thanked us for our purchase, and street vendors grinned in our pictures. They didn't seem to care who we were or how much we had.

After a day in the capital, we left early the next morning with a driver we'd hired to take us north through the mountains to Vang Vieng. We would stay there for a day and then move on to Luang Prabang for the remainder of our trip.

Vang Vieng is a quaint town of few, short buildings hidden in the midst of towering limestone cliffs and the rushing Mekong River. Its breathtaking views have been seen by only a small number of people.

Unfortunately, underage travelers had overtaken the town. Its biggest spectacle had shifted from the natural environment to a different kind of attraction, a thing called tubing.

Tubing consisted of renting an inner tube for about US$3 and starting at the top of the Mekong and riding down. There were various ropes and zip lines set up on the side of the river that allowed you to swing off of them into the water. To add to the danger, each of the restaurants along the way served not just food, but also alcohol and drugs. As a result, there were hundreds of drunken teenagers and young adults jumping from precarious heights into the river.

"I don't know about this, Viktor," I said as I watched bodies flinging themselves into the river. "Risking my life isn't exactly my idea of fun."

"Ditto," Viktor responded.

We were standing on something like a gigantic porch with a bar that had been built into the side of the cliff. Rap and R&B music blared while people sat with their feet dangling over the edge, cheering on the ones daring enough to jump. The rope was tied to an enormous tree hanging over the river, with a small plank protruding off a branch. The jumpers screamed in excitement. It looked almost pleasurable until you observed the surroundings. As the rope flew, the kids easily reached a hundred-foot peak in the air. Rocks jutted out at the base of the cliff.

Everyone was pressuring Viktor and me to jump. Viktor was strong enough to say no. I was stubborn enough to say yes. I wish I hadn't.

I climbed to the top plank of wood and looked down at Viktor. He seemed so small from that height, and I wished I were with him. When the guy in front of me stepped off the plank, my heart sank back down the stairs. Humans were not meant to do this.

The person in charge of fetching the rope was a Laotian boy no older than five—another sacrifice for a tourist economy. Small children could work the tubing attraction for more money than working with their families. We also heard that some got paid in the form of drugs, resulting in drug abuse and addiction at a young age.

The little boy used a stick to push me to the front of the plank, not caring at all that my hands were trembling. I stood there with my feet inches away from the open drop, leaning forward with my hands grasping the bar connected to the rope, like a trapeze artist in a circus—except without the skill.

When I stepped off the plank, fear took over all common sense. I immediately let go of the bar as soon as my feet left the plank. I didn't even reach the peak of air like I had watched so many others do, and since I interrupted the velocity and momentum by letting go, my body went in the opposite direction of the rope and I flipped backwards, face-planting into the water just a short distance from the shore. I was lucky I hadn't fallen directly on the rocks. The current was also running fast, so when I finally pulled my head out in confusion, I had already been carried well past the tree. My face and legs throbbed in pain. I heard voices yelling, but they seemed watery and distant.

Viktor came racing down the slope under the tree to help me. "Swim, Hilary!" he yelled. "Swim!" But I *was* swimming. I was swimming as hard as I could, but I wasn't moving. All I could think about was whether I was still alive or in a dream. I had just cheated death.

Someone chucked a rope with an attached tube into the water. The tube landed right next to my head. When I grabbed it, I stopped paddling and floated.

"Jesus, Hilary! Are you okay?" Viktor said. "You flipped completely onto the water. Are you all right?"

I wasn't really all right. I was in tremendous pain and shock. I could not believe how much of an idiot I was, and I was outrageously embarrassed. I wished I had just listened to my gut and stood up for myself like Viktor had. Rather, I had acted on peer pressure and against what I knew to be true: I did not want to jump off that plank.

But I responded to Viktor, "I'm okay," even as my whole body quivered.

One stranger came up to me with his camera to show me how he'd captured the entire incident on video. I couldn't look because I was so nauseous. He offered to send it to me, and I insisted that he not.

I sat for a while away from the water, trying to compose myself, but the image running through my mind did no good. I insisted that we move on. We floated in our tubes down to the next bar and rope contraption. As the day went on, I began to feel better, even getting the nerve up to try another zip line jump that was shorter and easier. We later discovered that the frightful jump I had fallen from was the highest of them all.

Toward the end of the day, we were floating in the water when we heard a sudden scream. Everyone turned back to see a local man standing in the water, beating a poisonous river snake with a long, skinny pole. By that point, I was ready for the day to be over.

That night, I had never been happier in my life to be clean and standing on sturdy ground. I vowed to never tell my mom about that stupid jump. She spent enough time worrying about my safety in Asia. That incident was the dumbest thing I did while living abroad.

We departed Vang Vieng early the next morning. The ride in the Toyota Land Cruiser was far from comfortable, but not because of the car. We had been warned of the winding mountainside roads, but they were far worse than we could have imagined. Viktor and I spent the day sliding in the backseat from the left to the right, falling onto each other's laps. We tried every possible arrangement to avoid moving and getting nauseous, but the effect was inescapable.

Yet the views grew more and more spectacular. I eventually insisted we stop to take a picture, and while we were doing so, three young girls walked past. The eldest could not have been more than five years old. She had dark skin and no shoes, a sack on her back and a two-foot-long machete in her hand.

"She must be collecting vegetables or something else from the wild?" I asked Viktor.

The other girls appeared to be two and three years old. All of their clothes were torn and battered, covered in dirt. This was the lifestyle in the mountain villages, dedicated to finding the food and drink they needed to survive.

At first, the girls wore harsh expressions, gazing at us with puckered brows. They spoke absolutely no English—not even "hello."

"The cookies, Viktor! Get the cookies!" I said. We had plenty of snacks in the car.

When he came back, the girls immediately recognized the cookies as food and snatched them out of our hands.

"Whoa, now!" Viktor joked.

When the sweet taste hit their tongues, the girls smiled and giggled, suddenly losing all austerity. They continued walking up the mountainside, waving good-bye as we drove past. I felt sad and enlightened at the same time—sad for their struggles, their lack of education and opportunity; enlightened by the simplicity of their lives.

We soon reached our next destination: Luang Prabang, a charming town that sits on a mountaintop and outlined by the Mekong River. Its architecture is much newer and brighter than that of Vientiane and Vang Vieng.

There is not much to do in Luang Prabang, but its tranquility is what makes the town so pleasant. People live and work as visitors come to observe the cleanliness, beauty, and peace of the neighborhood. Most of the tourist activities are outside the town, but if you stay within the town, your time generally revolves around eating padaek—lao fish sauce—and sticky rice, sipping Ol'Lien—Laos style iced coffee, getting a five dollar massage, and buying silk at the local night market.

One of the most intriguing people we met in Luang Prabang was Hannah. Viktor and I had decided to get fruit smoothies and entered a crowded shop when we saw a young blonde woman sitting alone. We asked if we could share her table, and found out that Hannah had just left Australia after high school for a yearlong journey around the world. Her next stop was Vietnam, where she was committed to work at an organic farm in exchange for housing and food. She was shocked that Viktor and I were both Western professionals living in Singapore. Many people we met traveling had similar stories to Hannah's. I wondered how she had the money to afford that kind of trip. She was the kind of traveler who promoted the Asian stereotype of Westerners: white and rich. At the same time, how many Americans did what Hannah was doing? Wouldn't the world be wonderful if more people had her courage and curiosity?

We stayed at the Souk Lan Xang guesthouse, hidden down an alley across from a temple. The guesthouse was run by Khankeo, a Laotian who was the grandson of the owner. Khankeo spoke English well because he was one of the more privileged locals that could afford a good education. He spoke like a laid-back, trendy hippy. Khankeo helped us plan our days in Luang Prabang and even helped with my birthday celebration.

My birthday in Laos was perfect. We started the morning at 8:00 a.m. with a visit to the desolate Kuang Si waterfalls and natural swimming pools, full of pure water, so blue that it didn't look real. The afternoon followed with an elephant ride in the forest. Suwannee was our tour guide for the day. He'd spent six years as a monk, from ages fifteen to twenty-one.

On the night of my birthday, we started with drinks at the guesthouse with Khankeo. Before dinner, he served Viktor and me an appetizer: a bowl of crickets mixed with dried chilies and some kind of leaf.

After sounds of crunching and a hesitant look on his face, Viktor responded, "Mmm, these are actually really good!"

"What? Ugh! I just can't do it," I said.

"No, they actually just taste like a pretzel or something. Hilary, you should try it."

"No, thank you." I tried to be as polite as possible and just laugh off my discomfort. Despite my ability to eat almost anything, I just couldn't bring myself to do it.

After our appetizer, Viktor took me to dinner at a restaurant called Blue Lagoon, where he gave me my birthday gift: a watch I'd been eyeing but hadn't wanted to spend the money on. Once again, Viktor surprised me with his consideration and generosity. He was always so good at noticing and remembering the small things people said or did. It made me so happy to think that we'd become best friends.

"You have a lot to celebrate for being only twenty-four, Hilary," Viktor said over our Laotian entrées.

"Thanks, Viktor. You know, I was remembering something the other day," I began. "Do you remember the Power Rangers cartoon?"

"Of course," Viktor said.

"Which one was your favorite?" I said. I took a bite of a fresh white fish fillet.

"I'm not sure I had one."

"I like the yellow one. The Asian," I said, putting my fork down. "But I don't know why."

"Because she's different," Viktor responded. He always seemed to understand me, but I don't think I was always listening.

After dinner, we returned to the guesthouse only to find Khankeo and his buddy still sitting in the same place. They were drunk by that time and insisted on taking us out.

"But first, you must blow out your candles!" Khankeo said. They had prepared a birthday cake covered in pink and white icing, flowers, a few rabbit-looking figures made of icing, and "Happy Birthday" written in a Lao language.

"This is so Asian. I love it! Thank you, Viktor."

Khankeo and his friend took us out, and we also met up with Neuk. Apparently, they were all friends in the small town. They took us to two local clubs called Utopia and Dao Fah. They were dark and full of cigarette smoke and loud music. Viktor and I were two of approximately ten foreigners there. Khankeo took us to a table of his friends where we found out that Khankeo was really popular in Luang Prabang.

I spent the entire night telling everyone, "Wan kerd kong koy," which in Lao means, "Today is my birthday." Everyone yelled and ordered drinks in appreciation of my attempt to speak their language. If you can say even one phrase, the locals feel comfortable to talk with you. I also knew how to say, "Chao seu yang?" What is your name? And if I were asked the same question, I'd respond, "Khawy seu Hilary." Lao is a beautiful language— similar to Thai—and most people in both nations can understand one another because there is so much overlap.

Our flight left the next day. Despite my headache, I woke up at 5:30 a.m. to watch the alms giving to the monks of Luang Prabang. Viktor chose to stay in bed. Only a few distant roosters disturbed the silence that morning. Walking up the alley to the street, I found Lao neighbors all kneeling on blankets in the street with bowls of rice in their hands. A procession of young monks with shaved heads stretched down the street, each dressed in an orange robe. They were all looking straight forward. As they passed the locals, they bowed and accepted the gifts toward their journey in Buddhism.

I sat behind some locals and took three quick photos before putting my camera away. Monks aren't supposed to be in pictures. Pictures had also become less important to me in my travels. Rather, I tried to observe each experience—to feel and understand its meaning. I didn't want to have framed photos of alms-giving that I couldn't explain if someone asked.

Unfortunately, there were other foreigners there that made a spectacle of the morning. One older couple with tennis shoes, knapsacks, and $3,000 cameras were trying to get the best shot. The husband ran up to a monk, waved his wife to follow, and took multiple photos just inches from the monk's face. The circumstance exemplified the ever-growing debate over international travel.

"The Lao citizens live such simple lives," I told my sister Elise through a phone across thousands of miles after I returned to Singapore. "It appears to be making them so happy."

"Simplicity is not what makes them happy," she replied. "We focus on achieving luxuries and forget what's important: character, how you treat people, and individual responsibility."

I had been walking around the room but stopped and stood against the wall for a moment, considering her words. I spoke so often to others about individual responsibility, but I had neglected some of my family's other values. In trying to be self-reliant, I usually chose to do whatever was easiest and most convenient for me; I didn't consider how my choices affect others.

In the two years I had spent in Singapore, I had kept the majority of my friendships shallow and watched many people come and go. Worse, I had missed opportunities to strengthen friendships with those who treated me with such generosity — Viktor, Alexandre, and work friends. I'd lost touch with what friendship meant.

"I gotta go," I said to my sister. I had somewhere to be but also didn't know how to respond and was still contemplating what the Laos trip really meant.

My family had become even more distant. My four siblings and my mother were facing their own challenges, but arranging times to speak was difficult. As a result, I developed a habit of calling only when I needed something.

Suddenly, I did not like the way I was seeing myself. I wondered if I had always been this way, or if the lifestyle in Singapore had changed me. As I thought back, I saw some patterns. I had worked hard in high school, making me unavailable to my friends. I had gone to school out of state, making me miss out on family gatherings and holidays. Then I had moved halfway across the world and created an even larger barrier between me and those I loved. I didn't know what to do.

I eventually realized the truth in my sister's comment. Happiness isn't about living a simple life but about staying true to your values. I'd been so caught up in the luxury of my privileged life abroad that I'd lost touch with those values. I was pretending. I was pretending that success in my job was enough to make me happy. I was pretending that being away from home didn't bother me. I was pretending that I didn't think about John. I was pretending that I didn't long for deeper connections with my friends, and I was pretending that I wasn't lonely. In my quest to become self-reliant and "individually responsible," I had pulled away from an integral part of my life: relationships.

Chapter 27
He Told Me in Privacy

"What country are you in?" Grandma screamed over the phone. Even she couldn't keep track of my travels anymore.

"Singapore, Grandma. Thanks for the birthday card. I just got it."

I opened up my cell phone to see what other calls I needed to return since my phone had been off while I was out of the country. Up on my wall, I posted her card along with my tickets from Laos.

The skies were black, and I couldn't see a foot past the bedroom window that usually offered me an excellent view of Chinatown. The thunder was so loud that it nearly overpowered the music in my room. I always loved the storms in Singapore.

I called my mom next. "You scared me! I didn't know you were going to Laos," she said. "I thought you were celebrating in Bali?"

"Sorry, I am. Laos was over my actual birthday with Viktor. Bali is later this month after I return from India. But it's just for the weekend with a huge group of friends."

"Oh my, Hilary. So much travel. You are quite fortunate. What is Laos anyway? Is that a city or a country?"

I took a breath of air. I wasn't annoyed, but this just made me realize how alienated I'd become from my family.

"It's a country between Cambodia and Thailand. It was absolutely lovely."

"What was your favorite thing about it?" she asked.

I paused and said, "The people." I didn't want to bother my mom with how lost and confused I was. She had plenty to worry about, and I didn't want to add to the list.

"Good. I can't wait to meet your friends in Asia. I cannot believe I will be there in two months!"

I smiled. "Me too, Mom. It's going to be so awesome." I was already planning our month together, including events in Singapore and a ten-day trip to Vietnam.

I also had a voicemail from John wishing me happy birthday. I listened to it over and over, lying on my bed. His voice made me feel safe. I held the phone against my chest for a few long moments, but I didn't call him back.

Upon my return to the office, I was welcomed with two gifts on my desk. The first was from Katie: an umbrella. I covered my mouth to keep from laughing too loudly, remembering how she was always prepared for the Singapore rain and I wasn't. I was too practical for the extra weight.

One White Face

The other package said "Royal Mail" on the front, so I knew it was from Peter. I was hesitant to open it, mainly because touching the box made me feel like I was right there with him again. It was thin and square, wrapped in cardboard-like paper and a thin rope. The tag read, "A package of love to my beautiful hilly billy xoxo." The black marker he used reminded me of the calligraphy pens he always carried on him and of his elegant handwriting that always made me feel like he was an older soul — one of the many things about Peter that enchanted me. I couldn't control my curiosity about what was inside.

My hands were shaking as I opened the package, afraid to tear anything. Peter used an old record case to display the gifts. He had covered the inside with Arabic newspapers showing through parts of flowers he'd sketched free-hand on translucent paper. Three CDs sat in pockets he'd sewn into the record case. After multiple conversations, he'd promised to send me music — typical of his artsy self, simply sending me CDs wasn't enough. He had to make an entire piece of art.

One CD was a documentary he'd created in school, and the other two were music, one entitled, "Beautiful reggae. Individually selected just for Hilary Corna." I laughed and cried at the same time. He was such a hippy and so romantic. I loved these things about him.

Hidden in a smaller pocket with a flap was a love letter — like something out of a movie. The note was written with his old typewriter on the same cardboard-looking paper wrapped around the package. In black font, typed slightly crooked, the letter read:

> To my dearest Hilly,
> I hope you accept my late offering of music. I was so happy
> to receive your package and all your gifts over the years. I
> am blessed to have you as a lover and a great friend.
>
> To set the scene . . . I am sitting at my seaside writing desk,
> cigarette in my mouth, tea on my table, sun shining, reggae
> playing . . . smiling. Because I have you in my life.
> Separated by oceans and continents, my love for you is an
> invaluable strand of my character, and a great
> reinforcement of all the beauty in the world. You are never
> far from my thoughts nor my heart. You are beautiful. My
> heart and mind bursts at a moment's reflections upon our
> memories and the possibilities of the future. I have learned
> endlessly from the insight of your character and your
> tenacity.
>
> Love always,

Your Peter
Xxxxxxxxxxxxxxxxxxxxxxxx

When my mascara hit my lips, I realized I wasn't breathing. I looked around the office and then released the tense breath slowly so no one would hear me. With my chin down, I walked to the bathroom — record case in hand — shut the door, and fell back with Peter's letter in my hands.

I missed him desperately, and his gift reminded me of what I wanted and didn't have: love. Despite our completely impracticable global fantasy of a relationship, I couldn't help my affection for him. Peter was a tease, but I'd never exchange him playing with my heart for not having him at all. Though we never shared a more traditional relationship, he showed me a kind of love that I'd never seen before. He showed me that my life was missing love. That lesson was worth every tear I cried over him.

I went downstairs to get some hot, humid Singaporean air. Only one other person stood with me in the elevator — the new ICT staff member from Pakistan. He stood tall and skinny with a long beard, mustache, and a turban on his head. To distract from my puffy eyes, I smiled at him in the reflection of the elevator mirror. He smiled back, but we did not exchange words.

I realized that this Pakistani man and I actually had much in common. I was also an outsider struggling to relate to the locals and Japanese management. For a moment, this thought was the only thing that comforted me. I wasn't alone. I wondered if he also missed his loved ones, and how he dealt with the longing. Right before the doors opened at the ground level, I looked at him again. If I could relate to this man — someone different from me in nearly every possible demographic way — could I relate to anyone? Are we all able to relate to someone in some way?

I mulled over these thoughts for a few days, but I didn't know what to change in my personal life to make me less frustrated

Then work got busy again. Compared to India, the Malaysia project required very little of my attention. My biggest learning experience occurred one day, unexpectedly. Goh, my counterpart in Malaysia, and I had been meeting with the Johor Bahru dealership for four hours. We'd been discussing how to rearrange the parts storage space, but when we finally went to the space, we realized that the shelves were actually bolted to the floor and ceiling. The local manager got angry. I had to hold in my laugh, as the incident perfectly reflected what our presentations preached: *Genchi Genbutsu.* This is a concept meaning, "Go to the worksite to see firsthand."

When I shared the story with Yoshida-san, he responded, "Treat kaizen like doctors. You need to gauge condition and after thorough inspection, determine treatment." Tanaka-san retold this story many times to other distributors. I eventually overcame my initial embarrassment and told the story as well, proud of the learning experience.

Malaysia taught me something else, but not related to work. Yoshida-san and I were on our commute one day returning over the border from Malaysia into Singapore. I had plans that night, but there was a heavy amount of traffic on the road.

I sat up in my seat and asked the driver, "Nanda-san, can you get in the other lane? This lane is going so slow. We are not going anywhere."

Kimura-san later revealed to me that Yoshida-san was disappointed in my request to Nanda. He thought that I was being rude, that my evening plans did not have precedence over disrespecting Nanda-san's role as a driver.

At first, I felt angry when I found this out from Kimura-san. In America, the other person would've understood that I didn't intend to offend or undermine Nanda-san, and that I didn't see my actions being at all related to my respect for him. I understood Yoshida-san's perspective on the conflict but felt that it was a Japanese viewpoint, and that he should also take some time to understand me.

"I wish Yoshida-san would've said something to me earlier rather than hiding it from me," I said to Kimura-san.

"Please do not mention it to him. He told me in privacy," he said. I agreed. Even if I had, it wouldn't have done any good.

I wasn't in America working for an American company where people worked the same way. I was the minority, and I needed to overcome my pride to understand their way and avoid further distancing myself.

This was one of my most humiliating mistakes during my time with Toyota. On the outside, the blunder appeared miniscule because it was unrelated to work and only one person saw. But it struck deep. The situation taught me that, no matter how talented or smart an employee is in Asia, a simple cultural misunderstanding has the potential to ruin everything. More importantly, I learned that I'd insulted someone I respected and, with a miniscule mistake, lost trust that had taken a long time to build.

Nearly a month had passed since I'd been to India. I found that the team in India had not updated the information we had requested as promised. Therefore, it wasn't being used to tell the management the status of the project. The management wasn't actually being told anything, which was due to the fact that there was no one person in charge. I wasn't looking forward to reporting the status to Maeda-san when he arrived the following Monday.

Even the daily commute to the dealership in India was aggravating me. The route was the same, on the same roads, looking at the same shops, thinking the same things, every single day. During one ride, I calculated the total number of hours I spent in commute and pouted in a gaze out the window as the locals walked the streets without shoes.

I was focusing all of my energy on the negative aspects of my job, blaming the downfalls for the unhappiness in my life. With an attitude adjustment, I could've avoided frustration in India and insulting my bosses, and absorbed more knowledge and experience.

One day, on the drive back to the hotel, my driver looked in the rearview mirror with a smile and asked, "How was your day, Madam?"

My lungs filled with air, irritated. "Madam! Why do you call me Madam? I am not Madam!" I had spent six months in the Philippines trying to convince people to call me "Hilary" rather than "Ma'am." When I arrived in India, I heard someone call me "Madam" and realized I'd have to start the battle all over again.

The driver looked away from the mirror and sank in his seat. With a quieted voice, he said, "Madam—a respectful word, Madam."

I immediately regretted my reaction, sighing and shaking my head. What was wrong with me?

We worked six days that week, as normal. When Maeda-san arrived, the day was just like every other. Everyone started working frantically without knowing what to expect. The team took more frequent smoke and phone breaks.

I sat down with Maeda-san in the obeya room and tried to verbalize some of my frustrations. I told him that I didn't like how the meetings were so irregular, and that they were only reactions to things going wrong.

"Can you visualize the difficulty you feel?" he asked. "Is it a numerical value? A picture? A movie? The target is to get management to understand."

Without saying it directly, Maeda-san was telling me that my method of telling management there was a problem wasn't working. I needed to come up with a better way to illustrate or show management what the problems were.

He continued, "If the target is achieved, what happens? If it isn't, what happens? If nothing, no importance is placed on activity."

I leaned back in my chair and crossed my arms. "But that is up to management," I said.

"Hai!" I began to think about his analogies and lessons, and attach them to my own thoughts and emotions. I still felt a responsibility to the team, a dedication to ensure the success of the project. He wasn't disagreeing with that. Yes, I had a responsibility to contribute given my position, but only to strive within the capacity of that position, and as a senior executive officer, there was no expectation that the capacity included being held responsible for the final success of the project. My focus should have been in the success of the team.

Maeda-san kept the same stern, bug-eyed expression that he always had when he taught. "First see if we can do ourselves. If yes, demonstrate how to do to others, and then let them do. We are a team." I bit my lip as he continued. "Instead of asking others to do, why aren't they doing? No time? So do for them to help?" He had raised his voice.

At first, I wanted to defend myself. I'd spent weeks helping them, and he didn't really understand because he hadn't spent the time with the frontline staff as I had.

Then I asked myself why he was getting so angry. His reaction was unlike him. I wasn't helping; I was just complaining, focusing on everything negative about the project instead of the good things that had happened.

Maeda-san then stood up and walked to the whiteboard. I remained seated in my chair, looking up. He drew a picture. On the left was a squiggly line; on the right, a straight one. He pointed to the left and said, "If I go like this," then shifting the marker to the right, "can someone else go like this?" He turned around, "Everything in between is my know-how."

I sat up straight and took a deep breath of air. My know-how was being built as we spoke. That day, Maeda-san became my favorite teacher, even though he was the hardest. I'd lost Kimura-san, but was thankful to have Maeda-san now as a mentor. Tanaka-san was supposed to replace him, but he was not as hands-on. I eventually learned that Tanaka-san only asked for you if something was wrong, so interaction with him was minimal. For the first time in almost two years, I had a real teacher and a real boss. Although that time in my Toyota career was the most challenging, it was the most rewarding.

That week, TMAP's senior vice president was visiting again from Singapore. This was the boss above Kom-san and below the EVP, Hamada-san. In an effort to show me an example from his lesson the day before, Maeda-san asked Kom for a list of the jobs to be done before the SVP's arrival. I had mentioned the disorganization of the group to him. His point was not that my observation was wrong, but that my handling of the situation was.

Kom began to draw out an agenda list on the whiteboard. I shook my head, thinking about how many times I'd seen these small efforts fail in the last few months. No one followed the instruction, and the tasks changed repeatedly. Also, Kom's authority level was unclear, so no one followed him consistently.

Once again, my negativity was keeping me from learning from Maeda-san. Even a small effort was better than none at all. The combination of small efforts over the long term would yield the final results. We needed to consistently try by showing through examples, not telling. The example reminded me of a saying from one Japanese kaizen expert: "You must show them minimum ten times." I was apparently the one needing to be shown ten times.

Another issue I later brought up to Maeda-san was Reshma's workload. Every day, Reshma showed up and got handed a number of different tasks from Prasanth, Kumar, me, or any one of the service guys. We each had something we needed her to do. Yet, because our project was separate from her normal responsibilities, she'd have to stay until 8:00 or 9:00 p.m. on many nights to catch up. Her workload became chaotic. I felt terrible watching the stress and aggravation build. She started to ignore my phone calls. At the beginning of the project, I was the only one in the team whose calls she answered.

Reshma was incredibly talented and had such high potential but was not motivated by our work. As a member of the frontline staff, she was the direct result of our poorly planned and managed project. I struggled to come up with a way around this. Her learning measured my success, but I was not in control of planning.

Reshma's challenge was that she never verbalized her feelings. On top of being incredibly selfless and modest, she was in not in any authority to complain. She was below the managers in the business hierarchy, and as a woman in Indian culture; she had little room for a voice. For a long time, I made the mistake of telling her to be more verbal and to tell her bosses how she felt, not understanding that she never could.

Despite my concern for Reshma, Maeda-san didn't see a problem. Now I see that he looked at her a lot like me: our struggles were good opportunities to expand our know-how. An environment is harder to learn in when nothing goes wrong.

When the SVP, Edmund-san, arrived and saw all the things we'd been working on, his question to the dealer president was straightforward: "What is your dream of e-CRB?"

The jolly, proud president, Jojo-san, took a moment and replied, "Every information is available for every employee. We can create a culture of continuous improvement."

I was relieved. Even in a short couple of months, his understanding of the situation had changed drastically. He'd gone from being a salesman to a caring boss and student; he'd opened himself up for learning and made himself vulnerable to risk, but we were all reaping the benefits.

Mid-management, however, was still trailing behind him. Nearly every morning, I reported to the sales room on the fourth floor to attend the daily meeting with all of the sales officers.

The room was dark, cooled only by fans. Keeping lights on in the room made it hotter. The sales manager stood in front of the seated teams.

"Let's make it clear," the sales manager said, shaking his wrist in the air, "we have to reach our target, and I don't know how you're going to do it." I sat in the back quietly, looking down at my papers and taking notes. He bobbled his head again and raised his voice, "I don't have to teach you sales anymore!"

The reality was that, despite the president's revelation with kaizen, he was not using the concept in the day-to-day jobs of his employees. I hoped that he would change that someday.

That same day, I stayed in the sales room observing how the sales officers followed up with their prospects. I noticed that one of their phones kept ringing. Someone was trying to get a hold of the salesman, but he was not picking up. I asked him why he wasn't picking up and if there was something wrong. He responded, "It's about stock, Madam. A customer's daughter is getting married, and the dowry was the Toyota vehicle, but Nandi has no stock. Cannot deliver. Sometimes this causes a marriage to be cancelled, Madam."

My jaw dropped. I knew arranged marriages were common in India, but I had never imagined a situation like this. I felt like he should tell his manager that, as a company, we needed to find this couple a car. He didn't feel the same urgency, though. He was afraid of getting in trouble because he had told the family the stock was available. I was not in a place where I could intrude, though, no matter how troubling the situation.

Yoshida-san and I met for coffee when I returned to Singapore. "Oh!" the café worker said to me, "No see, long time." I smiled.

The weather was still hot, but I enjoyed it over the dry, dusty Indian air. After giving Yoshida-san an honest update of the India project, he said, "Kaizen is like a love relationship. Sometimes the man loves the woman so much. The woman likes the man but will take time to feel the same about him."

I loved how the Japanese used analogies to teach. They make you think on your own. They made you absorb knowledge and determine how to apply it to your decisions and actions, thus forcing you to retain the lessons learned. Sometimes this style was frustrating because I wanted to be told exactly what to do and how, but this was just laziness on my part.

I never would have related kaizen to a relationship, yet Yoshida-san made perfect sense. I had to nurture the project and grow the India team's trust in me, which would eventually lead to a more productive work relationship. I could not expect them to love and understand kaizen from the beginning.

"It's like a double-edged sword," he continued, cigarette in hand. He leaned forward on his knee, "Same tool, same procedure. Sometimes protects, or can kill. How to use is important."

I nodded, thinking of the comment Maeda-san had made in India about me needing to understand my approach so that I could handle the situation better. Yoshida-san continued to say one of the most important things I ever learned in Toyota.

He said, "The key strategy is to learn to read minds. Kaizen is like knowing psychology — if you can read someone else's mind, you can make the correct decision on what action to take, and this is why taking time to come up with action is necessary."

His comparison reminded me of sales. In essence, we were selling the dealership an idea, that they could improve their operations and make more money if they empowered their employees. Our job was to understand the needs of each individual in the dealership in order to make that happen.

He then drew a figure on a red Toyota Post-it.

Fear — Kyoufu → Logic — Riron. Consideration — Jin

"When doing kaizen, must use fear to push the staff, but show logic to support. And must always consider them."

There were so many examples running through my head of how I'd failed to fulfill this image. With the GM in the Philippines, I'd shown him logic and fear, but no consideration. As kaizen leaders, we needed to make sense, but we always needed to show seriousness and respect for people.

The fear part reminded me of Kimura-san's statement, *Shinken Shoubu*, which meant "Do or Die." If we weren't going to do kaizen to the fullest, with all its components, why waste everyone's time?

On my morning commute to the office, I passed by the local fruit juice stand below my apartment. The shop owner was a Singaporean who had been serving me since I moved into Tanjong Pagar. She sold drinks like "Unbeetable," a mix of beetroot, orange, and ginger; "Land of Green," which was cucumber, ginger, and celery; and one of my favorites, "Road Runner," a blend of carrots, green apple, and ginger.

She always remembered my favorite: a banana smoothie with no sugar.

That morning, she said, "Wow, where did you come from? You have not been around."

I fumbled in my purse in my desire to quench my thirst. "Yeah, I just returned from two three-week-long business trips, and am leaving again soon."

"That is great. You must work hard. You have good job."

I stopped rummaging through my bag, and looked at her. "Thank you. Yes, I have a good job."

156

Her comment reminded me of how lucky I was to go through these struggles and to learn from them. If my job was easy, I'd be bored. Still, I felt inadequate and unsure of what to do to get better, but this desire to continuously improve myself was enough evidence that I *was* continuously improving. I hadn't been listening when my bosses said, "You are exceeding our expectations."

Chapter 28
God Bless Singapore

My second birthday celebration took place over a weekend in Bali, the epitome of luxury, much of a contrast to my birthday experience in Laos earlier that month. Twelve friends came on the trip including Viktor, Alexandre, and Chloe. The majority of them I'd met through Alexandre over the past couple of years and were French.

For forty-eight hours, we partied in a six-bedroom Balinese villa on the beach with its own chef, gym, garden, and full-size pool surrounded by a teak wood-carved bar and plush couches. With house music playing in the background, we worked on our tans and drank piña coladas made of fresh pineapple. For the birthday dinner, we sat regally at a long, covered table in the garden while our team of cooks served fresh lobster, king prawns the length of my forearm, and other seafood.

We decided to celebrate several birthdays at one time, and all of us received pink iPod docks for the occasion. As much as I struggled to accept my French friends' smoking, French speaking, and techno music, I admired their strong bond of friendship. Eventually, I learned that it takes time to earn French people's trust, but once you do, they'll do anything for you.

On our last day, we took motorbikes to Dreamland, one of the most famous beaches in Bali. I broke away from the group and walked the sand as far as I could go. The water was crystal blue, and the sand was white, disappearing softly between my toes. The place was pure paradise.

Yet, in the midst of our opulent weekend, I couldn't help feeling troubled inside. I looked out at the horizon beyond the ocean and imagined myself on a map, but this time, I wasn't excited about what I saw. There was so much separating me from the people I cared about: ocean, miles, and time zones. Meanwhile, I sat feeling alone, hiding behind this loneliness with the glamorous idea of global friends and a transient lifestyle. My continuous pretending wasn't fair to myself or to my French friends, who had been genuine the whole time.

Bali was known for being a place full of love, and I wanted to see more of it. I wanted to see more of the countryside, but on my own, so I could reflect in quiet and spend time understanding what kind of love I was missing.

At work, Maeda-san and I were already planning the next business trip to India. I only had ten days before I left. I knew I had to take some proactive measures to see my friends and branch out in that time.

TMAP arranged a tour of farms around Singapore in the hopes of building better relationships among colleagues and their families. This was the first time I'd seen any of my colleagues outside of work, interacting with their families. I also met up with some American friends on the way back from their honeymoon in Bali during this time. They told me stories about their journey, and I smiled, entertained by how fresh and novel their experiences were, like mine when I first arrived.

One night, I attended a barbecue hosted by a guy named Drew, whom I'd only met once at a lunch a few weeks prior. He was a lovely British journalist, polite, with a surprising sense of humor. The barbecue was a blast and I was able to meet a whole group of new friends. A sweet, bubbly British woman named Sarah spoke to me the whole time, and a handsome Australian named Anthony who was fairly quiet but hysterically funny when he chose to speak, as if he was constantly listening and waiting for one-liners. Then there was Fabian, an athletically fit, tanned, brunette Frenchman who had lived in Japan and spoke Japanese. We immediately got along. He was also good friends with a girl named Jessica, whom I'd met earlier in the year and joined in a few wakeboarding outings.

This was also the event where I met Lydia, a single British woman who had just moved to Singapore to work as a regional human resource manager for a branch of her London law firm. From the start, Lydia and I hit it off. She was beautiful, stylish, and a tremendous amount of fun. I loved her British sarcasm, and the fact that she was single gave her a freedom that a lot of expatriates didn't have.

I was a bit disappointed that I had not met any Americans, but meeting so many new young friends was refreshing, and going back to work made me bitter. Despite the significant level of commitment I had for Toyota, I felt like it tore me away from my friends and personal life.

Back in Bangalore, I found myself searching for things to do. Other than cheap market shopping, the city was a quiet one. The biggest happenings were at the Hard Rock Café on Friday nights. There were few restaurant options and everything shut down at midnight. I knew of a few museums and temples, but I had seen enough temples and never enjoyed going to museums. At the same time, I couldn't bear to sit at the hotel. My cousin was getting married and my twin brother was graduating from college without me. I knew I needed to distract myself, so I told Kom that we needed to do something in Bangalore.

We spent the day at the city's zoo, which seemed rather silly to me. It was like they had taken all the animals off the street and put them in cages: turtles, frogs, small birds, and even squirrels. In America, the more money a zoo has, the more exotic animals it buys, thus bringing in more customers. In India, though, zoos were still a new idea. This one had obviously just started, although it was bombarded with people. I was the only Caucasian.

The line to get into an exhibit reached hundreds of feet. We watched people continuously cut in front of others; there are few people in India that respect the purpose of forming a line. When Indian people move, they move in groups of friends or families. They move in groups when they enter doorways, even if there's someone coming from the other side. They move in groups down stairwells, even if someone is trying to get down. They move in groups while walking the streets, even if cars are honking behind them.

On the way out, Kom grabbed some corn on the cob from a street vendor.

"Ne?" he asked, holding the corn up.

I shook my head. I was hungry but wasn't going to risk my Western stomach by eating street food. Before Japan, my stomach had never tasted bone in a fish or anything other than a cleanly cut chicken breast. I'd grown accustomed to these things, but Indian food was different. Since it was common to get sick from street food, I avoided it completely.

I waited anxiously for nightfall at the hotel so I could call my brother and wish him congratulations on his graduation day.

"I'm so sorry I couldn't be there, James."

"Thanks, Hilary. It's really okay."

"I am so proud of you. It's incredible. Mom now has five kids that all graduated college," I said, sitting on my king-size hotel bed.

"Yeah, it's pretty amazing. Well, I have to go. We need to go set up for the party."

"Okay, I love you! Congratulations again!"

"Thanks, Hil."

I dropped the phone to my lap and closed my eyes as tears wet the crisp white sheets.

Every day went slower than the last as I waited for July and my mom's arrival. The project at Nandi had hit a halt, and management was visiting the dealership less to see the progress. We couldn't even hold a consistent weekly meeting.

"We still continue to work," Maeda-san instructed.

One of our managing officers, Miyagi-san, visited Nandi Toyota in June. This was a crucial visit as he was just under the president of TMC, Toyoda-san himself. Immediately, I sensed something was wrong. The dealership president approached me one morning in the hallway.

"What are the details of Miyagi-san's visit?" Jojo-san asked, no longer his jolly self.

Out of the corner of my eye, I saw the distributor staff either busy on their phones or not around. I gasped for air.

"Have you not been informed of his visit?" I said.

"Ne-ne," he responded.

"Okay, I will get the schedule and forward it to you."

The entire team of twenty people met later that day in the Indian headquarters office connected to our hotel. There was no other woman in the room. The tension made me aware of every laugh, every mannerism, and every expression.

"Do you have a working schedule?" one Indian manager asked his staff.

"Yes," the man replied. He opened his book, but the notes were all hand-written. He was the only one who had ever seen it. The conversation continued with questions from management, never a good sign.

"What was the objective of this survey?"

No one could answer. A team of kaizen experts from Japan had been running the show, but couldn't incorporate the local management.

Sitting against the wall behind Maeda-san, I didn't move. I didn't speak. I kept a straight face like I'd seen the Japanese do so often. I took notes, but quietly. I had my own ideas in my head about how to run the project, but I was determined to learn, not intervene.

One of the experts who had come from Japan was Oshiro-san. He generally worked more with the Japanese team than the TMAP team, although we naturally crossed paths given that we both wanted to improve sales operation. Oshiro-san was short and stocky, rigid with all of his movements. He'd walk with a perfectly straight back, looking forward and keeping his hands by his sides. He used hard writing strokes on the white board, stiff and controlled, just like his working style. Yet Oshiro-san had a soft side to him that he sometimes revealed.

During one meeting, he told us, "Please count young number to big number. Young to big."

I tried my best to hold back a smile.

"Hilary-san, you understand?" he asked.

"Hai," I said. A smile was still there.

"Why funny?" he asked. His English was poor compared to other project members.

"Oh, nothing," I said. I didn't want to make the mistake of insulting him.

"Please share with me," he said. He moved his chair forward.

"When you count in English, you don't say young. You say small — small to big. When counting age, you use young to old."

"*Maa* — I understand!" He pointed at me with his pen and said, "Thank you for improving my mistake! I must also kaizen my English."

"Daijobu," I said. This was one of my favorite Japanese words that meant it was okay. "Please continue." I didn't want to dwell on his mistake but move on to let him finish his lecture.

Unfortunately, pointing out his mistake was not okay. It was permitted at the time, since he was only with people below his position. That changed when there were people above him, especially his boss.

Later that week, Oshiro-san's manager flew in from Japan—a ten-hour journey with one layover—for only two days to hear the status of the project. Oshiro-san began the presentation and was explaining the new cars being introduced in India. EFC stood for Entry Family Car, which was the first small car in India.

As Oshiro-san began speaking, he mistakenly called the car EFI. In response, I giggled. He stopped speaking, turned around briskly and looked straight at me with his hands held together at his waist. His boss turned his head in my direction.

Oshiro-san's words were like poison. "You laugh like that, you make me feel ashamed."

I looked around the room to make sure he was talking to me. "Sorry," I stumbled in how to explain, "it wasn't like that—sorry."

He pivoted on his foot back to the whiteboard and continued. For the rest of the meeting, I tried to understand what had happened.

After the meeting, Oshiro-san went for a smoke with his boss down at the fruit market. I contemplated whether or not to tell Maeda-san and get his advice, but decided I needed to handle this on my own.

When Oshiro-san came up the stairs to the lobby of our working area, I asked him for his time. "Sumimasen, chouto iikana?"

He bowed to his boss, slightly ushering him to go forward alone. "Chouto matte."

"Oshiro-san, I am sorry for my mistake in the meeting. I did not mean to offend you. In America, we laugh to lighten the mood in the room. By giggling, I hoped Oshiro-san knows it was okay and that he may just continue."

He eyes were big and round, unlike most Japanese eyes I'd seen. They were scary when he was mad. "Laugh points out Oshiro-san's mistake. Not okay. Never do that again, Hilary-san." With his arms by his side, he turned and walked down the hallway back to his boss.

I was exasperated. That was my first time being scolded directly.

During the managing officer's visit, our unpreparedness was obvious. Different team members were answering management's questions differently. I watched in the background and saw how it all confused the MO more.

Problems that Maeda-san and I had been discussing over the past few months grew visible under pressure. Unfortunately, the root cause was so deeply hidden. To solve it would be difficult.

As Maeda-san advised, however, it was better for the MO to see the reality of the progress than not at all. I'd lost almost all motivation. I found myself in situations where the TKM staff was yelling across the table at each other, standing up and putting fingers in each other's faces, all while the Japanese staff and I sat there obediently.

My original objective was on-the-job training for kaizen. I didn't understand how I'd taken so much responsibility in implementation of eCRB operations.

"Through on-job training, whatever TKM needs is how you support. It is not our decision to make," Maeda-san explained. I rolled my eyes behind him. I'd just have to keep persistently working.

The second visit of another top officer from Japan barely improved from the last. Still, in Japanese fashion, he commented highly on the progress of e-CRB in India.

"Nandi is a pioneer for India market to implement activity," he said.

The Japanese way of always encouraging an activity was not being dishonest; rather, they believed that if you always showed support, results would come in due time. In theory, the approach was positive and ideal, but I felt that in actuality, it was not so simple. Also, there had to be some point where the company gave up if they weren't getting the results they wanted. The bosses did realize the problem, but knew they couldn't solve them all at once. My frustrations weren't calmed when Oshiro-san and his team continued to patronize me and my ideas.

"Schedule is not my matter," Oshiro-san said when I mentioned the need to plan out our activity. "Do not ask me that again. Please think for yourself."

I pulled back from him. I couldn't believe that he would say such a thing to me. It was our job to make the schedules and to teach the Indian team how to use them. Second, Oshiro-san was supposed to be teaching me, but such a comment made me afraid to ask questions or make mistakes. I felt like he just wanted to do things his way, and that we were just there to create little reports for his use. Everyone else noticed this too and talked about Oshiro-san during their lunch and juice breaks, but no one said anything to his face because they knew no good would come from it. He was from headquarters, and whether we liked this fact or not, headquarters had authority over us.

After two big visitors in two weeks, I was ready to return home. When I came out of the women's scanning line at the airport to get my things, my jaw dropped at what I saw. The Indian security guys were throwing around the massage ball that I carried with me for flights.

162

"Excuse me, that is mine," I said. The logical side of my brain was telling me how stupid I was for saying anything. They were part of the Indian army, linked directly to government. But the emotional and American side of my brain was telling me to stand up for myself.

One man stood tall with the red ball in his hand. He wore more badges on his chest than the others. "This here?" he chuckled.

"Yes, that's mine," I said firmly. "May I have it back, please?"

He tossed the ball to another guy, who laughed and tossed it again to a man standing near me. I turned to him and stuck out my hand. "That belongs to me, sir," I said. He looked worriedly to his boss, who shrugged and turned around. The man handed me the ball, and I walked to the business lounge. I was so ready to leave India.

On the overnight flight, I got a seat in the front row that had extra legroom. This only ever happened one other time because it was usually full of families with babies. I covered my eyes with an eye mask and put the blanket over my head. After an exhausting business trip, I couldn't wait to share a month with my mom. There was so much I wanted to show her so she could understand what my life abroad was really like. I also needed to get away from the cross-cultural challenges, from the race and gender issues. I needed to rest my mind from trying to understand. I'd gotten so wrapped up in thoughts and emotions that I didn't know what I was doing anymore. I was relieved I had Maeda-san but overwhelmed with all he'd taught me.

The plane landed and my eyes burned like the tires on the runway as I peeled off my eye mask. The time was 5:30 a.m.

I took off the airplane socks, put on my tennis shoes, and gathered my things. In the beginning of the India project, I always traveled in professional work attire for the overnight flights to Singapore, because I didn't want to portray a bad image of DOKD. At any given point in time, there were five to ten Toyota managers and executives on that flight. Also, the teams frequently crossed paths in the airport lounge before the flight and at baggage claim after the flight. Eventually, that concern subsided, though, and I wore what was comfortable — my soft pajama pants, a sweatshirt, and tennis shoes.

I had two months until another overnight flight. I turned on my phone, and waved good-bye to my boss several rows ahead of me. Blazing through immigration and grabbing my priority-tagged bags, I boarded a cab in less than twenty minutes from exiting the flight.

"God bless Singapore," I said to myself as I sunk into the back seat of the cab.

Hilary Corna

Year III.
July 2009 – August 2010

Chapter 29
First Vacation in Fifteen Years

"Now I understand why you don't come home more often!" my mom exclaimed as we hugged outside the baggage claim of the Singapore airport. "What a journey!"

It was nearly 2:00 a.m. and the airport was empty. Her eyes could barely focus on me as they recovered from the airplane that didn't claim bias to a particular time-zone. Coffee had spilled on her pants and she juggled bags on her forearms. Her purse exploded with things to keep her busy, although I found out she had hardly done any of them—typical of her even at home.

"Let me carry your bags, Mom," I said.

She laughed. "I made it all the way here. You don't think I can carry them the rest of the way?"

"Point taken," I said.

For the past day and a half, I had imagined her flying over the Russian and Korean skies. I remembered my first international flight and how discombobulated I had felt getting off the plane. Her first international flight was quadruple the distance.

"How do we get home? Is your place far?" she asked.

"Just another twenty minutes, and you'll be done with your travels! The city is very close and there's no traffic. Come, we'll take a taxi."

Within minutes we were in a yellow Toyota taxi with the luggage piled in. My mom sat next to me in the back of the cab. She pushed her toiletry case, a sewing kit, and two handbags to the side of the black leather seats, grabbed my hands with both of hers, and laid her head on my shoulder.

"I cannot believe that I am actually here." she said. "My dear youngest child. You are so strong."

I gripped her hands. I'd long waited for an opportunity to spend time with just my mom and I. Growing up, there were always four other kids around who had soccer practice, needed advice, or a car to borrow. Finally, I had a chance to grow closer to my mom and to share my life with her.

"Thanks, Mom. I cannot believe you are here either."

Outside the window, darkness hid the paradise I couldn't wait to show my mom. Remote in the ocean, specks of light flashed from the docked shipping boats for the evening. The cab didn't have air-conditioning, so we rolled the windows down manually. My mom arrived almost exactly the same day I had two years earlier—when I had taken my first taxi into the city, feeling the same humid air and seeing the same view.

This trip was my mom's first return to Asia since she lived in Japan as a child. To be a catalyst for this means more than I can communicate. But looking past the luxury of spending a month together in the tropics, this trip embodied much more. It represented my way to give back. Mom had accepted the life I build in Asia; now she just wanted to understand and be a part of it. My mom's four week stay in Singapore would forever change our friendship. For the first time, I'd see her in a new light that revealed a different woman—one full of curiosity, adventure and fun.

That weekend, we visited the tropical island Rawa. Rawa is heaven. Located off the southeastern coast of Malaysia, the island is unknown to most tourists because it only has two hotels, only one of which is listed online. As we approached Rawa by speedboat, we saw tall trees and a stony cliff side towering over a pure white beach with sapphire water.

"That is it!" I said to my mom. She was sitting upright on the boat with her bags wrapped between her legs so she wouldn't lose them to the ocean.

"Unbelievable," she said.

Only a quarter of a mile long, the island's one beach faces the west, making it perfect for viewing sunsets. The other side of the island faces the east and with a flat back, a steep cliff drops into crashing waves. Past it, the horizon combines the vastness and distance of the South China Sea to create a blindingly grandiose view.

The speedboat halted as it reached the sand of the beach. I grabbed my mom's bag and ran to the front.

"Come on, Mom!" I said.

"Thank you," she said to the driver and took careful step to the bow of the boat. "Oh my, Hilary. Oh my." She repeated.

I jumped into the warm ocean water with both duffel bags over my shoulders. Mom stood still with her chin up, staring at the outline of the island and cliff.

"The water feels so wonderful, Mom. Let's go!" I reached out for her hand and helped her down. The ocean splashed against our shins and was so clear we could see our freshly painted toes from pedicures we received the day before.

"Incredible. The sand is like powder! This is absolutely incredible," Mom said. We shifted our feet back and forth, deeper in the sand.

"Isn't it, though? Now you know why I love living in Asia! I can be at a place like this in just a few hours." I laughed and twirled in circles in the water. The sun beat down on our backs, but a soft wind from over the ocean cooled the air. Suddenly, we both got caught up in laughter—a by-product of our disbelief.

"This is unreal, Hilary."

"Okay, let's go check in!" I said.

We walked as fast as we could through the hot sand to the main building covered by a tiki-roof with ceilings just over my height. The back housed an open-air kitchen, an office, all contained in the home of the Malaysian prince who owned the island and lived there year-round. Near check-in, a rugged bar made of wood from palm trees received the most attention. Young travelers ate lunch at a few old tables in the sand.

Someone lay in a hammock taking an afternoon nap. The smell of ocean water was inescapable. Lining the cliff side, smaller tiki roofs safeguarded our individual bungalows from humid storms. We stayed in the newest bungalow just twenty feet from the beach, with a balcony facing the sunset

"Good morning!" I said to the bartender. My mom stood behind me. "We want to check in."

"Sure, you'll just have to wait a couple hours until the weekend crowd leaves," the bartender said. That was how it worked in Asia and at rugged beach hotels. Nothing was ever certain.

"No problem!" my mom said. "I want a drink! A fancy one!"

I spun my head around and laughed. "What? Mom, you never drink."

"Hilary, I'm on vacation in the middle of nowhere in Asia. I want a drink." The bartender watched and laughed.

"All right! Let's get a drink!" We hopped on some rickety bar stools.

"What's it gonna be, Mom? A Tequila Sunrise?" My siblings and I had a joke that on the few occasions Mom did drink, it would always be a Crown Royal on the rocks or a Tequila Sunrise.

"Yes!" she said. "And make it a strong one, with a couple extra cherries and oranges. Make it pretty!"

"Ha ha, all right, make that two," I said.

"You girls are silly," the bartender said. "What are your names? I guessing mother and daughter?" He was Malaysian, handsome, with leathery tan skin.

"Yes, sir, I'm the mother," my mom said.

"And I'm Hilary, her daughter."

"Wow, beautiful women. You look alike much. Not often we get moms here. Usually just crazy young tourists."

"This is her first vacation in fifteen years!" I exclaimed.

"Wow, Ma'am, welcome. Please tell me anything I can do," he said.

"Just a drink is plenty. Thank you."

That night, the young weekend crowd all boarded their boats home to return to work the next morning while my mom and I claimed the beach for ourselves. We were practically alone. My mom was used to being busy back home in her routine, so naturally, she was constantly asking me about activities to do on the island. She was still adjusting to the concept of relaxation.

168

One day Mom wanted to kayak around the island. Kayaking was one of her favorite sports, but I thought she might have had too many Tequila Sunrises that day.

"Mom, I don't know if you know this about me. I'm frightened of open water. It is one of my biggest fears," I said. We were lying out on sun chairs with our feet in the ocean.

"Oh come on, Hilary. You aren't going to make me go alone, are you? Because you know I will."

I pulled back my beach hat and looked at her. "Mom, you will not go alone. Why not just stay here where it's nice and safe and relaxing?"

"Fine, I'll just go alone." She stood up.

"Ugh, Mother. For heaven's sakes, let's go." The vacation was for my mom—I kept telling myself—so I'd do whatever she wanted to do. I didn't want to keep her from experiencing things.

Before I knew it, I was battling dark waves with a plastic paddle in a two-person, neon yellow kayak around the island of Rawa in the South China Sea. Halfway around the back, the water turned black. The sun scalded our backs as the waves tried to break open the cliffs.

"Isn't it beautiful, Hilary?" Mom asked.

"No! It is not!" I screamed, keeping my sight forward and not at the water. "It's scary!"

"No, it's not scary, it's beautiful, Hilary. Look at it." She lowered her paddle down to the kayak and peered out at the scenery.

"Mom! Keep paddling! What are you doing? I'm not looking. I hate this!" I screamed from ten feet ahead of her in the water.

Ninety minutes later, we were safely on the shore, and I felt like I'd lost five years off my life. But my mom was happy, and that's all that mattered. Forever, she would tell the story of paddling around the ocean waters of Rawa.

"Your scaredy-cat sister was screaming like she saw a ghost," my mom would joke with my siblings. "For such a fearless person, I couldn't believe that she let such a fear allow her to miss such a tremendous sight."

It was getting to be night. The owner, the prince, was usually working or fishing during the day, but he came out at night. He was tall and strong with bright blue eyes and long eyelashes.

"Excuse me," I asked, "is there a menu for dinner?" We stood in front of the bar—where we spent most of our time if not on the beach.

"Anything. You may join us if you want. You are our only guest," he said.

I'd heard the prince had his own food on the island, only for him and his fiancé to consume. One of his favorites was steak he shipped in from New Zealand.

When the prince and his fiancé sat down for dinner, we joined them at a square wooden table at the front of the patio under the tiki hut. The table was just as rickety as the bar stools. We'd already grown accustomed to the smell of salt everywhere. A light, warm wind traveled over our shoulders while the tide lowered and waves got stronger.

A friend of the prince also joined us for dinner that night. He was a retired Australian fisherman and had docked his home, a twenty-foot boat, on the beach just at sunset. The fisherman was six feet tall and had dark skin and a scruffy, dark-haired beard.

That night, the fisherman told stories of his travels as my mom and I listened in awe. One of his first adventures, after he sought his retirement fortune, was a *Survivor*-like challenge on an Australia island. However, this challenge was taken on alone, and the objective was to get off the island first, and alive.

"We were told," he began slowly, "that at one point of the course, we will have breached our need for thirst and will come across a pond. But if we do anything, do NOT drink from the pond."

In a circle around the table, no one else spoke. We sat upright with our full attention directed towards the adventurer.

After a pause, he continued, "There was one guy who didn't listen." We all gasped. "I found out at the end when his family was waiting in tears. The man was eaten alive by crocodiles in the pond. They couldn't find him during the search and were certain that was the only conclusion to be made."

Everyone gasped and looked away after the fisherman revealed the tragedy ending to the story. The prince's fiancé quickly switched subjects. Of royal blood in London, she apparently had family ties to the initial British business investments into Malaysia. Her vocabulary was superb and evidence of her private schooling. Our conversation led to Americans and the English and Australian peoples' opinions of us—a topic which often came up abroad.

"Americans are idiots," the fiancé said without hesitation. Her comment didn't surprise me; many Europeans disliked the American way of thinking and lifestyle and were frank about it. I heard a comment about us as often as once a week, sometimes even from friends. Colleagues and strangers did not hold back when they found out my nationality. But my mom had not been exposed to all that. She raised her eyebrows and looked at me. I shook my head, but neither of us said anything.

"They think only about themselves and will be destroyed because of it," the fiancé continued.

Well, that's a little far-fetched, I thought. After several minutes of her rambling, and her prince rolling his eyes—he wasn't necessarily fond of

Americans, but was less likely to say so in front of them—I was finally able to change the subject from the demise of America to her new Kindle.

After three days on the beach, and a nice glowing tan to show it, the time came to return to Singapore. I had to work the next day. My mom and I had almost two weeks to spend in Singapore before our ten day trip to Vietnam. I had to work, but my mom was easily able to fill the days. I showed her the public transportation system and helped her exchange cash into Singaporean dollars. Viktor lent her a key so she could visit the infamous River Place pool.

Every day, my mom took the local bus to my office to meet me for lunch. After a day at the pool, Botanic Gardens, or other tourist activity, she made sure to be at my office again promptly at 5:30 p.m. when I exited the Centennial Tower glass doors that had once so intimidated me.

I introduced Mom to all of my closest friends that week. It was important to me that she meets the people who played a significant role in my life overseas. Kimura-san was one of the most important. He took Mom and me to dinner at an exquisite Japanese restaurant. Mom shared how scared she felt when I first left on my one-way flight and Kimura-san shared the story of Carlos naming his daughter after me. So many stories had gone untold. For the first time, the two stories came together, interacted, and exchanged thoughts. I felt an overwhelming sense of pride to enable these two worlds to collide.

During Mom's visit, I revealed Sato-san's offer for us to visit him in Rome. "You overwhelm me with joy," she said. We were on the train home so we tried to maintain our excitement in public, but we couldn't help jumping up and down in front of everyone. My mom meeting Sato-san was crucial to understanding everything.

Another significant person my mother would have the privilege to meet that week was Peter. After John, he was the only man I'd ever loved. The three of us spent two nights together that week. On the first, we took my mom to the Chinese Garden—the only place far enough west in Singapore to watch the sun set. That night, my mom felt the first wave of jet lag and decided not to stay out.

"I'll come home with you, Mom," I said. Our time was limited and I wasn't going to prioritize Peter over my mom as much as I felt for him.

"No, Hilary," she said and nudged me. "Go and enjoy your time together. I'm just going to go to sleep anyway." My mom knew the basic story of Peter—how we had met and fallen head over heels for each other but could never pursue the relationship across countries—but none of the details.

"All right. Only if you're sure?"

"Definitely," she said. I turned around and smiled at Peter. He was only in town for a week, which fell perfectly between our trips to Rawa and Vietnam.

My mom left for home and I took Peter to one of my favorite bars in Singapore, Timbré. We sat on stools and listened to live music in the corner of the outdoor bar, covered by a canopy of enormous trees. We cuddled, held hands, played with each other's feet under the table, and kissed frequently completely ignoring the crowds around us. I wanted to be lying in bed with him, not out in public. Unfortunately, both of our parents were at home. I felt like school kids sneaking out at night with no place to go.

We left the bar and went for a walk around the paths of Fort Canning Park. They circle around and up a hill to the top, where an old British fort still sits. Although directly in the city, the tall and sturdy trees of the park protect it from the noise of urban sprawl. The humidity in the air keeps the foliage full of life and your skin fully hydrated. You can smell photosynthesis in process all around you.

After a couple walks around the brick path, we sat on a picnic table and laid back looking up at a row of tall, fanned palm trees. We held each other for a lengthy silence as if we would never see the other again. Peter's sensual and passionate touch made me fall deeper for him, until he interrupted the grip, along with everything else that ever defined us.

He took my chin with his big, soft hand and pulled it up to his face, just millimeters from his lips. "Hilary, I am in love with you."

My eyes closed themselves, and I garnered all of the breath possible into my lungs—and held it until I couldn't any longer. He'd never said this to me before.

"Darling, breathe." I did just as he said and collapsed closer into the hold of his body. "Oh sweetie, what's wrong?" he said.

Nothing was wrong. The man I loved was holding me under the stars. The man whom I'd always loved and wondered if he loved me back. The man whose thoughts and feelings about me I'd been waiting for almost two years to know. I'd been justifying the situation with logic but denying my heart since the day I met him. That's what was wrong.

I whispered into his chest, "I've loved you since the first day I met you." My tears had made a damp spot on his shirt

"Oh, Hilary. I've always wanted to say something, but it just wasn't worth the hurt it would cause the both of us. The situation never made sense."

"I know."

"As much as I wanted to consider—and did many times—I knew there was no way it could work. We are in different countries and living different lives," he said.

"I know."

He sat up and held my shoulders between his strong hands. "Do you know how much I love you?"

"Stop, Peter." I stepped off the table and turned away from him. The reason Peter and I had enjoyed each other's company so much over the years was because we'd never had to talk about it. Every visit to Singapore was like a getaway from reality. We didn't have to understand each other in our daily lives—only during the hours we were in each other's arms.

I'd known this from the beginning but ignored it because I was so lonely. To this day, I would never give up what we had. But I wished he'd never told me those three words; it turned everything upside down. It made our fantasy real.

After a few moments, Peter walked up behind me and kissed me on my shoulder. I can still feel that kiss. My crestfallen look denoted distress and I remained quiet until he turned me around.

"Hilary! Dear, what have I done? Why are you so upset? I thought me telling you this would make you happy."

"What can I be happy about? I can't have you. Why would I be happy when the person I love finally reciprocates the feeling and I can't embrace it? I have to ignore it and move on with my life because you're leaving and we'll never have a chance together."

"I'm sorry," he said.

"Why did you have to say that, Peter? It changes everything about who we are, and what 'us' is. You should have not said anything. I could have dealt with that."

"But you knew."

"But I could ignore it because it was never said."

"I'm sorry," he said again.

"I should go home," I said. We walked down to the street to catch a cab. As I climbed in, he grabbed my hand and yanked me into him, squeezing my chest against his and pressing his lips hard against mine.

The next morning he sent me a text saying, "You are amazing. I could spend a forever with you adventuring around. I love you and always have."

I didn't tell my mom what happened. The emotions were too raw, and I just wanted to forget them anyway.

Later that week, the three of us went to the theater to see the new Harry Potter movie. We didn't talk about the night in the park. I just wanted to enjoy what time I had left with Peter. When we reached home, I received another message from him that read, "Good night, Angel. It was such a pleasure to be with you and Momma Corna. I love watching you two together. You are so beautiful and I love you. Thank you so much for making time for me." I breathed, smiled thankfully for his love, but then turned off my phone and went to sleep.

Hilary Corna

At the time, I didn't know that that would be the last night I'd ever see Peter again. We were supposed to hang out one more time before I left for Hanoi with my mom, but something happened to one of his family members, and he had to rush to England earlier than expected.

The time had come to let go of Peter. I was ready. With the transient world I'd grown used to, I had confidence our paths would someday merge again. Just moments before his departure, he sent me his final words in a text. I was in my room and my mom was in the kitchen.

He wrote, "You are beautiful and I love you too much, more than you realize. I will, no doubt, be thinking about you in your moonlit bed wishing I was next to you."

I dropped my phone on the bed, and my hands hung by my side. In front of me, his memory wall engulfed almost the entire cement wall.

Chapter 30
Be Safe and Vibrant

My mom and I left the next morning on Vietnam Airlines bound for Hanoi. I tried to not think about Peter because I could not do anything about it.

Because I flew so many air miles with Toyota, I had obtained gold status in the Singapore Airlines frequent flyer program. It allowed me into airport lounges around the world. When we got to the Singapore airport lounge, my mom went exploring as if it was her first day in a new office.

"There is so much food here. How wonderful!" she said.

I traveled so much through the same lounges that I had memorized which lounges were good and what food they offered. The Philippines lounge served one table mainly full of triangle sandwiches on stale white bread. Meanwhile, the Thai lounge served four buffet tables of different cuisines from dim sum to pad Thai.

"It's pretty sweet, isn't it?" I said.

There was no jetway in the Hanoi airport. When we stepped down the stairs of the plane, we felt a gush of hot but dry air, unlike Singapore's humid air.

After my mom and I got through the snaking immigration lines, we found Gavin waiting on the other side for us. Gavin was my American friend from the dragonboat team who had introduced me to Viktor. Gavin's company had transferred him to Vietnam for a temporary assignment, so he invited us to stay in his condo.

"Hilary, welcome to Hanoi," he said. He gave me the biggest hug.

"It is so good to see you," I said.

"You, too. I am so happy you're here. I don't get visitors often, as you can imagine," he said. I knew exactly what he meant. It was hard to get visitors to Singapore, even when travel was easy, safe, and deluxe. It was much harder though to convince friends and family to visit Hanoi — the land of clamorous motorbikes, spicy street food and mysterious smells.

"It is such a pleasure to have you here," Gavin said.

Gavin was originally from Iowa but was living in Asia after meeting his girlfriend in China. His girlfriend was a Hong Kong–born Chinese-New Zealander, and was absolutely gorgeous. Being from the Midwest, Gavin was one of the kindest gentlemen I ever met while living abroad. He was polite and charismatic on top of being handsome.

"Be careful of the taxis," Gavin said as we drove to his condo in the city. "They will scam you if you don't make them put their meter on. If you ask and they still don't, get out. They can get mean."

There weren't many countries in Asia where I felt scared of taxi drivers. You always had to be aware, of course, but because of Gavin's advice and other stories I'd heard, Vietnam made me weary. Mom and I arrived in Hanoi on the perfect day. Although the day was hot, the skies were blue, and there was just a slight wind leading the dry heat away. Immediately, I noticed a difference from other Asian countries. The land was much flatter and less developed. Driving into the city from the airport in other Southeast Asian countries, I usually saw a fair amount of buildings and infrastructure. In Vietnam, agriculture mainly claimed the space of the landscape. It wasn't until we passed the main bridge into Hanoi that we saw its colorful, ornate architecture, like in Laos, due to long-term French control. The buildings stood tall, skinny, with little to no space in between. Murals of local cultural stories lined the freeway.

Gavin had to work during the days of our visit, but he spent a few hours walking us around town. Parallel with the streets, bunches of electrical cords hung from pole to pole. According to Gavin, the country never had the budget or organizational planning and support to put them underground. The cords looked like knots of hair you might pull out of a woman's brush, mixed and mangled, impossible to sort. There were hundreds, some hanging very low, others broken and dangling.

My mom and I were struck by the sight. "They could fall on us," Mom said.

"Don't worry. They won't," Gavin said, laughing.

All over the city, we watched as tourists got scammed into paying for ridiculously priced goods. Some tourists even paid to have their picture taken with women selling fruit or with a traditional pointed Vietnamese hat on their head. Meanwhile, the locals smiled because the one purchase made them enough money to eat that day. I knew because of my work in third world countries. Their monthly salary was probably close to what we spend on a pair of designer jeans.

"Do you want a photo?" I asked my mom. I wanted to give her the chance to have fun as a tourist. Gavin and I were used to it. We weren't tourists anymore. Although a citizen in Singapore, technically, my traveling made me feel like a citizen of Asia.

"No, I think I'm fine, Hilary, but thanks," she said.

Hanoi is famous for its shopping—also one of the reasons I wanted to go with my mom. I wanted to take her shopping and have fun buying stuff together. The city was known for many products including linens, furniture, and paintings. Stores sold hand-embroidered tablecloths, light fixtures, local handicrafts, and boutique clothing, and there was also a series of foreign stores. There was an especially large amount of Japanese stores because of a high number of immigrants.

After several hours of shopping one day, we left the central area with our arms full of bags. The sun was setting, but it was still hot. Gavin had just gotten off work, and we were on our way to meet him at a restaurant on a famous intersection in Hanoi. Within moments of walking, the skies turned black, and like ants coming out of their hill, locals filled the streets.

"This is insane!" Mom screamed as people, bikes, and cars sped past us.

"Walk behind me, Mom!" I screamed back. "I'll lead." It was easier to walk in single file than side by side.

We passed a food vendor on the street. Something large and dark, and apparently cooked, hung from a rod above the vendor's outdoor stove. Scattered tables and neon-colored plastic stools stood only a foot high.

"What was that?" my mom yelled.

"I have no idea. Just keep walking."

Twenty minutes later, our arms had lines drawn on them from the shopping bag handles, and sweat drenched our clothes and skin. Gavin was waiting with beer at a table outside for us.

"Are you guys all right?" he asked laughing.

"Beer! Amazing," I said.

My mom dropped her bags hastily and collapsed into a chair. I sat down next to her and propped by feet up on a stool.

My mom said, "I only drink beer when it is ice cold or it's really freaking hot outside. At least it's really freaking hot outside."

We all broke out in laughter. As aggravating as the situation was, the only thing you could do was laugh. I'd never known my mom to be so funny. Away from the chaos on the streets, we recapped our day with Gavin and told him about the pandemonium we'd survived to find him.

"You're right. People stay inside during the day because it's so hot and they want to protect their skin. You never want to be on the street when the sun sets," he explained.

"Thanks for the memo," I said jokingly.

"Hanoied in Hanoi," he said. This was a joke among foreigners about being "annoyed" in Hanoi.

After our adventures in the city, my mom and I traveled to Northern Vietnam to see the Sapa Mountains. Katie had insisted we go there—her last vacation spot before returning to the States. I booked the same cottage in the mountains that she had stayed in.

We left Hanoi on an overnight train that looked like it had been built long before my mom was even born. Rickety, brown wooden doors separated the rooms that held inch-thin mattresses. The beds were not made for Americans. Our feet stuck out far past the end. A small window the size of a tool box and barred with metal allowed us a glimpse of flat vivid green rice paddies.

"We are really sleeping on this thing?" my mom asked.

"Well, it's your choice to sleep or not, but yes," I said.

There were two other beds in our room. Unfortunately, the private rooms on the train were all booked up when I bought the ticket. We didn't know who would join us for the evening. I saw few tourists on the train so I hoped we'd get lucky that they would share the room with us instead of a local Vietnamese.

There was a knock on the door. Mom and I looked at each other. She raised her eyebrows and we both began to giggle.

"Here we go."

"Mom, shh."

I reached down and unlocked the small, tin-like contraption of a lock.

"Hi," I said. Two young Vietnamese businessmen stood in the hall.

"Mm," they replied. They smiled and nodded their heads. They spoke no English.

I looked to my mom who was bug-eyed.

"It's fine!" I mouthed to her without speaking, although the men probably couldn't understand anyway.

I believe strongly in giving people the benefit of the doubt. It troubles me when people say Asia is unsafe and warn me of food, violence, or theft threats. In three years of living in Asia, I could count on one hand the number of times I felt threatened—and they mostly involved westerners.

The men got up to use the bathroom down the hall.

"I can't sleep with them in here!" my mom exclaimed.

"Mom, seriously, they are just local businessmen. They are not going to do anything. What makes you believe they care about you at all?"

"Hilary, I don't like this. What if something happens at night? We have so many expensive items on us."

I actually had a friend who while riding the exact same train had all of her belongings stolen, including her SLR camera and passport. But I wasn't going to tell my mom that story.

"Mom, I promise you. It will be fine. I've never had anything happen to me before."

But I was a little scared. If I was traveling alone, it would have been different. I was used to keeping track of myself. Just before the trip, my brother had said to me, "You better not let anything happen to mom!" If anything were to happen to my mother, there were a lot more people that would be affected.

By any foreigner's perception, the situation appeared unsafe. Those businessmen could have done a series of terrible things if they wanted, and probably have gotten away with it. I didn't sleep the entire night. Lying on one top bunk, I kept my head turned toward my mother, who was lying on the other top bunk, and opened one eye every fifteen minutes or so to make sure she was okay. She was stone-cold asleep, thankfully, due to jet lag more so than comfort.

It was 6:00 a.m. when we arrived in Sapa, safe. Nothing had happened overnight. The men woke up and chatted briefly in Vietnamese together. We didn't know exactly where we were going, so I used a map and the little Vietnamese I knew to ask their help. They pointed us in the direction of our waiting bus and even led us out of the crowded train station.

"Cam on ban," my mom and I both said, thanking them in terribly broken Vietnamese.

The men waved but couldn't even say thank you in English.

I felt so guilty for judging them. They hadn't known, of course, but it bothered me how easily my culture is moved by fears based on stereotypes. In fact, they were just two men traveling for work—nothing more.

Still rising, the sun's beams just started to break through the clouds to warm the chilly air from the increase in altitude. Mountain peaks rolled in the distance and disappeared into the fog. We boarded our resort's bus and continued our journey.

"Are we ever going to get there?" my mom said. I felt bad. She had been using multiple modes of transportation now every day for a week. She was only still going because I was pushing her to.

The bus took just over an hour to reach the resort. We drove at what seemed to be a gradual rate of twenty-five degrees uphill, the engine of the bus revving with each press of the gas pedal. Fortunately, it was a Toyota.

As we wound our way through the mountains, Mom and I gazed out the window. I'd never seen anything so beautiful. Rice paddies had been carved into every side of the mountain. The seeds were just beginning to grow and the grass has sprouted in vibrant green. We also caught glances of azure-colored skies contrasting against the bold green; it looked like a child had taken the two primary colors and painted strokes of them directly next to each other. The roads were narrow, carved into the mountains, creating a steep overhang that looked down to the bottom where we had begun. I kept trying to take photos but failed because of the jerking of the bus.

"Oh, look!" my mom would say as we turned around each corner.

"Shoot! I'm not going to take anymore. I just want to enjoy it," I said. I realized that for twenty minutes I had been trying to learn how to use my camera instead of absorbing the moment.

Suddenly, the bus came to an abrupt stop. Everyone squealed and flew a few inches out of their seats from the momentum.

"What in the hell?" my mom yelled.

I slapped her leg. "Mother!" There were six other tourists in the bus and a couple kids.

"Sorry, sorry," the driver said to us all.

In front of us, water gushed down the surface of the mountain. It looked like someone had turned on a faucet from the unseen peak. The sound was so loud you could hear it inside the bus. The driver looked wary.

"You cannot drive over that," one woman yelled from the back of the van.

"This is insane," another said.

Then the children in the car chimed in, "Yeah, cool!"

I looked over at my mom. "This is one thing I have never seen before."

The driver began to inch forward as we sat in the back in silence except for gasps of air. "I'm sorry, Mom. I don't know what to say," I whispered, laughing.

"I'm not worried," she said. "I trust they know what they're doing." I looked at the floor. I couldn't watch the water. "Look, we're fine!" my mom said. "This thing is much stronger than the water. Look, it's beautiful!" I couldn't believe that in the last twenty-four hours I had put my mom in two threatening situations. She was handling everything so well.

We made it across the ten foot–wide stream of water and everyone broke out in applause for the driver. He grinned but kept his eyes on the road.

The bus dropped us off at a long stone pathway leading to a large cottage. The cottage was the main house of the resort and sat on the peak of the mountain encircled by individual solar-powered chalets, each with their own balcony and view of the valley below. Every view consisted of endless peaks of the Sapa range cutting their own shapes in the clouds.

"Talk about a getaway!" my mom said. "I don't think we can get any further than this!"

The staff carried our large bags of luggage on their backs as we walked behind them, still in our pajamas from our overnight train catnap.

"Wow. Wow." I had no other words.

"This is one of the most beautiful things I've ever seen," my mom said.

Hilary Corna

For three days, we didn't leave this mountain peak. We slept in every morning, ate breakfast at the main cottage, read books, played board games, and talked about the family and our coming addition, Ariana's boy. We traded off a cross-stitch project—a height measurer my mom was making for him.

Looking at the resort's guest book, I turned the page to April 2008 and found Katie's name. I knew her handwriting as soon I saw it. "Thank you for a great stay! This is a beautiful place and I hope to return someday!" Touching the page made me feel like Katie was right there with us, as if we were sharing the experience together. I missed her.

When our time at the cottage had come to an end, I felt like we had been there for ages. It wasn't often that I stayed still for so long. Like my mother, I had never been good at relaxing. The resort gave us the option of a van or motorbike for our route back to the train station. I didn't give my mom a choice and signed us up for the motorbikes. I wanted her to experience riding one in Asia. They were different from America—smaller and slower.

"Are you kidding me?" she said.

"Oh, come on!" I begged.

"Geez, I guess. Only in Asia!" she said.

There were two bikes and two drivers, a father and son. My mom rode with the father and I rode with son. I watched as Mom latched her legs around the bike and her arms around the driver to secure her safety. I was so impressed. She was being adventurous, courageous, and flexible, even though she had every reason not to be. She was fifty-six years old and riding on the back of a motorbike with a Vietnamese man in the middle of the Sapa Mountains. I couldn't think of many mothers like her.

When we finally made it back to home to Singapore, I had successfully run my mom into the ground. She only had one more day before her flight, so we spent it relaxing. It was grey and rainy. We went to a coffee shop and organized her notebook and turned it to a scrapbook. I then took her to my hair stylist for a cheap, Asian haircut. It had taken a year, but I had finally found a great stylist, and he was right under my apartment. I really just wanted her to get the extra service he always included, the ten-minute head massage. The hour-long appointment cost a mere US$10.

Then it came time to pack up Mom's things. As usual, Mom had her stuff scattered all around the room.

"Mom, seriously, do you have to spread it everywhere?" I asked. I didn't know it would spark a fume.

"Stop making me hurry! There is so much stuff! Can I please just organize it? Is that a problem?" she yelled.

"Sorry?" I said, standing behind her. The angry tone of her voice caught me off guard. She stormed out of the room and slammed the door. I didn't have any clue what she was so upset about.

A few minutes later, Mom returned.

"What was that about?" I said.

"I'm sorry. It's nothing," she said.

It wasn't nothing. She didn't want to go. She didn't want to leave her daughter, and she didn't want the trip to be coming to an end. We had spent almost a year talking about her visit and then planning it and then anticipating it. I also couldn't believe it was over.

We didn't talk about it that night, though. We just kept on packing. It wasn't until I spoke to her over the phone a few months later that she admitted she was just sad. We'd spent four weeks together every day. It was the most time we had spent together since I'd left for college.

My mom's flight was at 2:00 a.m. I had planned to take her to the airport to see her off but, caught up in my own emotion, I decided to get her a cab. We were exhausted and I needed rest, she advised, although I knew I wouldn't be able to sleep.

Finally, midnight came and it was time for her to leave. We loaded her taxi with two stuffed suitcases and multiple carry-ons. She was ready to go. Standing on the same curb that Katie once left me, we both attempted to hold back tears.

"Spark ideas — or help make other people spark ideas," she said.

I hugged her tighter than I ever had before. "I love you, Mom."

"I love you too, my youngest daughter. Be safe and vibrant."

She got in the little yellow Toyota taxi and drove off under the Singapore streetlights. Just as she turned the same corner, I fell against the post of my HDB apartment building in tears. I couldn't stand up. I couldn't walk. Sitting on the clean, gum-free sidewalk, my eyes swelled and I held my stomach.

Looking up, I saw one of the neighborhood stray cats, the one that always greeted me in the morning on my way to work. With slow steps, he walked toward me and brushed against my leg. Putting a hand on his back, I began rubbing the cat's dingy orange fur, and continued to cry.

Chapter 31
Challenge Your Team

I returned to work the next morning after only four hours of sleep. Our SVP, Edmund-san, had nominated me to participate in a panel discussion with one of the founders of The Toyota Way. The event started promptly at

9:00 a.m. in the same conference room as our promotion ceremonies. All two hundred and fifty TMAP staff persons were required to attend.

The founder sat on a small platform with an Indonesian manager, a Malaysian manager, a Singaporean manager, and me. I held my shoulders back, placed my hands in my lap, and crossed my feet below my chair like Japanese women do. The others on stage were highly esteemed within the company, each having served for well over five years; I was the only one who was not a manager, not in my thirties or older, and not male. Two years earlier, I would have been nervous in this position, but now these differences no longer intimidated me.

Edmund-san moderated the event strictly, allowing us each only one question. In the weeks prior, we had presented our top three questions to management, who had then selected the question they wanted us to ask. I saw this as a rare opportunity to ask a question that I'd struggled with for two years. When Edmund-san handed me the microphone, I gripped it so tightly that I could barely feel my fingers. The founder smiled and leaned slightly forward in attention.

Without wavering, I asked, "When conducting kaizen in the dealership, top management's understanding and commitment seems to be the most crucial, yet so difficult. Do you have any advice on how to build this?"

The founder's answer was so ambiguous that I don't even remember what he said. It touched on the need for communication and a clear purpose and target, but it wasn't anything we hadn't heard before. I walked away from the event frustrated—I'd wanted an answer to my question—but after talking with some of my coworkers, I realized that the panel had been more of a motivational tool than a learning opportunity. The company had faced a lot of challenges since the financial crisis and wanted to bring its employees back together. In such a case, I felt honored for the chance to serve a different kind of role in the company, helping to inspire the other staff.

Twenty-four hours later, I was on a plane to India; I hadn't seen Nandi in two months. Summer in Singapore was coming to end, and I couldn't believe that the trip I'd been planning with my mom for almost a year had already passed. I wasn't ready to reenter my fast-paced life, and I was beginning to wonder if I even wanted that lifestyle at all.

This time I traveled alone with the task of helping the team prepare for a visit from Hamada-san. Everything looked fine upon arrival, until I started asking questions. The distributor team didn't visit the dealership daily anymore, pulled by their bosses to work on other technology-related issues. Almost overnight, TMAP and the experts from Japan were leading the project instead of the local Indian team.

I wanted to do something, but my role was still unclear and I was unsure to whom I needed to report. Even though I was originally instructed to observe and study, I found myself leading Reshma, Mahesh, and Deepesh, becoming their only voice. No one else was working *with* them, only asking them to do things. One day in particular made me briefly lose faith in my leadership. Mahesh approached me in the obeya room and said, "This work makes me depressed. Making a list in the a.m. but then no progress. I hate this working style."

I tried to think back to what Maeda-san had advised—I needed to help support what TKM could not do. I would just have to persevere and continue to work despite the ambiguity of our tasks. I replied to Mahesh, "Thank you for telling me how you feel. I agree as well and am trying to come up with the best way to change the situation. Just trust me. It won't always be like this. We just have to keep following what we are told for the time being."

He reached out and shook my hand. "*Hai*, thank you, Hilary-san." I smiled. I didn't really have the answer, but all I could do was keep him motivated.

Kom-san asked me to help Reshma, Mahesh, and Deepesh practice communicating their part of the improvement process in preparation for Hamada-san's visit. Usually, the TMAP or other teams would converse with the visiting management. This was the first visit where the local team would do the explaining.

To start, we made scripts of what they would say—making sure to cover the main points—and even outlined their walking paths. We made visuals to support the explanation of the process, cleaned the areas being visited, and rehearsed the scripts in front of other teams.

Reshma was a pro at the explanation. She understood the logic so deeply that the script actually made her more nervous than speaking naturally, but she was so soft-spoken that we had to work with her to speak louder, especially with the Japanese whose English was already poor.

Mahesh was also very enthusiastic and understood the logic, but he spoke so fast that I could barely keep up with him as a native English-speaker. The Japanese would nod in agreement when he spoke, but later tell us that they couldn't understand anything he said. I also had to work with Mahesh to restrict his points to ones that would interest management. It reminded me of my first business trip reports that were over forty slides long; now I neatly covered the same points on one page.

Deepesh was very well spoken and at the perfect volume, but he had a hard time explaining the logic. He preferred a script that could tell him exactly what to say so he could memorize it. I worked with each team member for hours on his or her own needs, and I was anxious to see them perform when Hamada-san finally arrived.

During the observation, Hamada-san nodded and asked very few questions. Kom-san and some of my colleagues gave me thumbs up behind his back after each process was explained by the team. The Japanese management commented in particular on how impressed they were with Reshma's understanding. "She gets it-ne!" they said. I was so proud of how far my friends had come. Before kaizen, they hadn't attended meetings, much less spoke, and now they were presenting to the executive vice president of the regional headquarters.

At the end of the observation, we went to the main meeting room where the project had begun six months earlier. The management sat in order of their position around a long table with Hamada-san facing the door directly in front of the dealership president, who had a huge smile on his face.

Hamada-san's comments came as a surprise to everyone. He expected to see more improvements being made to the process rather than just an explanation of the process. "Thank you for Nandi's time and effort to pursue kaizen," he began. "But when I visit Nandi, I feel like I'm visiting a *kaiten-sushi* restaurant."

All of the Indians looked around for clarification. Kaiten sushi is served on a conveyor belt, and the food and service is of mediocre quality. I tried to withhold a visible reaction, happy that Hamada-san saw the truth but disappointed and shocked by his lack of positive support. It was uncommon for his level of management to pinpoint the dealership so openly.

Jojo-san, the dealership president, looked around, unsure of how to respond to the comment. Hamada-san sat back in his chair with his arms crossed.

Another Japanese top manager who noticed the president's discomfort added, "You can sell a car with or without a thank you. What is difficult is how to convince people and let other people feel there is a problem."

I heard from Kom-san and others that Hamada-san had the same feeling I had about e-CRB being too advanced for India. He felt that the operation supported the expensive technology rather than the expensive technology supporting the operation. This defeated the purpose of kaizen, which stated that tools are just tools to support the process. If you don't improve the process, it doesn't matter what tool you use; the problems will remain the same.

The Toyota executives shook hands and Hamada-san departed the room, concluding the meeting. It hurt to watch the dealership president searching the room for an explanation. He'd been in full support of the activity since the beginning. He was available when we asked him to be and provided the resources we requested.

Shortly after Hamada-san left the dealership, the president walked up to me in the hallway. I thought he was going to scold me, but instead, he said, "Hilary-san, I am embarrassed because I cannot tell Hamada-san about what I want to do. I'm frustrated with the past two to three months. The TKM coordinators have no communication. They are like ants pulling at the same insect in different directions. Whoever are the strongest wins."

I tried not to smile. I was shocked that he had approached me, relieved that he noticed the problem, and sad that I couldn't have done a better job to improve the situation even though I realized it was out of my control. I immediately thought of Reshma and the rest of the team. I couldn't wait to tell them that their real boss felt the same way they did.

Jojo-san immediately called the team together, and we met in the room where we always ate lunch. Reshma came rushing up, confused. She also thought the observation went well.

"Reshma, if anything is stagnated, you come to me," he said. Before the e-CRB project, Jojo-san and Reshma had barely spoken; he'd never asked her to report directly to him. Now, this direct contact showed his sincerity and strong intent to succeed in doing kaizen. Although I understood Hamada-san's desire to see more concrete results, I felt like he'd missed these little differences.

Jojo-san continued to tell Mahesh and Deepesh, "Challenge your team to find a solution—this is from Toyota Way. You should always ask questions, not give answers. Must solicit answers from different perspectives."

My team focused their entire attention on their boss, who shook his wrist in the air and said, "What happens when you mix salt and water? Salt dissolves or do you get dirty water?" Everyone shrugged.

"It doesn't matter. Neither answer is right or wrong. The value is created in having different ideas from different perspectives." I nodded. Even I was learning something from him.

Jojo-san reminded me of Gio-san, the general manager of the dealership in the Philippines who was so anxious to help but needed the right guidance to do so.

He continued to explain to the team, "We can still sell cars, but kaizen is to sell more cars and faster. Do you know how many ideas Toyota receives in a day? 1.6 million. Imagine how much we could improve?" I knew even then that I was witnessing sincere kaizen progress, and I wished Tanaka-san or Hamada-san had been there. They needed to hear it.

Finally the president ended his outpour of thoughts, "Like art of war, you provide weapons, food, and guidance, and then execute. Please think of problems—this is our weapon." Jojo-san taking lead from TKM, TMAP, and DOKD was crucial. Whether he succeeded or failed, the point was that he was taking ownership. This was the best sign we could ask for.

Upon my return to Singapore, I reported to Maeda-san and Tanaka-san, and they were thrilled to hear the good news. They decided to wait a little longer until they visited India again so that the president had time to take his own action. Also, Tanaka-san was nearing the end of his fifth and last year at TMAP, so he was busy wrapping up his responsibilities before returning to Japan.

I was ecstatic to have some time in Singapore. Soon after I returned, I scheduled a time with John to catch up over the phone. We'd only chatted online since our encounter the previous summer. Even though he wanted to keep in touch and maintain a friendship, his girlfriend didn't want him to have anything to do with me. After a year, she'd finally agreed that it was okay for John and me to talk.

I woke up early one day before work to accept his call on my cell phone. It was 7:00 a.m. — 6:00 p.m. his time. I wasn't nervous, just excited to have him as a friend again.

"Hey, Hil!" John said, as if we'd just spoken yesterday. The conversation was civil, small talk about work, his new apartment, and gossip about mutual friends. I prepared for work as we spoke. He told me about what was going on in his family, and I shared some stories about my mom's visit, making him laugh as he imagined my mom kayaking in the South China Sea.

"Flying her out there and having that time was such an incredible thing for you to do," he said. "I'm sure you will never forget it."

I stopped doing my makeup. "I'm just grateful that I had the ability to support her. I feel so blessed to have shared those memories with her."

Naturally, John's girlfriend came up in conversation. In the past, I never mentioned her when we spoke, because the thought of him with someone else disgusted me. I'd gotten over that, but still didn't have much to say on the subject.

"I want you to ask about her. And Hilary, I just want to be able to keep you as a friend," John said.

"I mean, it makes me happy to hear if you are happy, John," I said.

"That's all I needed to hear. It means a lot. Thank you."

"I've got to run. I'm going to miss my bus to work," I said. Our hour had passed quickly. It was hard to connect; we were so separated from each other's daily lives. But hearing John's voice was comforting. Even though I missed him — I couldn't help it, which was why I usually avoided contact with him altogether — I was sincerely happy for him. I didn't know when I would hear from him again, but I was just happy to know that he still wanted me to be a part of his life.

A social whirlwind of partying, eating, and drinking swallowed up the entire month of August. I finally connected with Lydia and Sarah, whom I'd met at Drew's barbeque, and Jessica and Owen, my wakeboarding partners, as well as their French neighbor Fabian. We'd created a small group of friends. Over the month, we saw concerts, went to barbeques, stayed out dancing, and slept in late the following afternoons. There were theme parties for birthdays, champagne brunches to celebrate engagements, and special VIP parties. I even had two dates. It was such a relief to have a normal life again. I could plan things with my friends and not have to cancel or back out. People no longer said to me, "I assumed you were out of town."

That month, I also began researching the process to apply for permanent residency in Singapore. Applying for permanent residency doesn't require you to surrender the passport from your home country, but you do get the retirement benefits of a local that you don't get as a foreigner. I didn't know how long I was planning on staying in Singapore, but I was beginning to feel comfortable, like I was finally finding my place.

One Saturday while I was in town, I met an old friend — Brandon — for lunch. We met at an outdoor restaurant on the Singapore River, right across from the River Place condos. We hadn't seen each other in almost a year. Sitting across from each other, but leaning in close, we talked for three hours, discussing everything from personal finance to work to love.

"You must know your value, Hilary," Brandon said. He had a beautiful British accent that complemented his good looks. Unfortunately, he was in Singapore with his girlfriend. "You are beautiful, smart, ambitious, and responsible — exactly what every guy wants."

I turned my head down to the side to hide my blush. Women don't receive such laud very often.

"You should hear how Kirk and I talk about you. You're like King Tut! You're top drawer, Hil."

"Oh shush, really," I said, smacking him on the shoulder. Although playful, the gesture made me think of John. I wondered if I'd have to find someone else before I could truly get over him.

"With all of your experiences at such a young age, I hope you know that you could be making a lot of money," Brandon said.

His comment brought my attention back to my career. I leaned forward and put my elbows on the table. "Yes, I know. But it's not about the money. I adore my job with Toyota." Glancing to the left I saw the River Place pool and smiled at the thought of Ren and Sato-san.

"People believe in me, Brandon. They have given me absolutely priceless opportunities within the company."

"I'm just saying."

"I know. It's just that nothing I've ever done has been with the objective of earning money. All of the sacrifices have been in exchange for experiences. The money will come."

The midday heat was beginning to subside, and Brandon left to meet his girlfriend. "She's going to think I left Singapore!" I could not have hugged him as tight as I wanted, in gratitude of his encouragement. Instead of going home, I sat on a bench by the river for an hour. Deep inside, I had the strange urge to cry, but I wasn't sure why.

It was Monday night when I found out. The workday had been positive, productive, and I left on time to meet Kirk for a cocktail, then Lily for dinner. Later, as I changed into my pajamas for bed, I put on my favorite T-shirt, a baby-blue Chicago Cubs shirt that John had given me when we were together. I had kept it because it was soft, but also because even after washing it so many times, it still smelled like the detergent he used.

I brushed my teeth and got my outfit ready for work the next day. I loved coming back to Singapore, because I could wear dresses in the office instead of my masculine dealership uniform. When I turned out the lights, my star night-light filled the room with a blue glow, leaving only my blue star night-light on to light up the room. I sat at my desk for a quick end-of-the-day peek on Facebook and froze when I saw the comments in the news feed. He'd done it. John had proposed to his girlfriend. And I was wearing his shirt.

Ava had warned me to be prepared, but there's not much you can do to prepare for something like that. I stared at the screen for several minutes, expressionless. Numb. I couldn't cry, though I felt like I should. I couldn't be angry, either. My emotions were at a strange equilibrium, just like they had been while sitting on the river a few days earlier.

I stood from my chair and covered my mouth with my hands. I paced my small room in a circle for several minutes, and then pressed my palms on the edge of my bed for support. I sat and tried to relax my legs. I took a deep breath in and fixed my eyes on the wall that represented everything I stood for: my hard work, my experiences, and my loves. The boarding pass from my one-way flight had faded so much that it was almost illegible. My train pass was there, in pieces, hung close together like a jigsaw puzzle. Peter's photo and pencil drawing he made for me hung nearby. Museum stubs from Beijing stuck to the wall next to my Olympics passes, and next to them, the same photo I'd given Ren for his birthday of the two of us in the pool. Then the most recent photo, a picture of my mom and me together in Vietnam. None of these things meant anything to me at the time, though; I think my heart had stopped.

As I looked down, I remembered that I was wearing his shirt. Standing up from the edge of the bed, I tore it off, balling it up in my hands and squeezing it as hard as I could. When I let go, my arms were shaking.

With a steadfast stride, I made my way to the kitchen. Reaching under the sink, I grabbed the handle of the trash shoot where the cockroaches hid that goes down to a garbage room for the entire building. I jerked the metal door open so hard that it vibrated as it slammed against the pipes. The smell of rotten food wafted past my face. I'd never been that close to the shoot before.

For a second, I stared down into the shadows. Then I tossed the baby-blue shirt into the darkness and let go of the handle. "Good-bye John," I said to myself.

Chapter 32
Anthony Is Waiting

I didn't sleep that night. I thought about the fortune-teller from years earlier during my trip to Bangkok with Katie. He had told me to keep communication; that the man would come back. I wondered if I hadn't kept enough communication, or if I should maintain communication now because there was still a chance. Or perhaps it was all a farce, and I was fooling myself into allowing a Thai palm reader to predict my future.

My mom had always said the opposite of the palm reader — to cut off communication with John. When I told her the next day that he was planning a May wedding, her only response was, "He must really like her, Hilary. He is marrying her. For the past two and a half years, he's been falling in love with her while you were having adventures."

In retrospect, I needed John to propose. I needed him to let go of me, because I hadn't let go of him, and it was plaguing my life abroad.

Now I really found myself wondering how long I would stay in Singapore. I'd never set a time period for it because I always imagined I'd know by instinct when I was ready to leave. Logistically, after two years of working in the Japanese business culture, I couldn't imagine what it was like to work with Americans again. The rules were all different. Emotionally, I had become enchanted with the idea of finding someone else and sharing our privileged lives abroad. What I would come to realize, though, was that I still had the same feelings as when I first arrived. I never went to Singapore looking for love — I had gone there looking for myself, so that I could give love.

I'd approached my two-year anniversary already and was having lunch with Kimura-san to celebrate. He told me that it had been an honor to meet my mother — that he could understand me better now that he had — and when we talked about the team's challenges in India, he said, "There are those that want to achieve more in life and there are those that are perfectly comfortable, as is, allowing it to continue as normal without disruption. Few others see this disruption as an opportunity." I admitted that I was one of those few others and promised to tackle the next ten-day business trip to the best of my ability.

That night, I spoke to Katie, and she reminded me of how overjoyed I was after my first day with the company. "You showed up to dinner with my father so proud," she said. I smiled, remembering the excitement, but I didn't know what to do now. I didn't know what the next steps in my career should be. I liked working in small teams, but I didn't like the control that big organizations like Toyota had on my life. The position doing kaizen perfectly fit my interest because the job allowed me to manage something independently, but I wanted to conduct kaizen on a more local level. Rather than visiting distributors from headquarters to convince them to do kaizen, I wanted to work in a distributor team directly. Sato-san had moved to Italy for this same reason; in a local setting, he had more hands-on responsibility and the management's understanding and support.

My goal, therefore, was to join a smaller Toyota operation or to someday run my own team and business. I now had the know-how and skills to do the same projects on my own if I wanted.

There was a lot of catching up to do during this particular trip to India. Maeda-san hadn't been there in two months. People from TMAP, the distributor and the dealership had questions for Indian management about the project as a result of Hamada-san visit earlier that month. His impression of the activity's progress was not as positive as anyone hoped. Word of mouth had spread his dissatisfaction.

Immediately upon return to India, Maeda-san understood the situation without my explanation. Again, the schedule hadn't been followed, and the key performance indicators we'd set were not updated. Yet, as we walked through Nandi's obeya room his first day back, he did not appear disappointed.

"They are not the minority," Maeda-san explained to me as we sat down. "We are. They think our way of thinking is abnormal."

He continued, "Don't worry. It's going to take ten years for them to realize." Granted, I didn't feel like waiting ten years, but his support calmed me greatly. I began to look at the India situation from a different perspective: a more positive one.

During one of our final days in Nandi, Reshma approached me in the hallway of the dealership. It was mid-morning, so it was loud, with many people rushing past us and bombarding Reshma with different tasks.

"Just a moment, please," she said turning her back to them. "Miss Hilary, here, these are for you." She held out a small white box with gold earrings in it. As Reshma pulled them out, they lay in her hand, delicate and light, with an intricate weaving design.

I held them between my hands and looked at her with a smile.

"I can't believe you did this," I said. "That was so thoughtful of you."

"Oh, it is nothing. Thank you for all you have done, Madam."

I stood there with the box in my hand while she turned to acknowledge the people begging for her attention. I couldn't stop smiling. It made me think of my team in Manila when they'd given me a matching necklace and bracelet for Christmas. My teams had become my friends.

I returned to Singapore in the best mood I had ever been in after India. I flew in on Thursday night and spent the entire weekend with Jessica and Lydia. I met with Lydia the most times and discovered we got along very well.

After a day at Jessica's pool with some of her neighbors, an unplanned evening turned into a late night in the city, resulting in one of the most memorable. Even though we barely knew each other, Jessica, Lydia and I laughed and danced under strobe lights until morning. For the first time in a long time, I felt like I had finally met my best girlfriends.

A few days later, I commuted to Malaysia to follow up with the project at the dealership in Johor Bahru. I was working on my computer in the back seat when the driver asked me why I came to Singapore. We'd never had the conversation before.

"So your work here is like a big adventure," he said after I finished the story.

I stopped typing. Amid the demanding work and travel, I sometimes lost sight of that.

"Yes. Pretty much, Nanda-san," I said to him in the rearview mirror.

"That must be nice," he said, smiling.

I smiled too. Living in Asia *was* a big adventure for me; I had nothing to lose and everything to gain.

An hour later, the car pulled into the dealership parking lot.

"See you at 4:30?" I asked Nanda-san.

"Yes, Ma'am. I will be here at 4:15."

My phone rang right as I was greeting Goh and the other Malaysian team members in the conference room. It was my mom calling from a hospital in Ohio. On that fourteenth of September, my sister had given birth to the first grandchild in my family, Anthony. I had become an aunt, but I was so far away.

"Mom, can you hold on a second? Excuse me, Goh-san; I have to take this call. It is my family back home."

"*Hai.* Of course," he answered.

I walked past the lobby quickly and exited through the side door. I sat on the curb of the sidewalk just behind a car so no one could see me. The smell of spicy Malaysian food being cooked in the dealership pantry drifted around the corner. The palm trees around the dealership stood still absorbing the harsh sun. I imagined the leaves that would be falling back in Ohio. At that moment, I would have given anything to be back there.

I brought my phone to my ear again. "I'm here," I said. I closed my eyes and held my hand over my mouth.

"Oh, Hilary, he is beautiful," my mom said. "And Ariana had a very easy birth. He has his dad's ears, but Ariana's eyes. Are you there?" she asked.

"Yes," I said softly under my breath. I patted my tears dry with the back of my hand as they fell down my face.

For months I had seen pictures of my sister pregnant, but it hadn't felt real. I didn't know how to comprehend that she'd brought another life into this world. I would have to wait for my upcoming trip home in December to see my nephew and understand what it really meant.

"We are waiting for you, Hilary! Anthony is waiting," my mom said.

Chapter 33
Shoganai

The next week, I attended a baby shower for one of my coworkers, Ein Ein. She had given birth to her first child within days of my sister. I had witnessed Ein Ein getting married and pregnant and becoming a mother, all during my time at Toyota. Her little boy's name was Axton.

When my coworker and I entered the Singapore apartment, Ein Ein's friends and family welcomed him, but stared at me in bewilderment. Once again, I was the only Caucasian in the room. Ein Ein immediately approached me and thanked me for coming. In Singapore, it's more common to give *Ang Pow* than actual baby gifts. *Ang Pow* are also referred to as red packets, which are envelopes decorated in red and gold with money inside. I handed her my envelope and she smiled in appreciation.

I immediately went into the baby room to meet Axton. He was sleeping soundly in his crib with Asian cartoon characters all over it. I pictured Anthony peacefully in his bed twelve time zones away.

Just a few minutes later, a small cry came from the crib. "Do you want to hold him now?" Ein Ein asked.

"Yes, I'd love to."

She gently lifted him from his crib and calmed his cry. I sat on the bed, watching her care so lovingly for her little blessing.

Ein Ein walked over and set his light, fragile body in my arms. I had to withhold the tears. It was as if I was holding Anthony. Although just as beautiful, Axton looked much different. He had pale skin, a head of dark black hair, and eyes the shape of tiny pea pods.

One White Face

"You're a natural, Hilary," Ein Ein said. I just smiled, rocking baby Axton. I'd never been opposed to having children, but it wasn't something I aspired to either. Strangely, holding Axton felt different from holding any other child. I imagined I'd experience the same feeling when I held Anthony.

I still had two big trips ahead of me before I could go home. November was the six-month progress report for the India activity. Immediately after, I'd travel to Rome for a week with Sato-san and my mom, a trip that Tanaka-san had just approved.

Maeda-san and I worked from Singapore to prepare for the progress report. A lot was changing in TMAP. Our office was moving locations as of next spring to Tanjong Pagar, just across the street from my apartment building. I also found out that a colleague and friend of mine, Yuko, was leaving the company. As we bid farewell, she said to me, "I remember our first day together at Toyota because of what you wore. Usually, on your first day to work in Japan, you just wear black, but you wore purple. I always remember that."

Yuko was moving to Germany with her boyfriend, following her heart rather than her career. Her action made me wonder how she came to her decision and if I would someday be forced to do the same. I associated Yuko with the excitement of my first days at Toyota; now I felt like she was moving on with her life while I was stuck behind.

Around the same time, one of my expatriate friends, Abby, returned to Canada after a decade of living abroad. I began thinking about how long I planned to stay in Singapore. I couldn't imagine living there for another eight years, but at the same time, I wanted to keep my options open to avoid missing any work opportunities. It wasn't hard to see that I was far from the person I was when I left home. I'd learn to navigate international travel alone; to communicate and work with people of many races, cultures, and religions; and made friends from around the globe. I'd learned to see, touch, taste, hear, and smell all over again.

I began to live in the moment, in the life I'd built abroad. My new friends and I ate scrumptious Sunday champagne brunches and attended plush VIP beach parties. We attended a white-collar boxing fundraiser and wakeboarded in Indonesia. A British guy named Eliot asked me on a date. Lydia and I called each other daily and wore matching costumes to Drew's birthday party. Things were finally going well, both inside and outside of work.

With John finally engaged, I felt ready to date again. After months of playing phone tag, I finally met Hiro, a Japanese guy I met at the club the memorable night that Jessica, Lydia and I went out. We dined at an outdoor patio in the middle of the city overlooking a shopping center. The restaurant was just high enough that you couldn't hear the crowds of people in search of the greatest deal. We immediately ordered beers because it was so hot, and because I knew Japanese men always started dinner with one or two beers.

We talked all night about everything from Toyota to how I dealt with Japanese bosses to America's portion sizes. I was instantly intrigued by trying to read Hiro's expressions. His gaze hid no lies. I felt honesty in every word he spoke. Free of wrinkles, his face indicated his focus was on our conversation the entire time, yet he seemed in a consistent state of introspection. He reminded me of Peter, who always had something going on in his head whether or not he verbalized it.

Hiro kissed me on the cheek as we parted. His gesture was so polite and gentlemanlike. It had been a long time since I had been treated so kindly.

"When will you be back?" Hiro asked. "After no more India, I want to see you again."

"Right after India, I am going to Rome. It will have to wait until I return from Italy."

"*Hai*, I will wait," he said. I couldn't help how giddy he made me feel. I had two other dates that month before Hiro, but I didn't feel chemistry with either of the men like I had with Hiro.

The seventh visit to India that year was for interim reporting to Japanese top management. The big bosses from all of the departments in Japan that sent members monthly were coming for only two days. After months of business trips worth millions of dollars, these bosses were expecting favorable results. They were expecting growth. They were expecting the impossible.

Yet surprisingly, I was feeling more positive about this business trip than any other. I'd finally earned Maeda-san's respect and confidence, which made me feel like I wasn't tackling the project alone anymore.

We met first with Jojo-san, the president, who had accomplished many things since we left and wanted to illustrate his newly found leadership. He invited me to meet with him and the customer retention team in the lunchroom. Deepesh, the CR kaizen leader, began the meeting by introducing Neraj, the supervisor for the call center, whom the president had never met. The two staff members sat across the lunch table from their boss while I sat to the side, actively trying to stay out of the conversation. I was an observer only.

After the CR team reported their progress, the president began, "Do you know the difference between culture and civilization?" Both of his employees' fixed their attention to him. "Culture is deeper. It's how we interact. Civilization is based on external factors." Jojo-san loved to talk. That was his strength. He continued, "Do you know the difference between obedience and discipline?" They shook their heads and he went on. "Obedience is accepting something from the outside. Discipline is something that you impose on yourself. Martin Luther King, Jr. was very disobedient and unconventional but very disciplined. Kaizen is culture and discipline, not civilization and obedience."

The team smiled at the president's personal definition of kaizen. "Kaizen is not a revolution. It's an evolution. Let's build the evolution of Nandi together." I tried not to get emotional, but I couldn't help but feel proud for Jojo-san's growth as a manager.

When Maeda-san arrived, I had a substantial amount of good progress to share with him. We went for a long lunch one day outside of the dealership. This was very rare since the dealership always provided lunch. We sat on an outdoor patio and splurged on Italian food, which Maeda-san loved. He began telling me about his history with the company.

"When I was young, I was searching for what I really wanted to do. Still today, I am searching." At first I was confused, but as he continued, I realized that he didn't want to leave Toyota. Rather, through Toyota he could test different skills he wanted to learn and better understand himself as a professional.

I leaned forward and listened. "My policy is three years," he said. "Give a company three years. The first year, just observe. Listen and watch. The second year, support. The third year is the hardest, trial and error of your ideas."

This made me think of the Philippines project and how I had fought so hard to lead the team, as if I was already in my third year with Toyota. However, in that early stage, my role was to simply observe and listen. This was what Yoshida-san had done when he joined the team, and what had upset me. I didn't understand. Now, I did.

When Tanaka-san had introduced me to the India project, he'd said that my purpose was to study. It was evident that I had the capability to support. That's why he had asked me to suggest recommendations in the business trip reports. It was all making sense.

Maeda-san's sudden openness was a surprise impetus to my work. I finally had someone paying attention and caring for me again. I had lost Kimura-san, then Sato-san. Yoshida-san couldn't fill the role, though he tried, and Tanaka-san had never wanted it. I had finally found another senpai in Maeda-san.

After the motivational lunch, we walked back to the office along the side of the road amid beeping horns and through the dusty air. Maeda-san and I were supposed to attend a committee meeting that day, but it was cancelled, so we used the time to review the presentation slides for the big bosses that Tanaka-san had asked me to prepare. I learned later that this was Maeda-san's idea; he knew I was one of the few people who understood everything that had taken place at Nandi in the past six months, and he wanted to see if I could tell the story well to top management. So he'd suggested to Tanaka-san that I be responsible for making the presentation.

I'd spent over thirty hours compiling presentations crafted by others from the past six months and trying to explain the activity progress in a concise manner—one of my biggest weaknesses. I began going through the slides with Maeda-san, and within seconds, he began to rip them apart.

"We must tell a compelling story to management. Where did we start, where are we now, and why?" he said. "Each slide should lead to the next like instructions on how to change your oil. You can't just jump to putting a new filter in without draining the old oil." There was something about the way the Japanese spoke that made them so easy to understand. Because their vocabulary was limited, their word choice was straightforward, logical, and clear.

"True meaning of SOP is set minimum and then ask all to improve. Take best improvements and share to level up. Others set standard very high, based on ideals, and then say to please find your way there." By others, he was referring to westerners. I nodded in agreement as so many examples came to mind.

I stayed up until 3:00 a.m. revising the slides so we could show them to Jojo-san the next morning. We had only one more day until the Japanese big bosses arrived. Maeda-san and I both slept during the hour-long morning drive.

Jojo-san paid close attention to the slideshow on the yellow drywall of the conference room. After I ended, he thanked me repeatedly. "Very easy to understand and positive. Thank you, Hilary-san."

I nodded, trying to hide my smile of relief. I looked back at Maeda-san and bowed slightly in thanks for his guidance and mentorship. The entire team was there except the service team.

The management left while I stayed in the room to make some final revisions. Within thirty minutes of the meeting's conclusion, the service team entered the room.

"Oh, hi!" I said, surprised to see them. They should have been in the meeting.

"Do you have the slides for tomorrow?" the service team's leader, Ajeesh, asked. He was average in height, about 5'8", and stood in dull khakis and a brown button-down shirt covered in dust.

"Sure, we just reviewed them and they're ready to go," I said.

Ajeesh started clicking through the slides. "*Ne-ne.* What is this?" he said.

"I'm sorry?"

He began talking to his team in the local dialect and twisting his wrists in the air like Indians do when they feel passionate about a subject. He said,

"You cannot show these figures. These are not the real figures. You must remove this."

I shook my head and squinted as if I'd just awaken from a dream. "What?"

"Where did you get these from?" he asked, standing and pointing at the computer.

"They are from your team's presentations," I said from my seat.

"That is not true. These are incorrect. We cannot show these to Yato-san," he said. Yato-san managed the Japanese experts we'd been working with in India since the start.

Blood began to rise to the surface of my skin. I stood up. "These came from your past presentations, so if they're incorrect, then you need to raise that issue with your team." I spoke slowly and sternly.

He walked away from me and took seat with his team. "They did not come from my team. Whatever figures you came up with, you need to check your math."

I took in a deep breath through my clenched teeth. "Ajeesh, if you look," I began slowly, "I can show you exactly which graph came from which presentation."

He wasn't even looking, and within the first couple of slides, he rotated his chair away from me slowly. In a mocking tone, he said, "I cannot work with you. You should not even be here."

A sweat bead fell from my forehead. I was speechless. I had never been in a situation like this before. My palms left sweat on my computer mouse, and I prayed that Ajeesh's team wouldn't see my eyes swelling up with tears.

I glanced over at Ajeesh's subordinate, Kumar. "Did these slides not come from your presentations?" I said, rolling my chair a little closer to him. Kumar looked away, turned his chair to his boss, and said nothing. Light from the one window in the room illuminated guilt on his face. I walked around the long conference table toward him, unable to contain my anger.

"Excuse me, but I'm here to help you. If these aren't the right figures, we need to discuss them one by one and identify the correct source." Ajeesh turned over his shoulder.

"Did you not hear me?" He said. "We cannot work with you. Your math is wrong. Maybe you should go back to mathematics class and study a little harder."

I took a step back as the service team laughed but avoided eye contact with me. Why had I even agreed to be a part of this project?

"Do not speak to me like you are my father, Ajeesh," I said. With that, I stormed out of the room. Some days I thought I was so strong, but that day, I felt weak. Running to the tiny bathroom at the end of the hall, I sobbed so loudly that the car washers must have heard me through the air vents. I slapped flies away from my face and held the cheap, rough toilet paper to my eyes. At least I didn't have to worry about my mascara smearing because I intentionally never wore makeup in the dealership, trying as much as possible to not draw attention to my gender. I already stood out enough as a Caucasian.

How could Ajeesh be so dishonest about the figures? Why should we even do the job if we weren't going to tell the truth?

Ajeesh's team was spending less time in the dealership and, as a result, our team from the regional office in Singapore had come in to save the day. We were never directly responsible for leading the project and the presentations; our job was to "support" the sales and service teams, but what did that word mean? Often, we were the ones doing the legwork.

I knew that Ajeesh's actions were simply a result of the underlying problem: his bosses, the Indian top management, had never viewed the project as a priority. They were feeling so much pressure from every angle of the company, even from President Akio Toyoda, that they were juggling too many projects.

Embarrassed by my lack of professionalism, I splashed brown tap water from the sink on my face, pinched my cheeks, clenched my fists, and went to find Maeda-san. He needed to know what happened.

I couldn't tell if Maeda-san was upset or proud of how I had handled the situation. His face was bare of emotion; he showed me no sympathy. I had gotten used to this style of management, but it was never easy for me as a westerner. He would show me how to handle Ajeesh, rather than telling me.

Looking straight ahead and barely even acknowledging my story, Maeda-san walked into the conference room where the presentation was paused on the differing slide. I trailed behind like a scolded kindergartener, unsure how Maeda-san would react.

Much to my surprise, Maeda-san greeted Ajeesh cheerfully. "Just wanted to check the status of the presentation. I heard the management was impressed."

Ajeesh smiled back. "Yes, we are just confirming some of the KPI now."

"Great. Thank you. We must absolutely confirm the KPI," Maeda-san said. He sat down and went through the slides with Ajeesh one by one as I'd tried to do. Within minutes, I understood Maeda-san's method. He approached the Indian team positively while respecting their authority.

Later that evening, he explained, "We are here to support TKM. If there is something they do not agree with, it is ultimately their decision to make." He wouldn't say whether I was right or wrong in the situation; our role wasn't to be right. Our role was to guide the local team to think and do what was right on their own without being told directly.

The Japanese expatriates were always more highly regarded by the distributor teams than those of us from the TMAP office. Their opinion or instruction was always followed above ours, and this made it very difficult for our office to ever earn the level of respect we needed. Therefore, I doubt I could have had the same impact on Ajeesh as Maeda-san did, because of his nationality. However, there was still a lesson to be learned from the situation: when conducting business, it was more important to know how to empower the workers to think for themselves than to tell them the right answer.

Despite the rush and last-minute changes, the presentation the next day went smoothly. Management had very few questions and was surprisingly pleased. They never saw the information that was cut from the presentation, but Maeda-san and I both just shrugged. *Shoganai.* There was nothing we could do. It was up to the India team now.

Chapter 34
Call Me "Antonio"

I arrived in Germany at 6:00 a.m. for my layover; I was on the way to Italy. Locating the airport lounge, I found a room full of tall, muscular, handsome men. Some were drinking red wine, while others stuck to coffee, and others ate large pretzels and dill pickles. The dark lounge held sleek modern furniture. Flat-screen TVs covered the walls playing the most recent fear-mongering news about the swine flu and other worldwide issues.

In pajama pants and a zip-up sweater, I sat in the plush leather chairs and watched the transient crowd move in and out of the room. It's amazing how different our world is from place to place, and I love it.

The week before I left for Rome, I had finally applied for permanent residency in Singapore. I thought I was ready to be a part of the transient crowd for a little while longer. "You can expect a reply in three months at the earliest," the woman at the immigration office explained. I didn't know what would happen in those three months, but I was looking forward to researching my options. I didn't tell my mom or my family about applying for PR, though; they wouldn't have been very excited about the idea of me staying longer, and there was no point in causing debate if it didn't even go through.

Singapore had become so normal to me. I no longer noticed the obvious things that had made me feel separated in the beginning, like eating hot food in hot weather, or carrying on a conversation while three other languages were being spoken. Yet, I was beginning to miss the

Western world. I still loved Asia, and my heart would always have a place there, but I felt a gap that couldn't be explained.

With all the men in the airport lounge, I couldn't help but think of one of the most significant things that I lacked: a man. I wanted someone to share Asia with. I wanted to feel like a lady. I wanted someone with bigger feet and bigger hands than mine. I wanted someone who would make me feel feminine. I was attracted to Asian men, but I often didn't get these same feelings from them, and westerners that were male in Asia were never in the mindset to start a long-term relationship because they were either just arriving or soon leaving.

I shifted my thoughts to what was ahead: a beautiful journey with my mom and mentor, who would be meeting each other for the first time. This wasn't my first trip to Rome, so I wasn't as interested in seeing the city as I was in spending time with Mom and Sato-san. But this trip wasn't about me. It was about my resilient mother who had given up her life to raise five kids. I was hoping Italy would be a time for her to relax and revel in the benefits of her hard work and commitment. I was also hoping that she could get to know Sato-san, who played such a significant role in my life, and that, by meeting my mom, Sato-san could better understand me.

I departed Berlin and flew over the Swiss Alps to Rome, arriving around 9:00 a.m. My mom wasn't arriving from the United States until lunchtime. When I exited the doors of the baggage claim, Sato-san was sitting right there on the plastic bench waiting for me.

"Sato-san!" I exhaled all of my breath as I hugged him tightly.

"Call me Antonio," he said.

He looked very different. In Singapore, he had rested well, golfed under the tropical sun, and even went running, but I could tell immediately that his lifestyle had changed. His skin was not as dark; he looked much more tired, and he had put on weight. Yet, he was still the same Sato-san at heart. He smiled big, laughed loudly, and acted like a gentleman, pulling my luggage and opening doors.

"We have so much to talk about," I said to him.

"Do not worry. We have a whole week. I want you to enjoy."

We had a few hours until my mom arrived, so he took me to his golf club for an espresso. He introduced me to the manager of the club and his golf teacher. It didn't surprise me that everyone knew Sato-san. That was one of his strengths: he was a connector of people. I wished I had looked a little more composed, other than in my pajamas from the overnight flight, because he was introducing me to his new life and the people in it. He wanted me to understand and continue to play a role in it. I felt honored.

When we picked up Mom from the airport, she looked like she had when she came to Singapore—tired and discombobulated after three

One White Face

flights. Overwhelmed with joy and a few too many espressos, I shrieked out to Sato-san, "She's here! She's here!"

My mom just started laughing, caught up with the fact that she was in Rome simply to meet her daughter's old boss.

"Hi, Mom!" I hugged her as we both tried not to cry.

"It is an honor to meet you," Sato-san said from behind us. I pried myself from my mother's tight grip.

"Yes, Mom, meet Sato-san. Sato-san, this is my mom."

With a jet-lag gaze, I jumped up and down as they hugged.

"Welcome to Italy!" Sato-san said.

Of all of the events that occurred during my time in Singapore—even my mom's visit—this was one of the most noteworthy. I thought of my father and thanked him for taking care of my mom and loving her vivacity. I wished he was there. I wished he could see Italy. I wished he could meet Sato-san and be a part of my life.

Typical of Sato-san, he had many events planned for us, from dinners to tourist sites and a weekend in Florence. One of my favorite memories from our week was from the very Sunday we arrived.

Sato-san took us to his home to meet Ren and Keiko, who was a gracious host, as usual. Ren had grown up so fast. Seeing him act like a boy when I'd only known him as a baby took me aback. My heart inflated with joy when he went to his room and brought down the framed picture of us in the River Place pool, the one I had given him for his third birthday.

For brunch, we drove to a small town thirty minutes away and ate at a local Italian eatery where we were the only foreigners in sight. The restaurant was overflowing with kids chattering and adults laughing and drinking wine. Meat hung from the ceiling and music roared from the speakers. Everyone was celebrating Sunday as if someone had gotten married.

We ate plates of antipasto and homemade bread and drank multiple glasses of Italina table wine. Sato-san told stories about my interview with Toyota and my first business trip to India, and my mom shared her fears during our overnight train to Sapa. Keiko was so kind to laugh and smile during the entire conversation even though I knew she couldn't understand much of our English. We didn't talk about work the entire day.

My mom and I spent the week in the city while Sato-san went to work. Keiko joined us one day for a small trip, but otherwise she stayed home caring for Ren and the house.

We spent an entire day at the Vatican and St. Peter's Basilica, saw the breath-taking Pantheon, roamed the Coliseum, and wandered through the Roman Forum. In between, we visited multiple famous piazzas to people-watch and rest our feet. We chatted with young, handsome male baristas and befriended locals. We made a point to eat gelato and drink wine every day. My mom was easy-going and full of energy, making her a fun traveling partner. By the end of each day, we were exhausted. Our necks hurt from staring up at the ceilings in the Vatican and our backs ached from walking miles to the next tourist destination.

In the evenings, Keiko would make us dinner and Sato-san would ask about our day. One night, Keiko made one of my favorite Japanese dishes, called nabe. The whole house smelled of chicken broth and fresh greens. Over his bowl of nabe, Sato-san asked my mom a question. "You raised five children. They are all healthy, happy, and accomplished. What is your biggest learning lesson?"

This was very common of Japanese men. They place so much respect on people who are older than them and often seek their guidance. My mom just laughed, like she did when she felt shy. It was not something people usually asked, nor was it something she often considered. Caring for her children was second nature; she was too busy to think about how or what worked best—she just did.

After Sato-san asked the question again, she responded, "My biggest learning lesson is to not worry so much and let them do what they want to do."

Keiko-san smiled, sitting across from my mom with her hands in her lap. She seemed to understand this comment from my mom.

Sato-san sat across from me but kept his attention on my mom. Ren was playing with a toy, unaware of his father's curiosity about raising him. "How do you not worry?" Sato-san was known for being a leader. He loved to plan and have control. This was his strength.

My mom was unable to answer concisely. She went on a tangent and told stories about my older siblings and how busy she got with the twins, me and James. But she never answered the question.

"Yes, but how do you not worry? What if something happened?" Sato-san continued.

I could tell my mom didn't really understand. She hadn't thought about it in so much depth before. I interrupted.

"You don't understand, Sato-san. I don't think my mom herself even knows how to not worry. She just couldn't because she literally had no time to worry." My mom sat still listening and thinking. I continued, "She worked and had five kids at home, going through five different stages of life at any given point in time. If she took time to worry about all of us, she wouldn't get anything done." I'd thought about it before. I'd thought about my mom a lot, how people often called her a superwoman. They praised her for her strength and courage. They admired her for her vigor after experiencing the loss of her husband and soul mate. The ironic thing was that she kept going, not because she sought pity or attention, but because she had no choice. She was forced to survive.

"You are bold, Ms. Corna." Sato-san said. "I am not as strong as you. I hope to someday be as strong as you."

By the end of the conversation, we were all in tears, including Keiko even though she tried to hide it. Ren continued playing with his toys.

Sato-san took off Friday and we left early Friday morning to drive to Florence. When we arrived, we went for a walk through the streets of the city. The air chilled our noses, but in refreshing way. Keiko and my mom were caught up in conversation, so I walked ahead, anxious to speak with Sato-san about TMAP and India.

I told him about the Ajeesh incident in India. "I was so ashamed, Sato-san. I just couldn't believe the Indian managers."

"Hilary, this is the situation in India. You know how they are. They were just verbal to you. It is a tough situation in India," he said, looking straight ahead.

I kept my attention toward him. "I don't know what to do. I feel like I cannot make progress. I feel like they do not have the intention. These core problems are out of my control."

"This is why I left. TMAP is not sure what they want to do with kaizen."

Sato-san began to tell me a story about the beginning of his career. He had been married before and was doing business with his wife's family. Sato-san was doing very well in the business, but his brother-in-law was not. His father-in-law wanted him to take over the business instead of the brother, causing a lot of conflict in the family.

"I was unsure what to do. My wife's father was like a father to me. I worked so hard and was going to be destroyed because of politics. Sometimes, you just can't do anything."

Keiko and my mom approached us from behind. "Onaka ga suita!" Ren said. He was hungry. Our conversation ended abruptly even though I still had questions. I still needed to know what I should do. I didn't know if Sato-san was telling me that I was bound to fail in India or that I should stick with it.

During our two nights in Florence, we went to the same restaurant for dinner. Famous for *bistecca alla Fiorentina*, a local steak, the restaurant was hidden down a dark alleyway, and you could smell the tomato sauce from outside. It was bright and lively inside, with people drinking and laughing loudly, and it reminded me of holidays with my Italian family.

We ordered a variety of homemade pastas, antipasto, and the famous steak. The wine went around quickly.

"To Hilary's mom!" Sato-san wished cheers.

"To Sato-san!" she returned.

Sato-san knew the family that owned the restaurant because he visited Florence often for work and always ate there. The owner came to the table and greeted us, bringing us a shot of limoncello with him. It was as if Sato-san himself had become Italian. I couldn't even understand everything he was saying. The restaurant owner accepted Sato-san like he was family, and thus, treated us the same.

"Welcome, welcome!" The other customers watched.

"Graze mille!" We yelled in response.

The next morning, we drove back to Rome.

"We'll go to Trevi Fountain first, and then I'll take Hilary to the airport," Sato-san explained. My mom's flight wasn't until the morning after mine.

We only had an hour or so to see the Trevi Fountain and get a quick bite to eat, and we soon realized that Sunday afternoon was probably not a good time to visit the world-renowned tourist destination. Surrounded by clusters of people, we took pictures quickly — my mom and me together with Sato-san, Ren, and Keiko.

"Rapidemente!" Sato-san yelled at us. "Okay, next, what do you want to eat?" he asked. "We have twenty minutes. Oh, Burger King! Perfect," he said pointing ahead.

"Yay, Burger King!" Ren said, and Sato-san started walking toward it.

Surprisingly, the fast food restaurant had a line all the way out the door. We ate quickly. Ren wore a paper crown that he got with his kid's meal.

"Hilary is leaving, Ren. She is going back to Singapore," Sato-san explained. "Do you remember Singapore?"

"Yes."

"Will you say good-bye? She came all of this way to see you."

"Bye-bye!" Ren said. He understood what was happening but was too young to care. I, on the other hand, held back tears. Tourists clattered their trays around us. The room smelled of French fries and Whoppers.

"Don't forget me, Ren," I said. "I will miss you and your family."

I hugged Keiko and thanked her. "You are a kind host." I spoke simply and slowly, "Thank you for everything." And then I looked to my mother. "Mom, don't miss your flight tomorrow!" We both needed something to make us laugh.

"I won't with Sato-san around," Mom said. Even Keiko laughed at this.

"I love you, Mom. Thank you for coming to Italy with me."

"Thank you, Hilary, for bringing me to Italy."

We didn't know what else to say to one another. I waved good-bye over and over as Sato-san and I walked out of Burger King, leaving Mom, Keiko, and Ren behind.

"Come on, Hilary. We cannot be late," Sato-san said.

The car ride to the airport was silent. I didn't know what to say. Sato-san parked and we walked swiftly to the check-in counter. The airport was busy, but I didn't have to wait in line because I had a priority account. Within minutes, the airport staff had taken my bag and handed me my ticket. I turned around back to Sato-san.

"All set."

"Be safe, Hilary-chan. I will miss you."

With that, my heart split and my hands began to shake.

"I will miss you too, Sato-san. Take care-ne."

"Do not worry about India. Focus on your job. Study and learn."

I still had so much to ask him, but I knew my time was up.

"Be patient. Your time will come."

"Thank you for everything. You have done a good job at being my guardian."

My comment made his eyes watery.

"Don't cry!" I said.

"I feel like I have done a bad job at being your guardian. I cannot take care of you here. Please seek help from Kimura-san for now."

"Please do not say that. You have. Kimura-san has taken care of me. Thank you."

"Sayonara, Hilary-chan."

"Sayonara, Sato-san. Totemo arigatou gozaimashita." Generously thanking him, I bowed and bid my farewell.

Sato-san waited behind the security line until I got through and walked to my gate. I waved the entire time. I didn't want to say good-bye. I didn't want to leave him. I was frightened, but I didn't know why.

As Sato-san's face disappeared from sight, I let everything go and broke down. My hands were so weak that I could barely carry my purse. I ran to the bathroom again like I had when we said good-bye in Singapore and sobbed with my forehead against the wall. I didn't care whether anyone heard me or not. I just cried. I cried so hard I could barely breathe. I wasn't sad about the trip coming to an end. I was sad about losing Sato-san again. Even though I knew that I could talk to him at any time, it just wasn't the same.

After twenty minutes, I left the stall and patted my face with ice-cold water from the sink. I kept telling myself to inhale and exhale. When I finally gathered myself together, I went to find my gate and depart from Rome.

Just as the flight took off and I thought I was going to be okay, the sorrow hit me again. The wheels of the plane took air, and all I could imagine was my map and how far I was getting away from someone so important to me.

The lady sitting next to me asked, "Are you okay? Are you leaving someone?"

I struggled to speak but mumbled through wet lips, "Yes, I am leaving a best friend."

"That is life, my dear. Be thankful you have a best friend."

I paused and considered this. I knew I shouldn't be sad. We had all shared a phenomenal week, a rare opportunity to merge families from countries far away from each other—both in culture and distance. I was upset, though, for not hearing the rest of Sato-san's story. I needed guidance from him for India.

But by thinking of his short example, I knew what I needed to do. I needed to follow my heart, which was not in TMAP at the moment. I knew there wasn't one "right" answer, that I could do anything with my career, but I had just one problem—I didn't know what I *wanted* to do.

The past two and a half years had changed my life, but did I want to live in Singapore anymore? Would I ever go home and be normal? Could I? Where was home, anyway? Was it a physical place or a state of mind?

I thought about my life and friends and experiences in Singapore; I adored them all. But more and more, I wanted someone to share these things with, someone to make me feel at home. One of the hardest parts about what I was doing was that I was doing it alone. I made decisions alone. I woke up and I went to sleep alone.

The new year was approaching, and with it, light began to shed on what I wanted. I wanted to be someone's something special. I wanted someone to look at me like Sato-san looked at Keiko. I wanted to fall in love.

Chapter 35
Genbarimasu

The month of December was always fairly quiet in TMAP. Activities slowed down, teams discussed the plan for the new year, and people took leave. Since I traveled so frequently for my job, people in the office just assumed I had been on a business trip during the past week. Very few of my colleagues knew that I had gone to visit Sato-san, and I wanted to keep it that way.

I had lunch with Kimura-san when I returned. He took me for sushi at the Ritz Carlton, just a few minutes walk from Centennial Tower. I told him about how wonderful the trip was and gave him an update on Sato-san's success. I refrained from telling him about my sadness upon leaving. That was between Sato-san and me.

"His life has changed drastically, but he is so very happy. Toyota Motor Italy really takes care of him."

"That is good news. Sato-san is a very strong man," Kimura-san said.

"It is the same for me now. India has not changed, and I don't feel like Tanaka-san cares about my well-being either in India or outside of work. He doesn't care about my opinion," I said. Tanaka-san had only one month left at TMAP before his expatriate term expired, requiring him to return to TMC in Japan.

"Hilary, they spend tens of thousands of dollars on your business trips. You don't think they care about your opinion?" Kimura-san replied.

"True. So then, what do I do?"

"They don't expect you to solve the India problems. Like *The Secret* said, an affirmative thought is one hundred times stronger than a negative thought." The book was the most recent one he had given me to read. "If you already believe they don't care, then what makes you think they should have a reason to care?" he continued.

I knew Kimura-san was right. I'd given them no reason to believe in me. Essentially, I'd given up. Still, I wondered how to handle the situation if my heart was no longer in the project. Unfortunately, I was so concerned about *my* performance that I wasn't focusing on the performance of the team and of the project as a whole. In effect, I was acting much like the rest of the e-CRB team.

I returned to India with the mentality that I needed to do something different. The last business trip had gone sour, and I was devastated by what I'd said to the India team and by the fact that I couldn't handle the situation on my own. I was traveling with Maeda-san this visit, but only for one week. We hadn't spoken about the Ajeesh incident since that day. Maeda-san expected me to persevere, not to make up for anything as long as I learned from it.

The first day in the obeya room, I met Oshiro-san, one of the kaizen experts from TMC. I raised the issue that had been bothering me. Why were we making an SOP if the sales people weren't using it?

He responded, "Use or not use, this is not my matter. From the original procedure, whether they follow or do not follow, this is not my issue." Jabbing his finger at the SOP manual, his eyes scrunched together as if I had offended his intellect. A ball of sweat dripped down his face from a combination of the heat in the room and his persistent energy.

The obeya room was full of people, but no one had heard this except me. I wished Tanaka-san was there. Oshiro-san had not been hiding this per se, but this was the first time he had said it out loud. His comment made me angry — angry because of his disingenuousness and his disrespect for Reshma and the rest of the team, angry because I understood and he didn't, though he was identified as a kaizen "expert." "Thank you, Oshiro-san," I said, choking on my words but trying to appear calm. "I understand."

He smiled and responded, "Oh, good! Hilary, you are very smart. Thank you for your hard work."

I turned around and gasped for air. It was hard not to defend my opinion, but I was slowly learning that there was a time and place for that. I was learning how to pick my battles, and this was not one of them.

Maeda-san spent more time than usual in the TKM headquarters during that visit. I didn't complain because TKM was adjacent to the hotel, which allowed me to sleep for an additional hour. All of the Indian top management now flurried to address the concerns brought up by the Japanese higher-ups. They were also tired of the disorganization and scheduled a meeting to rearrange responsibilities for the new year. This rare meeting involved nearly everyone in the project from each department from India and Singapore, as well as the Japanese kaizen "experts."

In front of everyone, Kom's general manager asked him, "Are you confident we can succeed?"

Swiftly and assertively, he responded, "No."

I thought of my recent conversation with Kimura-san and wondered how we could expect good results if we had no confidence in what we were doing. Kom was always very positive and happy, making him a fun colleague, but I could sense his dismay.

Then it hit me: the project was not fun anymore.

As I looked around the room, faces revealed weariness and uncertainty. Team members slouched and played Sudoku games on their phones. Many left the meeting early. We had lost a sense of teamwork.

We faced these problems even within TMAP. Maeda-san had a hard time speaking honestly with Kom because Kom was responsible for the project on a macro level. However, Maeda-san was aware that most of the problems were out of Kom's control. The underlying problem lay with the top management of TKM. Until they realized this, nothing with the e-CRB project was going to change.

At the end of the business trip, we drove to the airport under black skies to catch our evening flight home. The driver took the same route as usual; I had memorized every turn. Maeda-san was staring out the window. I could tell he was thinking rather than sleeping as he usually did during the ride. Suddenly, he turned to me, his face almost expressionless but content.

"Frankly, Hilary," he began, "we cannot achieve anything this year in India project. But you must know that the more important point is how to improve your skills. Your know-how from India project is what will be used for the future."

I smiled and nodded, saying nothing. I was beginning to understand Tanaka-san's comment from the beginning of the India project when he asked me to study and listen. Management at TMAP had never expected me to run the e-CRB project or even to attain as much responsibility as I had. I could have done nothing and been fine, but I had gotten close to the project—too close.

When I returned to Singapore, I let it all go. I let go of my fears, concerns, and frustrations and just tried to enjoy life again, both in and out of the office. I posted the business card from the restaurant in Florence on my memory wall and made a photo book of our trip for Sato-san and his family. When they received it in the mail by surprise, Sato-san sent an e-mail that said, "Your book. It bring tears. Still think of trip often. Miss Hilary-chan!"

December was full of parties before everyone left town for the holidays. I attended three different farewell parties, which was normal at the end of the calendar year. Assignments with companies were ending, forcing expatriates back to their homes. I was becoming numb to these good-byes now. I didn't cry anymore, just bid my friends farewell and wished them luck.

One of the biggest parties that month was called ZoukOut, a giant beach party held at Sentosa every year. It was the first time that all of my friends would meet Hiro. Even though I introduced him as a friend, I was nervous about how they would judge him and me. They knew we had been on a few dates but were not anything official.

Hiro and Fabian immediately hit it off. "I like him!" Fabian said. Since Hiro had traveled all over the world, he got along with everyone. The Kiwis loved him because he could ski; the French loved him because he smoked (though that factor greatly bothered me); Everyone loved him because he could cook.

"I don't know what you're so nervous about, Hilary. There's nothing to dislike about him," Lydia said.

Lydia was right. I enjoyed being with Hiro so much when we were alone, but for some reason I worried about other people's thoughts when we were in public. Maybe I was still getting over John and needed to take it slow with my next relationship. Or maybe it was the cultural difference. Though we meshed well together, everyone staring made me feel a kind of different that I didn't like.

"Just enjoy your time together. Don't try and define it so much," Lydia said.

"Yeah, you're right. I do have such a blast with him. There's just something more to it that I can't wrap my head around," I said.

Hiro and I hung out many more times before I left. One night, he took me to a concert of Lenka, an Australian singer that I adored. The music was upbeat and bubbly. Hiro held my hand in the dark, giving me goose bumps. Everything Hiro did, he did with intention. I adored his sincerity. He wouldn't be somewhere if he wasn't there entirely.

"She is cute," I said about the singer.

"*Maa*, so-so. You are much prettier," he said, kissing me on the cheek.

"Oh, this is one of my favorite songs!" I said. I sat up in my chair. *It's all up to you to do whatever you choose,* the artist sang.

"I thought of you when I first heard this song," Hiro said. "I knew it would be one of your favorites."

I couldn't hide anything from Hiro. It was strange, like he knew everything about me without knowing anything. He could read my reactions, my thoughts, and my body language. He had the inherent skill of seeing the true side of someone. I wondered if it was just me, or if he was like that with everyone.

I tried to monitor my actions while I was with him to see why I was so nervous. The same thought kept reoccurring, maybe I was afraid of missing out on someone else if I gave him too much of my attention? Thinking such things made me feel horrible. Hiro had been close to perfect to me. I had an enormous respect for him and hated to think that I was wasting his time. For the time being, I'd try to appreciate his company while I could. My flight home departed in a couple weeks. I'd use that time to take a break; I could think about Hiro when I returned, with a fresh perspective.

Before I left for the states, we had planned a farewell party for my general manager, Tanaka-san. Ironically, DOKD went to the same restaurant where Hiro had taken me on our first date, called Nanjya Monjya. It was very popular among expatriate Japanese.

Tanaka-san had always worked in an international context for Toyota. Japan would be much different for him. I often felt like we shared this trait: we often felt more connected with people of different cultures than those of our own.

"Please persevere in India-ne!" Tanaka-san said to me sitting across the table. His face had already turned tomato-red from the alcohol. We'd finished dinner and countless empty beer bottles littered the table. A Japanese waitress with almond eyes was clearing them away and bringing out bottles of whiskey for the next round.

"Thank you, Tanaka-san," I said.

"India is a hard project. But you are strong kaizen leader. Please, do not give up."

I started to feel guilty. It was evident that I was unhappy with the situation, and I was embarrassed that he had noticed.

"Genbarimasu," I said, promising to try harder.

Our department didn't go out together very often. Coordinating schedules proved challenging and the friendships in RDSD under Kimura-san were stronger than in DOKD. That night, we didn't discuss India, management, or kaizen, but ate soba noodles and played Japanese drinking games.

Tanaka-san's replacement had just been confirmed, and no one was very positive about the change. He'd be my third GM in two and a half years. Yamamoto-san was over fifty years old and had never worked outside of Japan on a permanent assignment. He had just five years of experience conducting kaizen, and his English language skills were minimal. I had never had a GM so challenging to work with.

Tanaka-san's party prefaced the next Dinner & Dance Christmas party, which was the following weekend. This year's theme was a little calmer than high school or mafia. The title was "Fashion Runway," and as usual, no one knew what to expect. I wore a gold dress. Packed in the hotel ballroom dresses ranged from elegant gowns to Indian saris, and even a Pokémon costume. Loud techno music played in the main hall. I could smell the delicious traditional Chinese food waiting to be served.

Maeda-san had planned a talent show performance with other managers from the service division. It was obvious from the moment I approached them that they'd already been consuming alcohol to calm the nerves. He and three other GMs, including Tanaka-san, had dressed as Egyptian goddesses. They wore gold, polyester dresses with mesh capes and beads around the crowns of their heads. The women in the office had done their makeup—blue and pink eye shadow, red lipstick, and all.

The talent show began, and my bosses made their way to the stage in their performance costumes: black miniskirts and silver-sequined tube tops. They had dressed up as a popular Korean women's group. Our dinner table cheered them on by clapping and singing.

I remembered my first D&D and how Elise and I watched the swan-man dance practically naked on stage. Two years later, the abnormal had become normal to me now.

I was having fun but I had a strange sense that this would be my last D&D. I had a hard time believing that I would stay with Toyota another year. I walked around the tables, visiting all of my friends, thinking about how my work relationships had developed over the past couple of years. We took photos together, and I even greeted the top management's banquet table, which I had not done before. I wanted to fit in a hello with everyone before I left. I wanted to remember the night.

My flight home was the next morning at 7:00 a.m. and I had scheduled time with Hiro after the party, but all of my colleagues were urging me to come out to the clubs with them. Torn by the situation, I decided to bring Hiro with me. I knew it would be one of the last nights I could hang out with my work friends, and I didn't want to miss out.

"Oh! Hilary-chan!" my managers all exclaimed. Practically all of Toyota was walking out of the party when Hiro showed up in a cab. "Kare wa handsomu . . ." They continued taunting me about how handsome Hiro was.

I noticed that I didn't get as nervous with him in public as I had in the past. We were with other Japanese, so I didn't have to worry about him being accepted.

"Hiro, do NOT let me sleep in! I set my alarm, but I have to get up at five," I yelled to him across the deafening techno beats and blinding lights.

"Do not worry. I will not let you sleep in," he said to me.

About four hours later, I woke up to Hiro staring over me. "My beautiful, Hilary-chan, *ohayou gozaimasu*. It is 5:05 a.m."

I flew out of bed. As I frantically gathered my things, Hiro took my arm softly, turned me around, and gave me a tender, passionate good morning kiss. He caught me in his deep brown eyes again like he had the first night I met him. The butterflies were still there. "Thank you for waking me," I said.

"Thank you for letting me stay with you," he responded.

"Why are you interested in me, Hiro?" I asked.

"Your personality is pure. Your smile too—your smile is pure." That made me smile again.

Within minutes, I was showered, dressed, and walking out the door with my pre-packed luggage bound for home. Hiro wanted to ride with me all the way to the airport.

"It's not necessary, really," I insisted.

"I want to, Hilary. It is no problem." Hiro was always so laid-back and considerate.

"You are too sweet, Hiro," I said. He smiled.

At the airport, Hiro hauled my luggage out of the taxi and asked the driver to wait. It was so early that the sun had not yet risen, but the air was already humid.

"Merry Christmas!" Hiro said.

"Merry Christmas to you too!"

"I will miss you."

I kissed him good-bye on those lips that I adored so much. "See you soon," I said. I waved as the taxi drove away and I entered through the airport's automatic doors. A rush of air-conditioning hit my face. I was thirty-six hours away from home and needed time to think.

Chapter 36
How Is Asian-Land?

I wasn't sure how I felt about the fact that I was memorizing the terminals in international airports. It had been fourteen months since I'd been home–too long. By the time the airplane door opened, I had no feeling in my feet and I felt like every ounce of blood in my body was stuck in my joints, but I took off running the moment I reached the gate. I ran past quieted gates, black windows, and closed coffee shops. I ran past other passengers who had been seated in front of me. I ran past the security desk and duty-free shops. It must have looked as though I was in a rush to catch a flight.

My entire family stood in front of me when I turned the last corner—all four of my siblings, my brother-in-law, my twin brother's girlfriend, my mother and her two dogs, and my beautiful new nephew, Anthony, who was in my arms almost instantly.

"Meet your nephew!" my sister said. I was so overwhelmed that I had to focus to see the spectacular life that lay in my arms. He was gorgeous. He fit perfectly on my forearm, no bigger than a stuffed teddy bear. His skin was smooth, like the Japanese, and his eyes were a dark brown, almond-shaped like my sisters.

"Ah! It's freezing!" I screamed as we walked out of the airport doors. The cold air burned in my nose.

That first night home, my mom made us a late-night snack—enchiladas, of all things—and we drank Baileys while playing Scrabble in front of a fire. I felt blessed to spend time with my entire family in one place. It was becoming rarer as we all got older.

I spent the whole week with Anthony and Ariana, insisting that she let me carry him everywhere. I didn't want to be apart from him even for a moment. There was so much of my sister in Anthony that it almost scared me. Their baby pictures looked almost identical. I had never placed much priority on having children, but that week changed my mind entirely.

"I must have my own children. I don't know what I was ever thinking not wanting to," I said to my sister. Her eyes went wide as she smiled, proud that she could have that impact on me. "This is just too special," I said, looking down on Anthony asleep in his baby-blue blanket. I couldn't explain my change of emotion or attachment to Anthony. He had inspired me in some way, though it would be a long time before he could understand that.

We spent Christmas Eve and Christmas Day at Ariana's home. It was the first normal Christmas we'd had in years. Growing up in a single-parent household with four siblings, there was usually immature fighting and yelling about who got what, who was late for Christmas, and any other drama going on in the family. There was none of that this year. We'd gotten over it. It was the most civil I had ever seen my family.

During our gift exchange, Ariana's husband Josh gave me a giant world map. I loved it. It looked just like the map that I always imagined in my head when I traveled. Furthermore, I loved that Josh understood me.

"One day, you can put tacks for all the countries you have visited and hang it in your office," he said. "I expect to see it full one day."

"This is ingenious," I said. "Thank you."

That evening, we all went to my aunt's house for Christmas dinner, like we did every year. You could hear the Italians talking loudly from outside the front door. Wreathes hung on every window, a nativity scene sat at on a table by the front door, and colorful bulbs lit up the house like neon signs in Tokyo. The smell of olive oil and tomato sauce filled the house, and I was elated to see antipasto, homemade ravioli, pulled pork, lasagna under preparation.

"Hilary, how is Shanghai?" my grandma asked. She and my grandpa sat on the white couch watching TV. She wore a maroon and black velvet suit and had had her white hair curled at the salon for the special day. She was a typical Italian woman, loud and demanding and loving.

"Singapore, Grandma. Singapore." Ariana and I smiled at each other.

"Oh, whatever. How is Asian-land?" she said. Grandpa shook his head at her. She just smiled back at him, giggling.

"Wonderful. Things are busy, but good as usual." I didn't really explain much. It wasn't easy to answer such a question concisely. Her eyes were fixed on me, and it was obvious that she didn't know how to respond.

There was so much I wanted people to know. I wanted them to know about Singapore, Laos, and other places I had visited. I wanted them to know about yong tau fu and thunder tea rice and how healthy they were. I wanted to tell them about how young Singaporeans stay home until they get engaged and how they take care of their elders. I wanted to tell them about things I'd experienced in person that they had only seen in movies and on television — like how my manager in the Philippines had given me coconut water for my health, two years before it got popular in the West. I felt like I could talk about Singapore all day, and nothing else. It had become a part of me.

Chapter 37
Smitten

"Where is Yamamoto-san?" I asked Yoshida-san. Everyone had already been back to work for a week since the New Year holiday and the new GM, Yamamoto-san, hadn't reported to the office.

"This week, he takes care of immigration and apartment issues," he explained.

"What is the status of the Malaysia project?" I asked. The project in Malaysia was very elementary, as we both knew.

"Management still has not planned for our visit, so for now, we will suspend the activity. Until they ask for our support, there are many other projects we can work on. We will have to wait for Yamamoto-san's direction."

We usually spent January and February making plans for the rest of the year, but there wasn't much we could do until Yamamoto-san arrived. Also, Maeda-san and I had decided not to return to India until Yamamoto-san gave us a strategy. The problems we now faced were out of our control and it was difficult to move forward.

"Let's go to Korea!" Yoshida-san said one day as I was reading news articles from the United States online. "I need to check on their projects and report to Yamamoto-san when he comes. Do you want to come with me?"

"Um, yes."

"You are bored-ne?" he asked.

"Very."

"Okay, I will show you Korea. Look up flights. If we can schedule it before Yamamoto-san arrives, I can make sure we go."

I was a little surprised at Yoshida-san's eagerness to give me another opportunity. I called the company travel agency immediately.

That same week, a friend held a barbeque to catch up with everyone after Christmas. When Lydia arrived, I almost trampled her with kisses and hugs.

"Lyd-ya! I missed you!"

"I missed you too, misses." She always called me that. "Don't ever leave me for that long again!" She'd gone to visit her father in Goa, India, and he was coming to visit the following week for the first time since Lydia had moved to Singapore.

"Merry belated Christmas!" I said, sweating beneath the setting sun.

"So when are you moving in?" Lydia said. "I cannot wait."

Lydia and I had been planning to move in together. My lease at Tanjong Pagar had one month left, but I was ready for a change, and especially ready to have access to a pool and gym.

"I'm ready whenever. Do you mind?"

"No! I'm lonely there ever since Drew left. I need the company."

"Okay, how about next week then, before I leave for my next India trip?"

"Done."

There were so many things changing, and looking forward to them distracted me from missing home.

New faces swarmed the barbeque that night, which was common at the beginning of the year. Companies had initiated their human resource plans, shipping people to Singapore for the first time. The newer people looked like they were walking on water: full of energy, talking about the food and the weather and asking questions about where to go out. They decked themselves out in jewelry and nice clothes wherever they went while the rest of us weren't trying to impress people anymore.

Almost protectively, I wanted to warn them about all the hard parts of life abroad. I didn't want to scare them, but they needed to know the things that people hadn't told me, like how dating was nearly impossible, and how you'd learn much about friendship, and how you'd feel guilty for missing every insignificant family celebration back home.

But no one wanted to hear that. People wanted to hear about the cheap vacations, and the techno clubs, and the celebrity parties.

I met someone in particular, though, who had been considerably different from any other at the party. Eliot was from England but had spent months traveling down the western coast of North America, from Alaska to Belize. He had worked since he was in high school and paid for his own college. Eliot flaunted blonde curly hair and bright blue eyes.

"I adore your American accent, love," he said. I laughed, wondering if that term of endearment wasn't making an advance.

"Most people hate the American accent," I said out loud.

"Ah! You make me smitten."

He had no idea that that's what he was doing to me.

That night we also met another newbie to the city who was surprisingly interesting as well. His name was Gabriel, and he was an architect from Minneapolis. We instantly connected because I always found architecture fascinating.

"Look at you, Hilary! On the game already, and we've only been home for one week," Lydia said to me.

"Thank God! I need it."

I spent most of the night talking with Eliot. His charm and gentlemanly persona had my attention.

"I still cannot believe how you got here," he said. "How bold!"

"I knew what I wanted," I said with a bit of a grin. "There was nothing I had to lose." He filled my glass of wine. The wind was picking up that night, blowing my hair away from my face. I couldn't get my eyes off him.

"I want to move here. This place is a paradise," Eliot said. He was only visiting to interview with a company. He sold yachts back in England, but the market had taken off in Asia, so he was looking at an opportunity to sell them there.

"Singapore is pretty fabulous," I said. For him, I emphasized the positive aspects of Singapore. I wanted him to come.

He leaned forward to kiss me.

"I'm sorry. I can't do this," I said. Even though Hiro and I weren't officially together, I still felt guilty.

"Hilary, you intrigue me. Please, don't go," he said. People kept bumping into us even though we had been against the wall. Our drinks had been sitting empty on the table next to us for a while.

"I have to. Please, keep in touch. And please, take the job," I said. I grabbed my purse and slipped into the crowd. I looked back just as I walked under the exit sign to see Eliot staring at me with puppy-dog eyes.

Lydia called me the next morning. "Where did you go last night?"

My head was aching. "What is wrong with me Lydia? Of course, I would go and befriend that guy that doesn't even live here!"

"Oh hush, he was adorable. I am a big fan. He's probably moving here anyway, so just wait and see."

"Yeah, we'll see," I said.

"Gabriel was cute too. Will you see him again?" she asked.

"Yeah, I think he's going to come to my friend's company's launch party next week. I really liked Eliot, though."

"Of course. We always pick the ones we can't have. What happened with Hiro? Does he even know you're back?"

"He's in Japan now visiting his parents. We're going to meet up when he gets back."

Lydia's father came the next week, and I planned to move in after he left. Like Lydia, her father was shy but observant around strangers. He was tall and skinny, with beautiful silver hair and stunning, cold-blue eyes. It was evident where Lydia got her good looks.

It was a Saturday, and we were sitting with a larger group of friends at an Australian bar. Suddenly, Lydia's dad said to me, "Thank you for being such a good friend to Lydia."

"Are you kidding me?" I responded. "Lydia has been one of the best friends I have had here in Singapore. Thank you for raising her the way you did. You have a phenomenal daughter."

Lydia was positive, gracious, kind, and overly giving. There was not a selfish bone in her body. I didn't want to tell him about my recent struggles, but she truly comforted me over the past few months. As expatriates, it was not often that we got to meet family members of our friends. Meeting Lydia's father made me understand so much more about her and deepened our friendship.

"Take care of her, Hilary," he said as he left the bar that night.

"I promise, Mr. Hardiman," I said with all sincerity.

I spent the following day moving my belongings two streets away to The Beacon, Lydia's condominium. Viktor came and helped me with his car while Margaret and her boyfriend helped me carry my things down our miniature elevator.

"It's not going to be the same without you," Margaret's boyfriend said. Margaret was never sentimental, but I realized that he was speaking on her behalf. Even though we didn't hang out much, she knew me as well as anyone else.

"Thanks. I mean, I'm just behind you, so come hang out by the pool with us!" I said. "I'll be around."

"You're never around," Margaret said jokingly. While I was out traveling and keeping busy, she generally spent the weekend roaming the house, cooking, and watching TV. I would miss having her around, though. There was something comforting about knowing that she was always there.

I went in my room for the last time before leaving the apartment. It was empty and clean — free of the cockroaches I had initially found. The bed was gone, because I had sold it, and all that remained was a blue desk, a cupboard, and the leaky air-conditioning unit. However, the star night light mounted to the wall shone as bright as ever.

The side of the room that once held all my tickets, pictures, and maps exhibited nothing now except clean concrete. All the memorabilia had been placed in a scrapbook.

"Hil! Are you ready?" Margaret asked. We had one last load.

"Just a minute," I said.

I went and opened the window of my room for the last time, soaking in the view of Singapore and Chinatown. Since we were on the seventeenth floor, we were blessed with a strong wind, keeping our place cooler than the ones lower in the building. That day, I felt the gush of the wind even more than usual. Whistling through the curtains, the wind had its own voice; its own presence. Bracing my face, it ascended my journey.

"Are you crying?" Viktor asked when I got in the car.

"Shut up."

He laughed and drove down the road to Lydia's. There was something more to this than just moving apartments.

Yamamoto-san finally reported the next Monday, although it took two days before Maeda-san called us into a meeting to introduce us to him formally. "*Sumimasen,* are you available? Yamamoto-san wants to make introductions now."

I quickly grabbed my notebook and pen and followed Maeda-san to the service obeya room. Yamamoto-san sat in the back corner facing the entrance of the room. He had a sinister smile on his face that made me a little uncomfortable. I wasn't sure what it meant.

"Welcome. Thank you for coming. I like to introduce myself," he said, speaking one word at a time like an old computer game. He told us about his career with Toyota and his seventeen years of experience working with domestic dealerships in Japan. "Please, tell me what your story is," he said.

By the time my turn came around, I had mentally rehearsed what I wanted to say. I was known for using too many words, so I practiced succinctness. "I began working with Toyota in 2007 under Kimura-san in RDSD. My main project was on-time delivery ratio in the Philippines. In

2009, the kaizen activity switched to the service division and I was assigned to DOKD under Tanaka-san. My project currently is customer retention in India."

"Yes, I know you. We see each other often at Nandi," he said. I grinned and nodded in confirmation. "Thank you all for introductions. Me, Maeda-san, and Yoshida-san will meet now about our activity. Then we will meet with you."

The meeting lasted ten minutes and we were back at our desks.

"That was weird," I said to the man next to me who was in charge of a project in Malaysia.

"Yeah, much different from Tanaka-san," he responded

Yoshida-san and I left for Korea the next day. Even though I'd had my fill of cold weather during Christmas, I couldn't wait to see Korea. I had heard a lot from Sato-san about the country and how it was very similar to Japan in food, people, and city life.

The business trip was very laid-back with only a few scheduled meetings. For once, I didn't have to prepare or report anything, and this was Yoshida-san's favor to me: a break and a time for motivation.

Seoul reminded me a lot of Japan. The streets were clean. The city was full of concrete skyscrapers hiding the grey and windy sky. People were courteous yet kept to themselves. The distributor in Korea was known for having very hard working and respectful staff, also like in Japan. When I walked into the office, they stared at me like they had never seen a Caucasian before, and being blonde would not have helped. Yet I didn't mind the signaling anymore.

People often asked me why I put myself in such a challenging situation, being a white female working in an Asian company run primarily by men. For a while, I didn't have an answer and even asked myself the same question. The reward was the huge adrenaline rush when I achieved approval from bosses and colleagues — when they finally liked and respected me. It felt like overcoming the impossible.

When Yoshida-san introduced me as the person in charge for e-CRB in India, it hit me. I had an enormous assignment. As I began to share about our activity in India, I felt overwhelmed by the title Yoshida-san had given me. I thought I was supposed to be a student. It reminded of my first interview at Toyota and how I had scared myself during the meeting, not giving myself enough credit. I was essentially leading the Nandi team for e-CRB. I knew everything about the project. I had come a long way since that initial interview.

Like the Japanese, the Koreans were incredibly efficient. Meetings always started and finished on time because it was important to respect everyone's schedule.

After our meeting, Yoshida-san and I continued to work out of the conference room. I commented on the differences I had noticed across Asian cultures from the Philippines to Malaysia to India, and now Korea.

"One trait that I see most common in kaizen leaders is *omoriyari*. Do you know *omoriyari*?" Yoshida-san asked.

"No, I've never heard it," I said. I sat across from him at the table, listening intently. Yoshida-san always had my attention when he wanted it. He was a good teacher.

"Selfless is what *omoriyari* means. It means that you put no discrimination on people. It is very hard."

This reminded me of one of the biggest lessons I'd learned from working with the Nandi team: I needed to see through their eyes. I didn't feel white anymore, and I no longer noticed a person's race. By acknowledging people for who—rather than what—they were, we could work better, together. Mastering this, though, would be a lifelong process.

Yoshida-san stood up and turned to the wall, entirely covered with opaque glass like a whiteboard. He drew a triangle with Japanese characters on each corner. "My senpai once drew this for me. *Kansha* means gratitude, *kenkyo* means humility, and *shinnen* means conviction. The requirements of a kaizen leader are these. They must be thankful but modest, and never lose their conviction."

That same day, we received notification that there would be another visitor to Nandi, someone of bigger importance. The president of Toyota Motor Corporation, Akio Toyoda, wanted to see the progress at Nandi and planned to come at the end of March. Urgent calls had been made and presentations started. The pressure on our team had increased yet again.

Chapter 38
-TA Not -DA

I returned from Korea just before the Chinese New Year and met with Hiro to tell him the truth, that I couldn't see him anymore romantically. We continued to hang out as friends over the next several weeks, and he consistently brought up why I couldn't feel comfortable with him. I told him I enjoyed our time together, but in public I still felt self-conscious.

The situation with Hiro perfectly exemplified my lifelong struggle for normalcy: I wanted to be accepted by the "in" crowd, yet I constantly did things that made me different. So what did I really want?

Just after the holiday, I got a call from Viktor. We hadn't seen each other in over three months because of our travel schedules. I was sitting on the balcony of my new apartment.

"It's finally set," he said.

"What's set? Oh no, Viktor. The company's made a decision?" His company had been telling him for over six months that they'd be making him move, but hadn't told him where.

"They are sending me back to New York!" Viktor said. This was exactly the position he wanted.

"Wow! Congratulations! That's huge, Viktor." I covered my mouth with my hand. "I'm so happy for you."

"The problem is that I have to leave at the end of next month."

My celebrating stopped. "Next month?" He had originally said the summertime.

"Yes. They want to make the announcement at the start of the fiscal year."

Two months earlier, the two of us had had a sunset dinner on the Singapore River. We'd made a bet about which one of us would leave Singapore first. I had insisted that I would win, and put down 50,000 flight miles as a wager.

"That is so much earlier than expected," I said.

"Yep. Looks like you owe me 50,000 miles."

Singapore and Viktor didn't exist without one another. Viktor had been there since the beginning. He had seen and been through everything with me. I couldn't imagine this life without him around. Had my time to leave arrived?

There was something else Viktor said about my next step in life that I couldn't let go. He said, "You'll never be rich." I was initially insulted, until he explained, "Not because you can't, but because money is not important to you."

My objective with Toyota had never had anything to do with money. I had joined the company for the learning opportunities, and with those learning opportunities subsiding, I didn't know what my next move should be.

Even though Viktor was leaving, I had finally found a group of friends with whom I felt comfortable. Spending more time together, the bond between Lydia and I had been growing, and I'd been focusing on building relationships with the friends around me. On top of that, I had a new fling to keep me busy.

"Tonight was so much fun," Gabriel said after our first night out. We'd spent the whole night laughing. "Can we do it again?"

"I would love to," I said. He kissed me on the cheek, drove me home, and immediately asked me on another date. The next week, he made me a homemade eggplant parmesan dinner.

I called my sister the next day. "You will never believe the guy that I met. He is an architect, plays the guitar, loves to cook, and had jazz playing when I arrived at his apartment."

"Um . . . He sounds perfect," she said. "What's wrong?"

"Nothing. He's actually wonderful."

The next morning, I woke up to an e-mail from Eliot, the other guy I'd met the same night as Gabriel. "Hilary, I got the job in Singapore. I'm moving there next week. I want to take you to dinner."

As if my life wasn't already complicated.

"Don't define anything yet," Lydia advised.

"But why does this have to happen after two and a half years?"

"Be happy it's happening at all."

That month, I celebrated my Canadian girlfriends' birthday at a VIP table in one of the hottest clubs in Singapore. Another friend threw a birthday party with a Bollywood theme, to which I wore a stunning sari that made me feel like an Indian goddess. I also joined an indoor soccer league with a friend named Lily.

For the first time, I felt like I had a normal life in Singapore. I had a manageable workload. I had a strong and growing network of girlfriends, and I was dating. Everything finally seemed to be balancing out.

I still talked with Peter now and then. He was back in England figuring out what he wanted to do with his life now that he had a degree. I refrained from telling him about the details of my love life, although he often asked.

"Actually, I don't really want to know," he said during one of our conversations. "I prefer to still think of you as mine."

I hated when he said things like that because I didn't have the will to tell him to stop. We were never the same since he'd told me he loved me.

So, I kept the conversation more focused on work. "I could stay in Singapore and switch companies or even start my own. I have some investors that have already expressed interest in my ideas. I'm still waiting to hear back about the permanent residency application, though. That will really determine everything."

"And what about Toyota?" Peter asked.

I exhaled. "My new boss is tough. Not in terms of work, but in terms of management. He doesn't seem to sincerely care about the individual improvements of the team members. He is entirely focused on the India project and on looking good while he is in this position because it will be his last before retirement."

"I know you, Hilary. You know what you need and want. What do you want now?" he asked.

"I think that's the problem. I don't know what my priority is. I've lost motivation in Toyota and don't see it improving. I'm going to give it a couple more months, though, to give Yamamoto-san a chance. Maeda-san and I are also working on a new project, so I will see how that goes." I sat hunched over my computer with my head propped on one hand.

"That's brilliant that you are alert to it and aren't letting things go dull, all the while not really knowing why," Peter said. "I love you, Miss Corna. Know that you are an important person in my life."

I rolled my eyes.

As I was developing a routine, I spent my nights distracted by men and my days reporting to Centennial Tower. I now had time to eat lunch with friends, instead of running errands for business trips, and I even began taking hot yoga classes in the morning before work.

Kimura-san and I were meeting more frequently for coffee or lunch to talk about the changes happening in TMAP and what they meant for me.

"I spoke with Yamamoto-san briefly in the hallway the other day," he said over his venti latte. "He is very impressed with your work and commitment in India."

"Do you believe that?" I asked.

"Hilary, he is trying. I know the situation does not look good right now, but you have to think positively. India has been very good to you. You have done some wonderful things there. And Toyoda-san was planning to visit your project. Do you understand how big that is?"

"You are right, as always. I need to be more positive."

"Things will happen as you need them to, Hilary."

That night, President Toyoda-san visited Washington, DC, for the congressional hearings regarding the recent quality accusations made against the company. Originally, he'd been scheduled to observe the e-CRB project at Nandi during that time, so I never got to meet him.

The hearings started at 3:00 p.m. (EST), which was 3:00 a.m. in Singapore. I woke up just in time to turn on my computer and boil a cup of tea while the live streaming began. I sat on a blanket on the cold tile floor of my apartment, still in my pajamas, with my computer on the coffee table. Singapore was silent, apart from my reactions and my small computer speakers.

Congress couldn't pronounce the name of the company. Every incorrect attempt angered me like nails on a chalkboard. "It's pronounced Toyo-TA, not -DA!" I yelled at the screen.

The senators sat in their chairs on pedestals above the defendant, pointing fingers and raising their voices, which are two of the most disrespectful things you could ever do in Japan.

"I would appreciate the courtesy of a direct response," one senator commented. My jaw dropped, and I could barely sit still. Japanese businessmen do not give direct responses, much less when the answer is indirect or complex.

I held my head in my hands and kept my voice low to avoid waking Lydia as the congressmen continued to attack Toyota. They'd speak for minutes and follow their commentary with a series of ambiguous questions, then wonder why the answer from the company was indirect and vague. The Asian businessmen were simply matching the clarity of the question, and they didn't want to risk answering incorrectly.

Watching the congressional hearings was one of the most challenging dilemmas I faced while living abroad. My nationalistic loyalty was in question, and I didn't know which side I was on. I sat helplessly as my country, which I always defended, fought the company that had given me opportunities and changed my life for the better.

I eventually had to stand up and pace the room to relieve my frustration. The hearings went on for three hours with repeated mistakes by the westerners. Their lack of understanding of Japanese culture was so evident that watching it made me feel humiliated. On Facebook, I commented live about the events. Many of my foreign friends from India, Japan, and Europe seconded the statements, saying that the American Congress was illustrating their obvious lack of cultural understanding. Peter even responded once, saying, "You are not happy, darling, are you?"

The verdict of the trial did not bother me as much as the handling of the situation. Congress had only confirmed everyone's stereotypes of Americans as culturally insensitive. I was scared to go into work the next day for fear that all I'd done to earn the respect of my colleagues had been ruined by the hearings.

"I feel embarrassed to be an American," I said to Kimura-san.

"You should never be embarrassed, Hilary. You are working to change it, and we know."

We received notices within the company from corporate management before and after the hearings. Everyone was surprised when we heard directly from Toyoda-san himself. He sent a few short sentences via a Word email attachment reflecting on the afternoon in Washington.

He said, "At times I was nearly discouraged by the severe questioning and dismissal of our claims. However, I was encouraged by our dealers and team members that traveled long distances to offer support." I began to cry as I read the screen, exhausted from the lack of sleep and touched by the sentimental and sincere words. I looked around briefly to see that no one was watching and hunched back over my desk to continue reading. "We are currently in a severe situation. However, I do believe that we will be able to restore customer trust if global team members work together."

Toyoda-san was a strong leader, and I hoped to play my own role in improving the image of the company and, concurrently, of the average American.

Maeda-san and I were planning our next trip to India to begin a new project on the side at Nandi. He mentioned that, since Yamamoto-san was still catching up with all the activities at TMAP, we should use the time to do some quick improvement. We wanted to use the existing data to do a small trial in the sales area.

Arriving to the Bangalore airport, a smirk came across my face at the sight of the skinny Indian drivers waiting amid a sea of signs with their patrons' names on them. I had more fun that trip than I had in the past, enjoying my time with each individual team member and noticing the small things about each one that made me laugh. Some of them used words that I would have never chose to describe leading a project, like *iteration* or *hand-holding;* sometimes they created their own words like *updation* and *anytinian,* which they defined as "to mean that anything." I wasn't aggravated by these differences anymore. I just laughed at them.

I knew I needed to tell Reshma before anyone else about my recent career thoughts. One morning, I stopped her in the sales hallway before her day got chaotic and pulled her away from coworkers bugging her with the usual questions about registration status, car delivery schedule, and the lunch menu for the day.

"I need Reshma for just a minute," I said.

"Hi, Hilary-san! Is there something wrong?" she said. Several people stood behind her with their arms crossed.

"There's something I must tell you, but quickly," I said. Reshma was smiling bigger than ever. For a brief moment, I felt bad. I didn't want to leave her, but I knew I couldn't stay.

"I think I might be leaving Toyota very soon."

Suddenly, the corners of her mouth lowered. She yelled back at the staff, "Go on! I'll be there in a minute! Hilary-san, where is this coming from? When? Are you sure?"

"I wanted to tell you first. I'm not sure yet, but I have a feeling I won't be with Toyota for much longer. I've been thinking about it ever since the interim report incident in October. There are a lot of uncertainties right now. I'm waiting to feel out the situation with Yamamoto-san and my new project with Maeda-san, but I don't see things changing."

"It's okay, Hilary-san. I understand. Please let me know how I can help."

"Don't worry. I'll keep you posted. You must know how much I have appreciated working with you. You have made this entire project worth it, Reshma." She smiled and turned away to help the others. I knew she would survive, with or without TMAP.

Our department finally had our first monthly meeting with Yamamoto-san as the new GM when we returned from India. After we reported to the group, Yamamoto-san said to me, "You are the boss. You should be able to teach us. You know better than us."

The room was silent and Maeda-san was looking at the floor, which is what he did when he wished to avoid people seeing his facial expression.

He and I both knew that Yamamoto-san's understanding was shallow. The boss in India had been undefined. Sure, I knew what was happening in India; I knew every story and every reason behind the actions that occurred. But the purpose of our business trips was often unclear, and had been from the start.

Among other changes that March, the top management officially announced the relocation of the office, inspiring a refreshed attitude throughout the company. The couple of years since the financial crisis had been tough. Most everyone shared the feeling that such a change would benefit the overall atmosphere of Toyota.

Viktor held a barbeque for his farewell party around this time. We lounged at the River Place pool patio, enjoying the mild night air. Food covered the table and a pile of alcohol rose from the cooler. Friends from all around the world attended and reminisced about good times with Viktor. Everyone loved him.

There was so much I wanted to talk to Viktor about. I wanted to know more about his job in New York, what his plans were when he arrived, whether he was really happy or sad. But we ran out of time.

"As my bosses always say, health is the only thing you have. Take care of yourself, Viktor. Don't work too hard," I said.

Singapore was such a transient place due to the many expatriates serving temporary assignments. I'd already bid farewell to so many friends, some after only a short time, and others after longer. Viktor was by far the longest. Our friendship had grown tremendously over the past couple of years with memories from clubbing in Hong Kong to spending Christmas at a spa in Malaysia to eating insects in Laos. Viktor consistently inspired me to be better person. I knew Singapore would not be the same without him.

Chapter 39
Opportunities in Disguise

Eliot put our dinner at the top of his to-do list when he moved to Singapore from England. We met for a steak dinner, an uncommon meal in Asia, at a quaint French restaurant I'd always wanted to go to. I explained more of my background, and even shared a little about why I left John.

"Wow. So what did you do?" Eliot said, sitting back in his chair. We hadn't even ordered our food yet, but only a drip of wine remained in our first glass. Even from our outdoor table, the street was silent and you could smell the meat cooking inside. Eliot was sitting upright across from me, listening intently. I felt like I was telling a childhood bedtime story.

"I bought a one-way ticket. I gave myself two months and a budget and said to myself, if either one runs out, I'll come home. I had nothing to lose."

"Mate, you just give me chills."

Most people were shocked when they heard my story but Eliot seemed to understand. He had made similar decisions, leaving college to travel, following a girlfriend to another country, and now chasing a career to Singapore on his own—not within a company. Our mutual sense of curiosity and adventure resonated with each other without an explanation.

Our series of story exchanges from our young lives continued through a French cheese platter, tomato mozzarella salad, and sirloin steak.

"So you and Gabriel, huh?" Eliot said.

"It's not exactly like that."

"Then what is it?" he asked.

"We are getting to know each other," I said, twirling the spine of my wine glass between my fingers.

"Why not get to know me?" he asked.

I looked up. "You weren't even living here. I'm sorry. I didn't know if you were coming back."

"I'm here now, though."

I shied away from eye contact and stared at a cleaned plate. "Yeah, we'll see."

At home, I told Lydia about the dinner with Eliot. "Why is this happening to me? Why do I meet all these great people right when I'm thinking of leaving?" We were sitting on our balcony, drinking a glass of wine. It was already past 11:00 p.m., but we needed time for a girl's recap.

"It doesn't mean you have to date them. Eliot seems like a wonderful guy. Gabriel is too. Even Hiro. But that doesn't mean you were meant to be with them."

I had distanced myself from Hiro. Gabriel and I had hung out a couple of more times, but when he told me he wasn't ready for a relationship, I backed away. I *was* ready. I did want someone, and I didn't want to waste my time anymore.

"You need to focus on yourself right now and figure out what you need. I don't think you need to be distracted by another man."

I propped my feet on the table and leaned back against the chair. "If I had someone here with me, I could stay—I think I could. I'm just tired of being here alone and not having anyone to share it with."

"It's most likely you will not find that person here, though, Hilary," Lydia said. "Even with Eliot, he just moved here. He doesn't want a girlfriend. He wants to explore and have fun."

I knew she was right. I'd tried for almost three years to date abroad, and it just never worked. There were so many conflicting factors from culture to jobs to time frames to location and more.

I sat up and hugged my knees. "You're right. And even more so, if I were to find someone—IF—do I really want that? I don't know that I want to live an international life forever, traveling across countries for holidays. It would be so difficult. It already is with one family."

"You said it yourself," she replied, staring off into the dark.

"Why do I always make my life so complex?" I asked, pressing my chin to my knees. "I can never just be normal."

She looked over at me. "That is you, Hilary."

I deliberated on her comment for the rest of the night, unable to sleep. As a result, I didn't wake up for yoga the next morning—further angering myself. I was missing something.

Later that week, I walked in the door from work. For the first time in a long time, Lydia was home before me.

"A letter came for you today," Lydia said from the living room, stopping me in my tracks.

I rarely received anything in the mail at The Beacon so I knew it must have been what I was waiting for: the PR status letter from the Singaporean government. It had been four months, and I'd been counting almost every day.

The envelope was thin and light, not a good sign, but I was willing to accept that I had done my best. At that point, it was out of my control.

The letter read, "We regret to inform you that your Permanent Residence Application has been rejected." One address, one statement, and one electronic signature—that was all the letter entailed. Just like that, my dreams were realigned.

"Sorry, Hils," Lydia said.

"It's okay. Really. It's just on to the next step. I'm glad to know now than wait longer."

We continued chatting about work, recent gossip, and boyfriends, but in the back of my head, I was drafting options. I knew Lydia was leaving at the end of the year. Viktor had just left. Did I want to stay around to find more friends again? Did I want to find a new job and a new apartment again? No. I was tired. I wanted stability and normalcy. But what was stable? What was normal?

Lydia and I stayed in that Friday night. Neither of us was in the mood to party despite the many celebrations going on. I hoped an early morning run would clear my head, but the next morning, I still felt confused and overwhelmed.

I went on Facebook to escape my nervousness for a little while. Thanks to Facebook Chat, an old college friend arriving home drunk from the bar asked me how "the freaking hell" I was. There were so many Americanisms I had forgotten.

He then asked me a very simple question: "What's on your mind, Hilary?"

I pondered his question for several seconds, thinking to myself how few times we ask this question to people. I decided to respond with the truth, "I'm afraid I'm going to regret leaving Singapore."

"Why? You've done so much in such a short period of time and have so many memories to look back and be thankful for. What are you afraid of?"

I typed, "I'm afraid of what I don't know. I'm afraid of not knowing."

He responded beautifully, "That's what life is about. You cannot plan everything and should not expect to. It is exciting not knowing what's going to happen. You should embrace it." This guy was just a drinking buddy in college. I could probably count on two hands how many times I had ever actually carried on a conversation of substance with him. Yet, here he was, giving me advice and making me feel better about such a significant decision in my life.

It was that curiosity of the unknown that had brought me to Singapore, and to Toyota, and now was not the time to lose it.

I met Kimura-san for dinner before the next trip to India. We had our usual discussions about the project, Toyota, and having a positive attitude. He'd gifted me a book a few months earlier by Dr. Tina Seelig called, *What I Wish I Knew When I was Twenty.*

"What did you think," Kimura-san asked.

"I want my children to read it," I said. "Her Chile story gave me chills. It's so similar to the story of Ren—same parallels of being aware of opportunities in disguise." Dr. Seelig's book couldn't have come at a more perfect time for me, thanks to Kimura-san.

Suddenly, my phone began to vibrate and Lydia's name flashed on the screen. I apologized to Kimura-san and answered the phone to find Lydia sobbing on the other end.

"I was right, Hilary. Hilary, I was right," Lydia said.

"Right about what, Lydia? What's wrong?"

"Paul—he cheated."

A few days earlier, Lydia had turned to me and said, "I have a very ill feeling, Hilary," in her strong British accent. "I just don't feel right." I had insisted that she relax, but she'd been through this before with another man, and her instinct had been right.

"I'm coming home now," I said, and hung up the phone. I looked at Kimura-san apologetically. "I'm sorry, I have to go. It's an emergency."

"Of course. Please let me know if I can help," Kimura-san replied. I stormed out of the restaurant and hailed a cab from the street.

"Tanjong Pagar, please, as fast as possible," I said.

Lydia was outside on the balcony, exactly where I expected her to be, puffing away on a cigarette. The ashtray was overflowing with butts. She was looking into the distance with her leg propped up, shaking.

"I am so sorry, Lydia," I said. I hugged her, but I didn't know what to say. I felt so bad for trying to tell her she was wrong. I felt even worse that her suspicions were entirely true.

"He is a bastard," she said. Apparently, she had called him out on his cheating over the phone, saying he sounded strange and asking if there was something wrong. Then he admitted it. Paul and Lydia only started dating a few months before she left for Singapore, and Lydia had known she was taking a risk. "But I'm thirty, Hilary. And I really liked him," she said.

We didn't sleep that night. I couldn't leave her alone. After so many times I had needed her, she finally needed me. I kept thinking about the promise I'd made to her father to take care of her. I was all she had. I had to make sure she got through this.

We stayed home that entire weekend, leaving only when Lydia needed cigarettes or if I went to buy her food. She wasn't eating. Paul called many times, and they fought every time. At one point, I was so disgusted that I wrote him a message: "You are a coward. Lydia deserves a prince. Leave her alone or I will personally fly to London and kick your ass."

Jessica came to visit for a while, and Fabian too, but Lydia really didn't want to see anyone. She was devastated and embarrassed. I felt awful because I had to leave again for India on Monday night.

"I'm so sorry I have to leave tomorrow, Lydia."

"Hilary, please! Are you kidding me? You cancelled your whole weekend for me. You have been an amazing friend."

"Still, it has only been two days, Lyds. It's still fresh."

"I know. But Jessica is coming over tomorrow, and then Fabian is coming over Tuesday, and I have a work dinner Wednesday. I'll be fine."

Lydia was so strong. Sometimes I wondered if it was a good or bad thing.

I left the next day for India. Maeda-san and I had one week to gather some final data before I could complete the summary of our findings. We weren't traveling as much, so I had an eerie feeling that this might be the last visit to Nandi.

Chapter 40
Be Home

Maeda-san received an abrupt call from management when we returned to Singapore on Friday morning. There had been a bombing at the cricket field across from our hotel and the TKM office. Everyone was sent home.

We hear about terrorist bombings all the time in the news, but it's difficult to grasp when you don't have any association to it. My eyes closed and I pictured the exact dusty street outside the field that I walked by nearly every day. My heart pumped faster. I couldn't imagine what I'd do if something had happened to a colleague. Fortunately, everyone was safe.

Lydia had to travel to Hong Kong that week for work, so I was home alone. I had so many things going through my mind that I wanted to discuss with her, but my problems seemed miniscule compared to hers. I was overwhelmed with emotion and confused by the opportunities in front of me. I could start my own business in Singapore, expand someone else's business, or work for another multinational corporation. But none of these choices really thrilled me, reproducing the same feeling I had after college.

On Saturday morning, my friend Lily was supposed to come over for tea to catch up. I hadn't seen her since one of our soccer games months earlier, but I wanted to speak to another American in Singapore who could understand my situation. Lily not only led a successful career in international affairs but was an honest and trustworthy person, so I valued her advice.

Lily had told me beforehand that she could only stay for thirty minutes, so I was nervous that I wouldn't be able to tell her everything. I boiled water for tea and put a plate of cookies on the table. I sat tapping my finger on the table, thinking about how best to utilize the little time I had with her. I wasn't sure exactly what I wanted out of the visit. I just felt like I needed some guidance, maybe inspiration.

The doorbell rang and I jumped from my seat.

"Hi!" Lily was a petite Korean-American woman, with an infectious energy level. I loved her relentless optimism.

"Thank you so much for coming," I said, hugging her tightly with my eyes closed.

"Oh, don't be silly. I love seeing you, Hilary!"

At my kitchen table, I poured her a cup of black tea. The day's sun rays grew stronger with every minute and beamed through the wall-length window to warm our forearms and the glass table. Immediately, I began my rant. I told her about the Singapore jobs, the India jobs, and all of my other options. I told her about my concerns, my thrills, and everything in between, until I had nothing more to say.

"I just don't know what to do. For the first time in my life, I don't know what I want," I said, falling back into my chair.

Lily nodded to everything I had to say, smiling the whole time, with glinted eyes that looked nowhere but on me.

The first words she said changed my life forever.

"It sounds like you need to go home, Hilary."

My body trembled. All of my energy and internal heat and nerves that had been building over the past few weeks fell on me like an avalanche. The clouds of thought in my head dissipated immediately, and within seconds, light shone on the answer to my question. Everything was clear. It was as if I'd been waiting for someone to tell me that it was okay, that I had done enough, and that I could return to the States — that I didn't have to prove myself anymore. The funny thing was, I had never needed anyone else's approval. I'd been waiting for my own. During that afternoon tea with Lily, I finally gave myself permission to go home.

People can tell you what you need to hear, but you have to be listening. For six months, I knew I needed a change but didn't know what form that change would take. I didn't know because, even though the answer was inside me, I wasn't listening.

"You are right," I said to Lily.

My thirty minutes had run out and I hugged her good-bye with every ounce of energy I had in me. Lily rushed on to her next appointment with the same remarkable smile as when she walked in. I waved good-bye to her from my door as she entered the elevator. I couldn't help but wonder how I would have reached the decision without her. Though she'd never understand it, Lily was a godsend that day, and for the rest of my life, I'd be grateful to her.

Lydia came home from the airport an hour later. I ran up to her, with her arms full of luggage, and hugged her tightly.

"I'm going home," I said.

"You're what?" she said, pulling my shoulders back.

"I'm moving back to the States!"

I shared the entire conversation with Lily.

"Okay, slow down. This is a big decision," she said, dropping her bags to the tile floor.

"Oh, I know, I've only been thinking about it since last October. It's been six months now, Lydia. Don't you see? I knew I needed to leave Toyota. I knew it. But I wasn't happy with anything in Singapore." I took a deep breath of air and continued. "Why? Because nothing was going to make me happy here anymore. I need to be home to be happy."

"I mean, it makes sense, Hil," she said, and smiled.

"I have never been more certain," I said, hugging her even tighter.

Chapter 41
Hugh Hefner & Highlighters

The next day, Lydia and I met Jessica, Fabian, and our other friends for a champagne brunch, followed by a party for Australia Day. The day was perfect and one of the most memorable of my time in Singapore. Knowing that I had made a decision was one of the most comforting feelings I'd ever had. I didn't need to question my intent, purpose, or goals anymore. It just was. And there was no going back.

At work, I prepared a 3 x 3–square drawing on a Post-it and kept it hidden in my drawer. Each of the nine squares represented a week of work. I was planning to submit my resignation letter in five weeks, just in time for my one-month notice. I decided to leave the company in June because of the vacation time I had left, the project with Maeda-san, and my sister Ariana's visit, which I arranged to begin just two days after my last day.

For my birthday, Lydia and I were planning a party with the theme "Anything that starts with *H*." In Europe, they call theme parties "fancy dress," which only sounded right when Lydia said it. Following the party, we planned to stay awake in order to catch a 5:00 a.m. taxi to Rawa Island. Yet again, another glorious tropical paradise beach party.

Before I left for my big birthday weekend, Yoshida-san nominated me to attend an external training entitled "Master Your Mind for Breakthrough Results." It was the Friday of my party, so I was already in vacation mode. I had very few expectations as my mind pictured what costumes my guests were planning.

The training took place just across the street from my condominium, so I woke up later than usual. With my makeup and hair undone, I arrived at the meeting room with my coffee in one hand and two-liter bottle of water in the other. The room was bare like a hospital ward, just an open space with some folding tables and chairs. On the walls, motivational posters and phrases, communicated messages of hope and inspiration. The florescent lights overhead made my eyes burn. A computer and projection screen sat at the front of the room. I was not thrilled about what the day would entail.

Normally, I sat in the front at things like this because I wanted to be involved, but that day, I sat in the back next to Utako-san, the admin to Yamamoto-san, hoping to get out as soon as possible for my party.

Suddenly, loud techno music began playing from the speakers behind the projection screen and an Indian man entered the room from behind us. He wore frameless rectangle glasses below black hair that curled up in the front, complementing a big smile and a sleek, formal suit. He spoke quickly, but powerfully. "Welcome to Mastering Your Mind!" If we weren't awake before, we were awake now.

The man immediately started making jokes and telling us about himself. "I talk fast—I'm warning you now. If you don't understand me, stop me. If you don't, your loss!"

"My name is Ranju," he continued. "Yes, I am Indian. I've been doing this for over ten years, and it's my passion. I've traveled the world doing this and have won awards doing this—even in the United States. I see we have a Caucasian here." He pointed over to me. "Where are you from?"

"The United States."

"Bam! I have won awards in your country. Have you?"

"No," I admitted.

"Now you must listen to me . . ." he said. He had my attention for the rest of the day.

For eight hours, Ranju essentially taught us psychology and the reasons why we do what we do. We took a personality test and reviewed each category, showing us our strengths and weaknesses in all areas of personal and professional life.

At one point in the day, we did some role-playing, and I partnered with the Japanese colleague sitting next to me. The situation painted a patron riding in the back of a cab in Singapore, and the driver was lost. We each had to act out how we would respond to the situation.

When the "uncle" gave me attitude, I responded, "Stop the car and let me out. I'll get another cab. And I'm not paying!" I'd actually done this before in Singapore multiple times.

Meanwhile, when we switched roles and my Japanese colleague rode in the cab, she apologized to the cab driver and sat quietly in the backseat while he looked up directions and found his way.

"This is the first time I've ever had a Japanese and an American woman on stage together," Ranju commented, "This is fascinating. Do you know why I picked on you in the beginning, Ms. Hilary?"

"No," I said, sitting in attention.

"I could tell from your mannerisms, the way you dress, and where you sat, what you would answer." Everyone else stared at him in awe. "You are an extrovert. You are intuitive and make decisions based on your feelings. You are a judger—you like to have a plan and manage your time efficiently."

"Yes! Kom-san always says I plan too much!" I said. Ranju didn't know who Kom was but that didn't matter. What I expected to be just a day out of the office turned into an eye-opening experience.

I did not want to leave the training center at 6:00 p.m., which was already an hour later than the seminar was originally scheduled for. Something in me had clicked into place. I had more questions to ask Ranju, who had taken control of my world for those few hours and overwhelmed me with curiosity and ambition. My mind was racing with thoughts about how I could utilize what I had learned to make the critical decisions I was facing.

"This explains so much!" I said to Ranju as I gathered my things.

He laughed. "Oh yeah?"

"Yes! I need to see you again." I wanted to tell him more, but I was around all of my colleagues who didn't know I was even considering leaving the company.

"I would love to answer whatever questions you may have," he said calmly.

"Can we . . . I don't know . . . meet for lunch or something?" I said. People were going to be arriving for my party at any time now, but I desperately wanted more answers.

"Of course," he said. He gave me his business card, and I went running out of the training center across the street to my apartment, my legs fueled by the excitement of what I had learned. I stormed into the apartment to find Lydia and some friends already there.

"I need to go for a run," I said as I switched clothes.

"What?" Lydia and Fabian both asked. "People are going to be here any minute," Lydia said.

"I can't explain it. I'll be right back." I went down to our gym and sprinted on the treadmill for twenty minutes, hardly feeling the weight on my toes.

My birthday celebration lasted seventy-two hours. The Friday night, "H" theme party brought the likes of Hugh Hefner, hippopotamus, and Lydia, Jessica as highlighters. The next evening in Rawa, while the moon gazed at us and the South China Sea, we ate a stupendous seafood buffet dinner and danced under the tiki roof until morning.

My department had purchased a birthday cake for me when I returned to work the next week. Everyone left their desks without warning and started walking toward the pantry for the surprise. I knew what was happening, because I saw it every month.

"Hilary-chan, can you come for a moment?" Yoshida-san asked.

I went along with it.

"Surprise!" The team surrounded the table where a delicate tiramisu held a single candle lit. Someone had discovered my favorite dessert.

I couldn't help but feel guilty. I was planning to submit my resignation letter in just a few weeks and was already looking at one-way flights to the States.

They all smiled and wished me a happy birthday. I took one photo with just the men in the office and one with just the women, then all together. This was the common procedure for birthdays. In the photo with the men, Maeda-san had a huge grin. He was the one I was most nervous to tell.

The team joked about some new positions opening in our department. "Please, Yamamoto-san fill new hire space with female," Alvin commented. Everyone laughed. The profession of operations was primarily dominated by men.

"Are you going to forget me?" I teased.

"You are special," he responded but neglecting to look me in the eye.

"Too high," Yoshida-san said with bug eyes and a teeth-bearing smile.

I was realizing how much they valued me in the office, and I hoped they would not feel remorse for the change I was about to impose upon them.

I knew I had to tell Yoshida-san first. He was my manager on paper, but was more like a friend. He knew I wasn't happy, but he consistently told me not to give up and that he wanted to work more closely with me on a project.

On Thursday, I met Ranju for lunch at noon. My nerves were at their highest. I had a 2:00 p.m. meeting with Yamamoto-san, but I didn't care if I was late—being on time for meetings didn't matter anymore. I felt like I had Ranju-withdrawal for the few days that had passed since "Master Your Mind". I couldn't drink coffee that morning because the anticipation of his guidance was so overwhelming that I was already shaking.

We met at the sandwich shop at the foot of Centennial Tower where Sato-san first took me before my interview. I waited outside because the air-conditioning was so strong. Ranju was late and my stomach was growling. When he came around the corner in another sharp suit, I let go of all the tense air in my lungs and my stomach subsided.

"Hilary, please accept my dearest apologies for being late," he said, giving me a tight hug. It was bizarre. In his arms, I felt relaxed and comfortable, as if I were safe around him.

"Don't be silly. Thank you for coming to meet me," I said.

"Thank *you* for asking. I often sense that people want to ask but never do. It is my absolute pleasure to see you again." He opened the door of the sandwich shop and ushered me in first. As I stood in line to order, I tried to organize my thoughts. I'd lost my appetite completely and only ordered the chicken sandwich because it was the first thing on the list.

We sat down at a table in the corner with our sandwiches. The room smelled of freshly baked bread, for which the shop was most famous.

We spoke frantically and energetically for an hour, responding to each other's comments as fast as possible without losing too many points as the direction of the conversation changed. Ranju took a napkin and began to list out tasks for me to do.

He explained to me the von Oech theory that breaks the decision-making process down into four stages: Explorer, Artist, Judge, and Warrior. The explorer stage is the learning stage where you receive all

236

information available, followed by the artist stage where you process, interpret, and draft the information into your idea. From this stage, the judge helps to weigh out the options and prioritize. After which, the warrior takes bold, decisive action.

I was confused as to where I was in this process.

"You are mixing your explorer and judge," he said. "They are bumping heads because you are unable to properly see one stage through completely."

I shook my head. It was such a simple but true way of explaining what I'd been feeling. "This is the fun part," he insisted as he leaned forward, "Hilary, go back to being an explorer and learn. You are only twenty-five and have already accomplished so much." This sounded so old to me, but then he said something that I'd never forget: "Without acknowledging what you've done in the past before moving on to the future, you will never be satisfied with your achievements."

I nodded, gazing at the napkin. I'd accomplished nearly everything I'd ever wanted but had a tendency to immediately move on to the next thing without taking time to celebrate my success.

"In order to execute your explorer mode, you need to focus on the moment. Find where you resonate," he said. "What is it that makes you feel right? Hone in on this," he said.

"Grasp it and breathe into it." He held his hand to his chest like an opera singer about to let go. He ended, "You have so much energy and I don't know where it's coming from." I didn't know either.

Jessica, Lydia, and I were leaving for Langkawi, a group of islands off the coast of Malaysia, the next morning, so Ranju gave me clear instructions to take many pictures of small detailed things that I found interesting. He told me that he wanted to see me again, maybe two or three times.

Suddenly, the smile left his face. "But through this process, we cannot be friends."

"Why?" I asked, shocked.

"Because I'm going to be very strict with you."

Even so, I felt comfortable around Ranju. He understood me. He also had what I'd been seeking for so long: answers to questions I'd had about myself, and answers to the question of why I'd really come to Singapore in the first place.

After our lunch, I sent him a text message saying, "Thank you so much for your time. I can't explain easily in words, but have you ever heard of a bodhisattva? I feel like I just found one."

He responded, "I am inspired by your voyager spirit. To discover, one must depart the near shore. Now it's time to rest a while. Eat well. Sleep.

Nourish your spirit. Honor your path. I am blessed to have met you as well."

It was almost impossible to relax in Langkawi. As much I wanted to enjoy the days that were dwindling, there were many tasks I had to do. I was getting sick of vacations.

"We live such privileged lives here," I said to Lydia and Jessica as we watched the sun set over our resort. "It's like what happens to the rich — luxuries become normal, and it's easy to lose what's important to you."

I did as I was told by Ranju. I went around the entire resort taking pictures of the small things: insects crawling on the ground, cats drinking leisurely from the infinity pool, the hand carved flowers in walls of the hundred year old building. I tried to think of things that resonated with me: live music, moving crowds, and helping people with directions. I didn't see a link, though. What did it all really mean?

Lydia returned to Singapore to find a series of missed calls from her ex-boyfriend. She'd improved drastically, but it was still difficult for her to keep her mind off of him.

"Why is the heart so fragile?" she asked me as we unpacked our things.

"Because it's the heart," I said.

"Well, it should just stick to pumping blood," Lydia said, laughing. "You know what I love about you, Hilary?" she asked.

"Not my jokes. They're nowhere as good as yours."

"No. I love how you get so inspired by people."

Chapter 42
Five Vodkas and a Cigarette

Sato-san called me from Italy that week. I told him about Yamamoto-san and the lack of direction in TMAP, how I had many career options. "But all I can think about now is going home," I said.

"Hilary-chan, you have a brilliant future ahead of you. You will find a good man because you are a good person," he said. I couldn't help but be skeptical. I couldn't help but think of John and what I had given up. I'd sacrificed my first love in order to follow my dreams to Singapore. That weekend, someone else was claiming his love. That weekend, John was getting married.

It was the only weekend that month that we were not out of town. I had wanted to be doing something breathtakingly different to distract me from what was taking place. In the end, I didn't want to be doing anything at all. I constantly checked his Facebook status. The rehearsal dinner on Friday had gone perfectly. Meanwhile, on the other side of the world, my Friday night had disappointed. Jessica, Lydia, and I ended up sitting around. There wasn't much going on and no one was out. Saturday night's plan wasn't any better; just another party that I predicted would be full of drama and gossip in the small city-state where everyone's paths cross. I felt like someone was telling me to just sit down and face the facts — there was no going back. He was getting married.

On Saturday afternoon, Lydia returned from the salon to find me in my favorite maroon dress with my hair wrapped in curlers. In one hand, I held my second glass of wine, almost empty, and in the other, a box of tissues. I was crying.

"I don't want to go, Lydia."

I didn't want to be in that environment of surface-level conversations about work and recent luxury vacations. I wasn't in the mood to be social. In fact, I didn't want to talk to anyone or be around anyone.

"Oh, Hils." She came over and wiped my face with a tissue. We sat down at the table and she held my hands in front of me as my chin hung to my chest.

"I keep telling myself this is normal and that I'm not still in love with John or even desire to be his wife."

"You don't," she said.

"But to know that part of my life is really coming to a close — it's heartbreaking," I said. She squeezed my hands.

I had once imagined our wedding while we were still dating; walking down the aisle to find him at the end, his big smile, and how proud I would be to be his wife. I had pictured our wedding party and colors — how the whole night played out. Those thoughts had not crossed my mind again until this night.

"He planned the wedding almost exactly like a wedding I attended with him once. The church, the hotel, the reception hall, and even the band are all the same." It allowed me to imagine exactly what was taking place.

"When was that?" she asked.

I looked up. "It was the last time we saw each other. I'd broken up with him, but we had already made plans to go together. During the first dance, we were sitting at the dinner table watching when he told me it was me he wanted to be in his arms someday for that dance."

My tears dropped to the clear, glass table. Lydia cleaned them up with a tissue.

"What did you say?"

"I said nothing."

The sun was setting in Singapore and rising in Miami, Ohio, on a stunning bride preparing for her wedding day. Meanwhile, red wine drizzled down my throat, and with curlers in my hair and a dress of jealousy on, I sobbed on the shoulder of my British roommate.

Hilary Corna

It was so hard to break up with John when nothing was ever wrong with the relationship. We loved each other so much, but it was just bad timing. For that part of my life, I loved him as much as I could. But as a young woman, I still had exploring to do; I still had to discover what love truly meant. I also knew that I needed to love myself before I could love him.

"All right, up and at 'em," Lydia said, shaking my hands and standing up. "We are going to at least make an appearance at this party. You cannot sit here."

"I really don't want to go, Lydia. I just want to face the situation and deal with it. I'll be all right."

"Nope. Let's go." She pulled my arms so that I lifted from the chair. "We are going to go enjoy Singapore. We only have so many weekends left, anyway."

"I'm not sure this is a good idea."

"Hils, what happened when I was in my slump? You wouldn't let me just sit and mope around about Paul. You know what you need to do."

"All right, all right," I said. I thought maybe I could distract myself from thoughts of the marriage kiss and first dances.

After five vodka sodas and a cigarette, I had told at least four guys that my ex was in the process of getting married "as we speak." Gossip and drama filled most of the conversations at the party, while the shallow introductory chit chat irritated me further. I was miserable. It wasn't difficult to say yes when Lydia suggested we leave to get McDonalds and go home.

At least the vodka sodas helped me sleep. Stuffed with a double cheeseburger and fries, my makeup still freshly prepared for a night out, I crawled into bed. I tried not to wonder whether or not she had walked down the aisle yet. I left that imagery for the certainty the morning would bring.

Unforgiving construction started behind our apartment promptly at 8:00 a.m. the next morning. The sun had risen in Singapore and set in Ohio. I woke with dried makeup and a throbbing head to an image of the wedding party making their grand entry in the reception hall. What was their song, I wondered, lying in my bed. Rather than pitying my jealous heart, I did what I do best: pulled out my to-do list that included laundry, cleaning, and packing, and began to check them off. Productivity always made me feel better.

Chapter 43
Beautiful

The past few months had been a whirlwind of emotions, like the sinister Singapore skies during their infamous storms. I used to watch them from the office window, changing from murky black to dazzling blue in mere seconds.

It was time to listen to Ranju. I needed to slow down and live in the moment. I was going to Bali for a week by myself — my third and final holiday in May. I wanted to see the other side of Bali that I hadn't seen during my birthday weekend the year prior. With the encouragement of Lydia, Ranju, and my yoga instructor, I agreed to leave my iPhone at home and resort to my old phone from 7-Eleven, just in case of emergency. It wasn't until I boarded the train to the airport that I started to freak. What if I go to the wrong terminal? If I had my iPhone, I could double-check. What if I get lost in Bali? If I had my iPhone, I could use my GPS feature. It's pathetic how dependent we are on tools that make things so easy for us that we don't even think for ourselves anymore.

I sighed as I stood among the real Singaporeans. It was 4:00 p.m. and I had lost patience with my boredom. Usually, I'd read Reuters or listen to podcasts or browse Facebook. I didn't know what to do for the forty-minute commute to the airport.

Then, I started to watch, and I suddenly felt a sense of separation, like some big hand had just picked me up by my back like a cat and told me to look down on everything. I almost wondered if everyone else could see me watching. Chins were all focused on their iPhones and Blackberries. Arms were full of designer bags. Sunglasses covered eyes and, though so close in proximity, no one exchanged communication. Each person was in their own world, on their own mission, with their own thoughts.

An old friend was picking me up at the airport in Bali — Betsy, an American I'd met on the plane during my first trip home. She lived in Bali with her husband and had offered for me to stay with her for the first night. It was amazing to think that I could go to an Indonesian island and have a friend with whom I could stay.

As soon as I got into Betsy's car, it was like we were back on the plane again, talking over one other all the way back to her home, which she had built when she married her husband over twenty years earlier. With all contemporary materials and embellishments but traditional architecture, Betsy's home encapsulated the atmosphere of Bali. Teak wood outlined the frame of her home and marble floors cooled the ground. The living area didn't use air-conditioning; only the bedrooms.

Betsy told me more about her family and life in Bali as I looked at her photos. "It must be so hard being away from the rest of your family," I said to her.

"This is my home now," she set a family portrait back down on the table.

I was just two weeks away from telling Toyota and announcing publicly that I was leaving. Singapore was a small town, so I had kept my decision fairly secret. Betsy made me wonder if living abroad permanently was something that I could actually manage if I gave it a chance. She had done it and was very successful.

But I was looking at all of her benefits without seeing the challenges, the family disagreements and personal struggles. I had a new sense of what it meant to spend an extended period of time overseas, and these were all things that you couldn't see on the outside.

Betsy's nephew had been living with her for the summer while he interned at her catering company. He had just graduated from college on the West Coast and had only been in Indonesia for a few months. Betsy had helped him find a full-time job with a major multinational corporation in Thailand.

I felt as if I had the right to advise him, despite only being three years older. I didn't want to patronize him or be negative, but I wanted to help.

"I'm an expat boy now," he said, laughing. I thought to myself that this was not a laughing matter. It was a huge decision that would change his life. I wondered if he really had enough information to know it was what he wanted. I wondered if he was prepared for what he was getting himself into. Yet I kept quiet, having learned not to give advice unless people asked for it. His decision had already been made, and I supported it, telling him to email me if he ever needed anything.

I left Betsy's place to explore while she worked for the day. I had lunch at a restaurant overlooking a range of rice paddies. I had my own covered table and waiter to take care of me. When he first walked up, he asked me, "Sick?" I told him that I was not. He responded, "Broken heart?" I laughed and asked why. He said, "Because you don't look fresh."

I happened to be in Bali during a major religious holiday. An Indonesian friend of Betsy's asked me to join him for the day to visit the local temples. His name was Bedu. He instructed me to wear something that covered my legs. I arrived at our meeting point ready for the day's adventure. He was standing by his motorbike in a kain sarong and headpiece.

"You look beautiful in that sarong, Hilary," he said with an immodest grin.

"Thank you." I was wearing a long skirt I had bought in college. I was pleased that he found it suitable.

"Here, this is for you," Bedu said. He handed me a white and yellow flower and told me that all the women wear it behind their ears.

"Okay, sit like a girl," he said as I climbed on the motorbike. He first took me to his village and to his home, which was about a thirty-minute ride from the touristy town in which I was staying. I felt like a local, sitting gracefully on the side of his bike. I forgot about my white face. From the moment Bedu pulled onto the main street of his town, people started waving hello to him from the side of the street.

"Welcome to my village," he said.

"What are they saying?" I asked.

"Oh, nothing much. They are just joking with me and asking why I have a white person on my motorbike."

I wondered what it was like to have neighbors that knew you so well, and I wondered what people would say if I brought a foreigner from Asia to visit my home. Most likely, they'd find it strange.

We pulled up to Bedu's home, which had an entrance directly on the narrow street. We walked under a small archway and I saw that the entire property consisted of four small buildings. He explained that his parents lived in the main house, while he and his brother lived with their families in the two buildings on either side. The building in the middle was specifically for prayer.

I was amazed by how the structure of their homes revolved entirely around their family, three generations living side by side, eating and praying together every day. Back home, families were separating, moving across towns and states, even across the world. Religious practices were losing priority over careers and other tangible commitments. Westerners consider this "success" an improvement in quality of life, but looking at Bedu's family, I questioned it.

"We will go inside so I can quickly take a shower before going to the temples," Bedu said.

"Okay," I said, caught up in the fact that I was visiting a local villager's home. In all my travels, this kind of situation didn't happen often. I was either traveling for leisure where I treated myself to luxurious surroundings, or I was traveling for work, which treated me to nice hotels and transportation. Even though I often worked with locals, I rarely visited their homes.

"You must have a clean mind, heart, and body to enter the temple," Bedu explained. Then he asked me something that I was not expecting.

"You know that thing girls get every month?" he said.

"Yes," I said, a little taken aback by the question.

"Are you on it?" he asked.

"No."

"Because the temple is a very holy place," he said.

He left to take a shower, and I sat on the edge of his steps. It was a strange moment, reflecting on where I was, both physically and mentally. I had come to Bali with few expectations. I simply wanted to get away and have time to think by myself. I didn't expect my thoughts would root back to ideas of home and family.

I left my new friend that day with a deep new sense of respect for him and Indonesian culture. In his village, he was just another young man working to provide for his family. He was no one of special privilege. Yet, his perspective provided me with a new notion. Family had played a substantial role in my life, but always having it there may have led to easily losing sight of it.

Bali is a tourist trap, full of overwhelmingly gorgeous things to buy. Yet I soon realized that I had no desire to own them, and therefore had no reason to walk the shops. All these objects and all these items . . . what did they all mean? Giant mirrors with colored glass that framed your reflection, hand-carved statues of giraffes, and countless gold Buddhas were sold around every corner, and in the past, I would have taken many photos of them and purchased my favorites. But life was what I now found beautiful—animals and plants and people—and I wanted to remember less of the objects, meals, or buildings.

At the end of the week, these ideas of values, goals and life's purpose besieged me. I went to Bali to relax and find clarity. In fact, it only made things more blurry.

On my last day, I was sitting in a coffee shop and struck up conversation with a man next to me. After several years in a good position at Google, he had left the company and was spending six months in Bali. He said to me, "I'd rather be at the bottom of a ladder I want to climb than the middle of a ladder I don't want to climb." His comment confirmed that I was doing something right.

Chapter 44
She Has a Dream

It had been over seven months since I first decided to leave Toyota. After discussing my thoughts and feelings with Lydia and other friends, I was finally able to make the decision wholeheartedly.

But when I walked into Centennial Tower on June 10, 2010 to give my one month notice, I felt like I was suffocating. My breath was not circulating as it needed to be. This day was going to transform my life, and my body knew it. I had skipped breakfast. My stomach was too busy digesting emotions.

There is an unwritten protocol for the quitting process at Toyota. First, I needed inform my managers, Yoshida-san and Maeda-san. This was primarily out of respect, to give them a chance to manage the situation and potentially retain me. By informing them beforehand, I would give them enough time to manage the impact and take action to minimize the consequences. Simply put, it would be disrespectful to surprise them in front of their boss.

After gaining the consensus of the managers, I needed to communicate the decision to my big boss — the general manager, Yamamoto-san.

I had informed Yoshida-san of my decision the day before over coffee and a smoke break. We had sat for three hours while he went through an entire pack of cigarettes, staring at people walking in and out of Centennial Tower's glass doors. The sky was dark with clouds that day, and it rained on and off. I could smell the humidity.

Yoshida-san's forehead wrinkled as he sat back in a lattice chair with his legs crossed. "I feel sorry for your mom — for Sato-san and Kimura-san," he lamented, "because it is my responsibility and I didn't take care of you."

I avoided eye contact to hide my smile. His considerate comment was exactly what I loved about the Japanese — their caring and sincere way of managing people.

"Give me one week, Hilary-chan. Let me speak with Yamamoto-san and try to find a new assignment. Then we can finally work together."

I contemplated the idea quietly for a moment. I'd always wanted to work with Yoshida-san more closely, but I knew it was too late.

He paused. "Hilary, tell me one thing. What is the real concrete reason?"

I didn't hesitate with my answer, "It's not fun anymore."

He shifted his crossed legs and put out his cigarette. "I want to cry but cannot," he said. He looked as though I had just broken up with him. Yoshida-san's wrinkles and thin waistline always concerned me. He was addicted to work. "Company is like a creature," he explained. "It's born, grows up, and dies."

We spoke about my plans and schedule in the coming months. Then he admitted, "I'm afraid they will blame me for you leaving. I failed in developing you."

My relationship with Yoshida-san had always been a friendship. We had never worked in-depth on a project together, but because the organizational chart visualized him as my manager, he was still held responsible for my performance.

"I promise to make clear to Yamamoto-san that you were a good boss," I said, even though I knew what I said could do very little. In Japanese corporate culture, if someone quits, it's the fault of the manager, regardless of the circumstances.

It didn't matter anymore what opportunity presented itself. I was going home.

That Thursday presented a bigger challenge. I had to tell the boss that had shown the most care for me, which would make him feel that he'd fallen short. I will never forget Maeda-san's dismal face that day.

It was 4:00 p.m. I wanted to do it at the end of the day so I could leave soon after. It also allowed my bosses the weekend to let the news sink in. It was one of the most difficult working days to get through.

"*Sumimasen*, Maeda-san, do you have a moment?" I asked, choking on the words.

"Hai," he agreed and followed me to the meeting room. We swerved through the aisles of the office, avoiding tall stacks of packing boxes.

The Prius room was cold. The Singapore rain had conquered the skies, making it nearly as dark as an Ohio winter. I laid my notebook on the table, closed, and seated myself at the corner nearest to the door. I crossed my legs, sat up straight, and breathed in deeply, even though all I wanted was to sink over in my chair and pray for support.

Maeda-san entered the room, cheery as ever. The air was stale. It almost hurt to breathe. I stared at my boss, realizing that he had absolutely no idea. He was so innocent. My actions were about to ruin his day, destroy his ego, and make him lose face for not performing as a manager. I knew I needed to speak fast before I let my nervousness inflict my rehearsed script.

"I have bad news to share with you," I said. The elongated moments in between each word brought even more awareness to my decision. "I am leaving Toyota."

His stare was blank. I could feel his foot begin to tap, like it always did when he got nervous. I continued quickly, "Looking back on almost three years with Toyota, I will forever be grateful for the opportunities granted me by our company. However, I need to make a change."

His face was still empty of emotion. I was always taught by my bosses to say what you want first, and then follow with the details. I was never able to clarify if this was for efficiency or the language barrier. Typical of Maeda-san, he proceeded according to protocol.

"Are you already decided?" he asked, moving only his lips and keeping his eyes narrow facing the table.

"Yes, I've been considering for months."

He had confirmed the decision and would now try to understand my level of preparation.

"Do you have a plan?" he asked and then paused. "A dream?"

"Yes," I said and continued to tell him exactly what I wanted to do next.

Although refraining from eye contact, he pulled his head up and nodded with a smirk. "Shoganai," he said. "There is nothing I can do." This was the last thing I had expected to come from his mouth.

The corners of his mouth turned up and he finally looked me in the eye. "If you have a dream and have been thinking for six months, there is not much I can say. That makes me happy. I must be happy."

I exhaled. I could breathe again. I felt appreciated, valued, and respected. I admired his way of thinking because he could acknowledge my personal path and journey outside of the company and that it was about me, not them.

"My dream was never to work for Toyota," he admitted. "I wanted to be a technician or a musician." He explained that he had always wanted to pick something up, be able study it, and then do it. While studying to be a car technician, he'd been selected to take an entry exam into Toyota. "I didn't even do well," he said. But here he was, more than twenty years later.

"Why did you stay?" I asked him.

"Toyota is my life."

What I assumed Maeda-san meant was that he placed pride in being loyal to Toyota in exchange for all the company had provided for him, and that he had stayed true to his decision. To look back in regret is futile because our current state is only a result of our actions, but looking forward and taking ownership of our actions in order to learn, improve, and grow — this is empowering.

Despite his support of my dream, I could tell that Maeda-san was hurt. For a brief moment, his emotions overpowered his logic, and he lowered his head, sighing and repeating "Ma . . . ma . . . ma . . ." as his deep brown eyes filled with tears. He shook his head back and forth and rubbed his eyes. "Ma . . . Ma . . ." He reminded me of Hiro when I had ended things a few months earlier. They both seemed so innocent, and my profound sense of respect for them made me feel so guilty.

Maeda-san had executed the professional response in the correct operational manner. He was realizing, though, that accepting it meant he was losing more than just a colleague. He was losing a friend.

My heart felt like someone had reached into my chest and squeezed it until it burst. We both started crying. I closed my eyes and blinked repeatedly but couldn't hold them back.

"Choto-mate," he said. Wait a moment.

I knew he was going downstairs to have a smoke. My arms no longer had goosebumps from the cold room, and I was relieved that he had reacted with appreciation, not anger even though I felt bad for Maeda-san; I knew I was doing the right thing.

He returned from his smoke in a much better state. I asked if he had any questions for me. With a straight face and dried eyes, he leaned forward on the wood table and said, "Just one. Tell me, what was your happiest moment?"

I smiled and lightly closed my eyes, thinking immediately of Anna and Reshma. Both women were highly capable, but their talent was being capped. Kaizen helped expose and utilize their potential to improve the company. Anna revealed to me in Starbucks that kaizen had changed her entire perspective on life. Reshma challenged the gender bias in her country, making small but progressive steps towards change, and had earned the trust and respect from her management. Both of them had impacted my personal and professional growth. They were my proof that I was changing something in Toyota — and not just the numbers.

Maeda-san listened intently as I explained this to him.

An hour had passed. The meeting was unplanned so I imagined Yamamoto-san at his desk looking around for Maeda-san and I. The worst part was over, though. I had informed the people whose feelings concerned me the most, and I found myself overwhelmed with their support and handling of the situation.

Maeda-san's hands smacked the table. "All right. I'll go get Yamamoto-san and Yoshida-san. Please wait here."

He gathered his things and promptly left the room. I sunk into my chair with my head in my hands. It was done. There was no going back now. I took air into my lungs as slowly and deeply as possible, in and out.

Yamamoto-san entered the room, expressionless, but that was not abnormal. It had reached 5:00 p.m. already. The room had become cold again.

Yamamoto-san sat down at the corner of the table facing the door. I sat at the corner with him. Maeda-san, cross-legged with a stern look on his face, fidgeted with the dividers of the calendar he was holding. It was no longer just the two of us where he could speak openly. His boss was there now, and he was going to have to defend himself and me.

"Where is Yoshida-san?" Yamamoto-san asked Maeda-san, like a schoolteacher to his assistant.

"I'm not sure. I could not find him and he is not picking up his phone."

I knew Yoshida-san was downstairs smoking. I imagined him holding consecutive butts, burnt down with angst.

"Okay, please start," Yamamoto-san said.

I tried to repeat what I had said to Maeda-san, but failed. My first mistake was that I began the discussion with an explanation instead of getting to the point.

"Thank you for your time this afternoon. I have been giving this a lot of consideration over the past six months, considering both my personal and professional goals. As you know, my home is very far from here, and I think it's time I need to go back. Therefore, I should show you this. It is my resignation letter for the company."

One of Yamamoto-san's worst nightmares was having a team member resign on him. Kimura-san told me that likely I was the first employee to ever do so. Since he had never worked abroad, he was used to staff who spent their entire lives with the company. My actions would make him lose face.

"Huh?" Yamamoto-san responded, his cheeks sunk. "Really?"

His vulnerability was almost tangible. He shook his head quickly and lightened his reaction, retaking control of the situation. "We worked hard in India but still didn't get the results we targeted," he pointed out. "How can you leave without our project being finished?"

I raised my eyebrows and shook my head, wishing I could pause the moment like a movie and ask Maeda-san for guidance. Yamamoto-san's comment was focused entirely on the impact of my decision on the company instead of my career.

"It depends on how we define finished," I finally responded after a moment of deliberation. "My goal was to share my know-how with the dealership team so that they may continue the project on their own. The team has now taken responsibility of the activity and is running the meetings. I believe we have been successful in our initial purpose in India, which was to make them self-reliant."

I probably should have just said sorry instead of explaining. That would have been the Japanese way. But I am not Japanese. I am American.

Yamamoto-san's expressionless face considered his next question, "You told me you wanted to be a manager in two to three years. Why?"

"That is what I wanted. I wanted to grow and to learn more, which I have." What I really wanted to say was that I don't place my value or self-worth in my title like other people at Toyota seem to.

"But, still, I need to go home," I said.

He continued to question the sincerity of my resignation, checking with me that I had really "thought about it" or if I was just "overreacting to the project's obstacles."

"I've been thinking about this for six months now," I said. Yamamoto-san's eyes opened wide. I had truly caught him off guard. It had only been six months since I'd started working with Yamamoto-san. He was not the reason for my leaving, but I'm not sure I did an adequate job of presenting the resignation that way.

"She has thought the process through," Maeda-san said. I jerked my head in his direction, shocked. It was unusual for him to interrupt a conversation. "She has a dream and is going to pursue that," he added.

I grinned, happy that he was defending me, and bit my lip to avoid tears of relief. By speaking on my behalf, Maeda-san was actually standing up for himself.

Yamamoto-san was uninterested in my plans or the reason for my departure; it was irrelevant. From his perspective, I was giving up on the mission of the company. I never blamed him for my leaving, but he was a strong example of why I needed to go.

The conversation with Yamamoto-san was over within minutes. Yoshida-san arrived just as it was ending. He kept his attention to the floor, walking with loud stomps, and took a seat farthest away from us behind Maeda-san. Yamamoto-san didn't even acknowledge his appearance before ending the conversation. "Ma . . . we will talk later," he said, stacking his papers and zipping up his pencil case. "Thank you for your time."

Yoshida-san followed directly behind him. Maeda-san remained holding the door open for me as I cleaned up my things.

"Arigatou Gozaimashita," I said, bowing and thanking him. I returned to my desk, grabbed my purse, and practically ran out of the office.

The humidity seemed to hit my face differently that day as I exited the heavy doors of Centennial Tower, gently embracing me back into the world. I stood tall, walked briskly, with shoulders back and eyes wide. I had control over my life again. I could do anything. You could've asked me to climb a mountain that evening, and I would have accepted the challenge. My destiny was in my hands again, and it was up to me how I wanted to shape it. Whatever I did for the rest of the day was my choice. Choice. What a fabulous gift. For a long time, I thought Toyota had taken it away from me, only to realize that I'd taken it away from myself.

That night, I went to meet Jessica, Fabian, and Lydia for a drink at a bar on the Singapore River. "How'd it go?" Jessica asked. I felt like I was on a high but still in some shock.

"I did it. I have officially resigned and will have no job in one month." For the first time in my life, I experienced what it felt like to leave a company. Despite the common belief, the world was not going to end.

My friends went on talking as usual about who had left town, who was new to town, and where they would take their next vacation. I sat on the stool, listening with one ear but staring at the floor. I'd actually done it. After nearly nine months of analysis, I'd left Toyota. Ranju had been right—I needed time to think through such a big decision.

"I am now one of those expatriates," I said under my breath.

"What, Hil?" Jessica asked.

"It's weird. I'm finally that person that people gossip about when they leave. I've been watching for three years, wondering when it would be my turn."

"Yeah, no one thought you'd ever leave. You've been here longer than almost everyone." We'd all grown accustomed to losing friends by now. It's just that, with me, the return to the states came as a surprise because, unlike many expatriates, my term had been indefinite.

Chapter 45
I Needed Twenty Years

I was overwhelmed with things to do over the next several weeks — things like cancel my Singaporean credit card, find someone to take over my cell phone account instead of incurring an exorbitant fee of SG$600, and plan a farewell party for Lydia and me. On top of all of this organization, I had to plan Ariana's vacation and my final trip, to Cambodia.

People began to ask me why I was staying in. They said I should be going out and enjoying the last of my time in Singapore, but I had enjoyed enough. It was time to work hard toward figuring out my next step. Play time had ended.

At the office on Friday, everyone acted like nothing had changed. Yamamoto-san was extra friendly, as was Maeda-san. Maeda-san told me openly that Yamamoto-san was going to try to convince me to stay. I warned him that I had already made my decision. I was relieved to finally be able to tell people, but at the same time, I was hesitant to reveal it to everyone in the office.

A week or two passed, and I started to get a little concerned because none of the top management had said anything to me. A friend who also worked on the India project stopped me in the hallway. "I'm proud of you, Hil," he said.

I looked around to see if anyone could hear. "Thanks. I don't get it, though. None of the top management has approached me. Do you think they even know?"

He leaned back in laughter. "Of course they know their only American is leaving."

An Indian friend of mine from the e-CRB project said, "It is a beautiful decision. That is just lovely. I am so happy for you." His smile bore only sincere support. "You cannot dot the path forward into the future, only backwards."

These comments helped to build my momentum. Nearly everyone was encouraging, which made me wonder if what I was doing — standing up for what I needed and making risky decisions — was really that rare.

Another friend from outside the office commented to me, "That is your strength and the strength of the best leaders: they don't lose who they are."

But I still had a job to finish. A few days after I formally submitted my resignation letter, I asked Maeda-san what I could do in my final days to help with the India project.

Maeda-san had requested me to make a summary paper of the past sales kaizen activity in India. The purpose was to share the know-how from our experience so that the next person who joined the team could learn at a glance what had taken us over a year to learn, thus preventing them from making the same mistakes. With all the company had given to me, it was my responsibility and duty to complete the report with full energy and effort. It was the least I could do. I needed to end my service to Toyota with dignity.

I had only two weeks left. Maeda-san and I met for several drafts and discussions before the final review.

We sat next to each other at the corner of the working table. I held the paper in front of him and went through it with a pencil, reviewing the project's history, accomplishments, current situation, and future steps. He nodded in agreement during the entire explanation. It was because of him, and that one day in the Indian pantry when he showed me how to present a story, that I was able to refine these skills.

When I finished presenting, he smiled. The final paper was clear, comprehensive, and concise. "I needed twenty years to get knowledge," he said. "Maybe whoever reads this doesn't need twenty years."

He sat up in his chair and said, "My purpose is not to change operation. That is easy. But my task is how many people I can touch and share the difficulties faced." I thought of my team in the Philippines and India. This is exactly what I was trying to say to Yamamoto-san when I resigned.

Maeda-san continued, "Even if they rush, they cannot achieve the ideal situation—they will make mistakes—but we can help minimize those mistakes." Even though I was leaving, I knew Maeda-san would not let my story and impact in TMAP vanish. The purpose of the paper was to teach others, but it also served as my value add to the e-CRB project and to Toyota.

Maeda-san held my paper tenderly in his hands, rough and worn from his experience in the service division. He handled each of his words with seriousness and passion, yet openness and consideration. I wished I had more time to work with him. He was one of the few people that truly understood what we were trying to do with kaizen.

"Sales kaizen in India jumped too high. We were missing the step-by-step because the lack of intention and understanding was not there. Like a traffic light—people still don't follow because of lack of intention." I listened attentively. "Sales operating procedure or a manual is just how to use. The reason it exists is behind it—and this is know-how."

Often, it's so easy in Toyota, and in life, to just do as someone says. But to listen to many perspectives, backgrounds, and opinions—to digest them and determine your own—this is one of the most difficult skills.

"Hilary-chan, I have many senpais. But they are not all right. I take little things from them all."

On June 29, our office officially moved locations to Tanjong Pagar, allowing me ten days of walking to work. Luckily, the change served as a distraction from my leaving. It was in this new office that I received my final bonus check. I put it straight into my desk instead of running to the bathroom to open it. I didn't care how much it was. I stood up from my chair when Yamamoto-san approached my desk.

"Do you have a moment?" he asked.

"Mochiron." Of course.

We walked over to the new side table in the office and sat down. It was lunchtime so the office was almost empty.

Yamamoto-san's perfect posture didn't allow his back to touch the chair. With his hands in his lap, he said one last time, "I want to know you are sure about this decision."

Again, I didn't hesitate. "I am," I said.

"Is there anything I can do to make you stay?"

"I'm sorry, there is not," I said. I had already booked my flight home.

Lydia and I decided to sell our things at a local flea market. Even with the transient lifestyle I had lived for the past three years, I was shocked with how much junk I'd accumulated. Our combined load took up eight suitcases, requiring us to take two taxis that evening.

The outdoor market was packed with local vendors selling their stuff on rented tables and clothing racks, with a tent overhead to protect us if it rained. We were the only expatriate vendors. Our table was in the corner, giving us extra space to lay open suitcases on the concrete with more stuff. It was particularly hot that night.

Our piles of belongings slowly diminished. Lydia and I were juggling people with bids over each shoulder, getting rid of almost half of our table within the first hour. We had Singapore's two-dollar bills falling out of our pockets. After the first wave of patrons passed through, we finally had a brief moment to hydrate.

"I'm going to get some water and grab us some dinner. Do you want anything in particular?" I asked. My stomach growled. It was already 8:00 p.m.

"Something local—you know, we've only got so many days left to eat Singaporean food!" Lydia said.

When I returned, I stopped for a moment with our plates of chicken rice in my hands and watched Lydia handle our table. Swift and business-like, yet kind and quirky, she sold our stuff to bombarding customers. I was going to miss her.

I walked up from behind her. "I got us chicken rice! I haven't had it since I first arrived three years ago!" I said. Lydia turned around with money in her hands and a pale face. "What?" I asked.

"I'm so sorry, Hils," she said.

"For what?"

She fumbled over each word like we had been fumbling the things, not moving fast enough to keep up. "A girl was here—she gave me five bucks for them . . . I didn't know what to do."

"Them? What's them?"

She dropped her arms. "Your capri pants."

I had an expensive pair of capri pants that I bought several years prior hoping to fit into, but had never worn once. They were made of high quality black linen with white balled trim. Earlier in the night, I'd been consistently getting nervous about letting them go—refusing to sell them for anything less than five dollars.

I set the food down and gazed at the table. My appetite had disappeared. I couldn't believe that they were gone. I'd carried those from college to work in Chicago and then to Singapore, hoping to one day wear them, and I'd never gotten the chance.

"Hil, I'm sorry. You'd wanted five bucks for them all night," she said, with her coin purse on her hip bulging gold one dollar coins.

"It's okay, I think."

"Are you sure?"

I looked up at Lydia, who was definitely being unnecessarily apologetic. "You are so sweet, Lydia. It's okay. It's really okay, actually," I said with a smile.

She reached into her coin purse and handed me the money. "Here," she said.

I held the Singapore five-dollar bill in my hands, looking at the prime minister on the front of it. For years, I'd contemplated and worried about those pants. I'd hoped and wondered if they'd ever fit. I had literally carried them across the globe.

"Sorry!" Lydia kept saying before returning to the table. I sat just behind her with the chicken rice, still smelling delicious, although getting cold. Our table emptied of nearly all of our belongings that now had new homes. What was I thinking? I needed to let go of those pants long before that night. I needed to let go of many things long before that night.

We zipped up our eight empty suitcases. Everything seemed lighter; the old things had been weighing us down.

Fortunately, we were able to fit everything into one taxi on the drive home. At the apartment, Lydia opened a bottle of wine and we sat on the balcony. I propped my feet next to Lydia's on the table.

"I feel rejuvenated," I said, shaking my hands at my sides. "Like I'm free of all my emotional ties or concerns."

"Walking away with just a handful of items—it's cleansing," Lydia said.

"It makes you realize how little we really need to survive," I said.

"It makes you realize *what* we really need to survive—and it's not things," she said.

Chapter 46
Toyota Dress

The next week, I made my life-changing decision known to the public. I sent an e-mail out to friends, family, past colleagues, professors, mentors, and others. The response was overwhelming. I don't think I've ever felt more loved in my life.

People wrote, "You have hands down one of the best and most significant post-university experiences."

"Your brave approach to endeavors that you take on is envied."

"I have often told people of your adventure to Singapore, your determination and general zest for life."

An especially unique mentor wrote, "Visionaries are rare in this world. I can't wait to see what you do."

I couldn't believe that I'd had such an impact on people, when for so long I had felt alone.

My heart fluttered as usual when I saw that Peter had written from England. "It really reflects your priorities squarely," he said. "And so, it makes anyone that cares for you really happy to hear. That's incredible self-discipline."

I had only one day left at Toyota. The last day of a business trip was always the most productive because of the anticipation of returning home to Singapore, and I also remembered counting down the hours for my annual trip back to the States. This countdown was different and more significant, marking the end of my time with Toyota.

A colleague was arranging my farewell party at Nanjya Monjya—the restaurant that had become one of my favorites ever since Hiro had introduced me to it. I accidentally got the e-mail to the rest of the office about the party. It read: "Please send one of your photo to me for arrangement of token of the memorial, even if you can't attend the farewell party."

Memorial? Token? I wasn't sure what was transpiring for my farewell gift, but I was certainly going to miss the poor, broken English.

With one workday left, I thought about what I would wear ever since Yuko had said she remembered my "abnormal" outfit from our first day, I thought people would probably remember the last day too. I was searching through my closet when I came across an old dress hidden in the back. It was my "Toyota dress."

The dress was fire-engine red and sleeveless with a sharp collar, and fell just above my knees. Pong-san, my Thai boss, had branded it the first day I wore it to the office: "Oh! Red dress, oh! Your Toyota dress!" To me, it had just been an old red dress, but after that it always reminded me of Toyota.

The day came and went as quickly as a holiday. Between saying good-bye to numerous friends, filling out the final paperwork, and turning in the company's supplies, or assets as they called them, it came to an end before I even had time to write my farewell letter.

One Japanese friend couldn't attend the farewell dinner that night and asked to meet me earlier so she could give me a gift. It was a pair of earrings that she had made by hand. I still don't know why it struck me so deeply, but I got very upset.

"Oh, please cry only happy tears," she said to me.

It wasn't the earrings or the situation that made me cry. I was crying at the thought of someone who cared so much that she'd take hours out of her day to hand-make something for me. It perfectly represented Japanese culture. The Japanese are gracious and value that kind of personal touch. I was going to miss that.

When I finally sat back down at my desk for a short period of time, Maeda-san, Yoshida-san, and I began reminiscing about funny stories. I shared about Yoshida-san's "elements of smell," and Maeda-san joked, "I have to be honest, you've change a lot since our last meeting. When you go back, please don't eat fried chicken. Please eat tofu and vegetables." We sat in our chairs — mine still with a low back — and simply talked and laughed.

Whenever someone left Toyota, they e-mailed the entire company a "farewell" letter. Sometimes people were short and brief, but more often, people extended their deep thoughts and emotions in the letter in a very informal way. I always thought it was a strange idea and had planned not to write one myself. That last day, though, I felt a pull to do so. I drafted mine multiple times but waited until 5:25 p.m. to send it. I had the same nervous feeling I'd had the day I pressed the "BOOK FLIGHT" button to purchase my one-way ticket to Singapore.

Dear friends and colleagues,

Today marks my last day with TMAP. These past three years with the company have been priceless, and I will forever be grateful to Toyota for giving a young female American woman a chance. I just hope I've given back as much as the company has given me. My sincerest thanks to my managers: Maeda-san and Yoshida-san for truly practicing The Toyota Way through their daily work with me. Without their consideration and modesty, I could not have grown to where I am today.

Many thanks and God bless,
Hilary

The return e-mails began arriving within minutes, and they blew me away. I tried to hide my face behind the computer screen while I read others' overwhelming support. Apparently, many people didn't know that it was my last day.

The box of things on my desk reminded me of the new journey I was about to undertake. I knew I could not plan what would happen, but Toyota had taught me a skill even more valuable than planning: how to be flexible and adapt.

Another friend tapped me on the shoulder as I leaned over my computer, reading. She was also Japanese, very independent, and still single in her thirties. We'd always gotten along well. She said, "Hilary-chan, I want you to know, my image of an American is a big spoon in a tub of ice cream on a couch watching a movie. But that has changed since I met you." We both laughed.

I hadn't moved to Asia in hopes of changing the way Asians thought of Americans, but I ended up doing that in a small way.

I cleared my final e-mails and saved my documents on my flash drive. For one last time, but this time not to schedule a meeting, I checked my bosses' calendars. On Maeda-san's calendar, I saw "Hilary Farewell Party" and choked up. I'd seen so many other people's farewell parties noted in calendars over the years and still couldn't believe that I was finally staring at my own.

Despite the upset of my departure, my friends and coworkers were all excited to go out for my farewell party. But before we left, I had one last thing I needed to do. After my own internal debate, I knew I had to e-mail the big bosses.

Hamada-san hadn't approached me or said anything to me that final month. It was hard not to take it personally. I wanted him to reach out and tell me to stay like Hayashi-san had when I switched divisions. I later realized the desire had been narcissistic. Because I was no longer within his sales division, he was not obligated to say anything.

Since there was so much talk in the office about me leaving, it was crucial that the top management hear the reason directly from me. I waited until moments before shutting down my computer and handing it over to IT. It was my last sent e-mail as an employee of Toyota.

Dear Top Management,

Two years ago, when faced with the decision to move from

Sales to the Service division, I strongly requested to stay with DOKD to expand my kaizen know-how. I am aware now that seems questionable. However, it was through this experience that I was able to identify my true passion: helping others improve their jobs and overall happiness in life.

I will be forever grateful to the company for helping me realize this passion and dream. I know this is unlike the TMC way of thinking, but I want to ask you to please consider the situation. TMAP consists of many cultures that all have their own way of thinking that should be understood.

I cannot express my gratitude in words, but thank you for giving a young female, American woman a chance. The past three years serving Toyota have been priceless in my growth as an employee and human being. I hope what I have given could account for even a fraction of what I've received.

If ever you are in America, I welcome your contact.
With the utmost respect,
Hilary

This kind of outreach between the staff and top management was unheard of, but I was different. I will never know if the e-mail made any impact to our relationship. One top management responded, though, three weeks later; It was our senior vice president, Edmund-san.

Hilary,

Thank you for your mail and apologies for the late acknowledgement. I was, to say the least, a lot surprised and not a little regretful to learn that you decided to leave TMAP. I always considered you a valuable member of our Kaizen group, of Team TMAP and Team Asia. As well, you were an invaluable testament to the diversity that is essential to building a true regional organization. I don't mean only diversity in terms of nationality but, more importantly, diversity in terms of thoughts and ideas. I really appreciate your individual and team contributions during your stay with us. I especially thank you for your great efforts in the two countries that are closest to my heart—the Philippines and India.

In fact, I was in Manila just last week and was speaking to "Ma'am" Ona. When I informed her that you had left us, her immediate comment was that she missed your regular presence in Toyota Makati and your patience, persistence and doggedness in promoting kaizen in their organization. Although their activities continue, she feels that the absence of your clear "ownership" in driving kaizen activities has somewhat diffused the energy in their workplace when it comes to things-kaizen. She asked me to say hello to you and extend her appreciation for all you did for Team Toyota Makati. I told her that the best way to thank you would be to make sure that she continued to fan the flames of kaizen and to make sure that what you started blossomed fully into a more mature kaizen organization and culture.

In any case, I wish you all the best in your new endeavors. Of course, there is no place like home. Writing a book on "following your dreams" and furthering the cause of studies abroad are very personally fulfilling and spiritually gratifying engagements, I am sure. As they are borne out of your own personal experience and from your heart, I am sure the sincerity and passion that will infuse your new adventures will not escape those whose lives you will touch through them. Bravo! I hope to get an autographed first edition copy of your book.

Hilary, your joining TMAP was almost "movie like" in the way it unfolded. It could not have been better scripted . . . a chance meeting with a strange Japanese named Antonio, enjoying the sun by the poolside in a place far, far, away . . . what were the chances? Ha ha ha. It was serendipity and a most fortunate accident, indeed.

I always like to say when we find ourselves at a parting of ways, please don't be a stranger. You know where our (new) offices are. You will always have friends to welcome you here. When—not if—you find yourself in our neck of the woods again, please drop by and say hello.

Life is short. We have to enjoy the moments . . . Give, Live, Love.

All the best. God bless.
Vince Edmund

The honesty and sincerity of Edmund-san's e-mail amplified my appreciation for Toyota's style of management. The workplace was unlike any other. I spoke with Sato-san the day I got the e-mail.

"I'm jealous of Edmund-san's English skills," he said. "I'm also jealous you received an e-mail."

"What do you mean?" I asked.

"Edmund-san never wrote me any words like that when I left last year." Sato-san commented.

"Currently our know-how is very special," Sato-san said. I smiled on the other end of the phone. "Your know-how is not applicable to just Toyota dealers but any business."

Sato-san's mentorship during my time at Toyota was an invaluable asset. The learning I'd acquired from him, Kimura-san, Yoshida-san, Maeda-san, and my other bosses made my experience more than just my "first job." They'd changed my entire perspective, not only of business, but of leadership; how to treat people, how to motivate them, and how human beings work.

Chapter 47
Fist-Sized Eyes

The more popular you were, the more farewell parties you had. The big bosses—VPs and above—could have two weeks straight of evenings full of sake, noodles, and karaoke. I specifically requested only one farewell that combined all the teams with whom I'd worked. I also asked that it be on my last day. I didn't want to bid farewell and then see everyone back in the office the next morning. My farewell party at Nanjya Monjya began promptly at 6:30 p.m.

The dinner began formally and started with beer, as is tradition in a Japanese corporate dinner, but the evening developed into an uncontrolled and informal one as we moved on to sake and shochu—a Japanese whiskey. We played Japanese drinking games that required us to remove a piece of clothing with each loss. We joked about office crushes and revealed secrets that—mutually understood—will never be revealed again.

The company always presented a gift for the person departing, and it varied depending on how popular the person was. I was given a gift card to Amazon along with a brilliant photo frame entitled "Rainbow Bridge's Friends." It was an 8 x 10–inch frame with a collage of mini-pictures of my colleagues, including a "Special Guest" who was known around the office as my Japanese crush from a domestic dealership in Japan. At the top, it listed all of my projects in Toyota. I also received a beautiful silk business card holder from Kyoto, handmade earrings, and a photo/scrapbook. I felt so blessed.

On the walk to the taxi stand, my dear friend and boss Maeda-san admitted his true feelings. "I was so very excited to work on our new idea for India sales, but you didn't even give it a chance," he said, stumbling over his feet.

"I'm sorry," I said. There was nothing I could say to make him happy. It's never easy telling bad news to someone you respect so highly.

My last day reporting to work at Toyota, together with the farewell dinner, sent me off with memories of laughter and an equal amount of awkward moments that made us laugh further. The night reminded me why I so much enjoyed working with the Japanese. It also reminded me of the things I'd miss, but would refuse to forget.

In addition to a stomachache, I was also greeted the next morning with a longing to return to the office. I'd broken my three-year routine, but there was no time for sulking. Sunday arrived, and I went to the airport to greet Ariana and head out immediately on our trip to Thailand.

Her flight was earlier than expected, so when I arrived, everyone was already exiting the plane. I ran down the terminal with my bags like a crazy woman but didn't see her. She knew to wait for me at her arrival gate like I instructed. I was so worried something had happened.

"Pardon me," I said, catching an airline attendant getting off the plane. "Is everyone off the plane already?"

"Yep, that's everyone."

"Shoot!"

I ran down the terminal again, yelling thank you over my shoulder. Because of the way the flight schedules worked out, Ariana and I were taking separate planes to Thailand, and there was only about twenty minutes left until my flight boarded. I had barely enough time, but I wanted to see Ariana, so I went to find her next gate and see if she was there. When I arrived, she wasn't.

The last chance I had to find her was through the information desk. I managed to get my words out between gasps of breath. "My sister is coming from the U.S. She's never been here. I was supposed to meet her. But she wasn't there. Can you page her?"

The attendant agreed to do so, and within seconds a message went out. "Ariana Seguin, please report to the information desk in your terminal." God bless Singapore for being so efficient.

I kept checking my phone frantically to see the time. Even if she did show up, I was going to have to hug her and run. My flight was nearing five minutes to boarding and it was in another terminal.

"You called me on the intercom?" I heard her say from down the hall.

Hilary Corna

It was something straight out of a love story — but between sisters. We ran down the terminal and caught each other in our arms.

"That was a ridiculously long flight," Ariana said. She now understood why I didn't come home more often.

"Yeah, no kidding."

"What happened? I thought you were supposed to meet me at the gate?" She surprised me with her level of energy and enthusiasm after so many hours in the air and four flights from Columbus. Ariana was completely composed and alert.

"I know! Sorry, your flight was early, so I didn't get there until you guys were already exiting. Then I didn't see you. I was running up and down the terminal looking for you."

"You probably ran right past me."

"Oh geez, that's probably so true."

Although only at a brief glimpse, it was wonderful to see my sister in my world. We had talked about it for three years, sometimes jokingly but sometimes seriously. Finally, we had committed to making it happen, and she was the third sibling I shared my Asia with. I was looking forward to our adventures in Thailand.

"Okay, I have to run and catch my flight. Let's take a picture!"

The attendant watched in glee from her desk as she helped reunite sisters. She took our photo with my phone, and I immediately sent it to the family.

"You know where you're going?" I asked.

"I hope so. I've gotten this far!" Ariana said.

"Okay, love you, see you in Thailand!"

I took off running to the gate. The last thing I wanted to do was to miss my flight and leave her stranded in Bangkok!

Our seven-day trip in Thailand was epic. It strengthened our bond as friends and as sisters. We traveled from Bangkok to Chiang Mai to Pai, about as far into the northern countryside as you can get. There, families grew what they ate and children walked without shoes.

The first day of the trip, we stayed in Bangkok for one night. My old boss Pong took us for a seafood dinner cruise on the Chao Phraya River. He picked us up from our hostel in his Toyota van. I hadn't seen him since we took the Philippines team to Bangkok right before the financial crisis. It was incredible that my sister and I were meeting my old boss from Singapore in Thailand.

The river cruise was the perfect way to spend our first evening together. It was pitch-black out, but the boat's Christmas lights flickered on the water. We ate enormous king prawns and all sorts of fish and fresh vegetables, and I spoke with Pong about my decision to leave the company.

262

I apologized to my sister for boring her, but it was important to me that he knows my reason for leaving and to have his support.

"There is a very big problem in India. I can feel it. You made the right choice."

I exhaled and let my tense shoulders loose.

We didn't speak too long about work. He wanted to enjoy his night just as much as we did. He began asking my sister about her story and family. Ariana showed him photos of my nephew.

On our first day in Chiang Mai—a much smaller version of Bangkok— we saw a young boy lying in the street. He was probably three years old, naked except for a T-shirt, covered in dirt and sleeping in a cardboard box on the curb. I knew it would upset Ariana, but I had no idea how badly. She looked away from him in tears.

"Oh my God. Why?" she asked. "Why would any mother ever allow that to happen to her child?"

I felt terrible for becoming numb to it. I had seen it so often now, and I tried to tell her how India was worse. I also felt terrible because I couldn't understand her perspective as a mother.

The highlight of the trip was the one thing Ariana wanted to do the most: ride elephants. I had ridden an elephant with Viktor in Laos, but the flattened, roped off path had made the experience feel incredibly commercialized, like a circus.

This time, the elephant camp sat right at the foot of a mountain. The establishment had been in operation for over twenty years and was now run by the granddaughter of the original owner. They took incredible care of the elephants, fed them regularly, gave them a safe place to sleep and grounds to roam, and even brushed them. They were like children to the owner.

Boarding the elephants, we began our journey around the valley. We rode for an hour through a landscape that stretched green for miles. It was humid, but clouds hid the sun that day. Ariana and I were both speechless.

Elephants moves slowly and shift their massive weight from one side to the other when they walk. When you are riding on top, you shift with it. We had to grasp tightly to not fall off.

"This is amazing. That is all I can say," my sister said. "I could have never imagined this."

The handlers stopped the elephants at the top of the hill and offered to take our picture. They said I could stand on the elephant, insisting that it was strong enough.

"Is he crazy? No way," I said.

"Be careful, Hilary!"

You only live once. I stood up on the animal just long enough for the photo and sat back down.

"That probably ranks as one of the dumbest things I've ever done," I said.

We got back on the elephants and continued into the river. The elephants dunked us in the water while we sat on their thick-skinned necks, and then flipped their trunks so we would slide down their backs into the warm river. Their fist-sized eyes stared at us as we pet their coarse hair.

On our flight back to Singapore, Ariana thanked me for planning our trip: "I'm so happy I came, Hilary."

We had two days in Singapore before she left. We met up with friends, had foot massages at my reflexology Chinese doctor, and ate lunch with Kimura-san. Kimura-san had now met almost my entire family.

Our final dinner was with Lydia. We went for dim sum at a famous Chinese restaurant. Out of all my friends, it was especially significant for Ariana to meet Lydia.

I wasn't sad when Ariana left. I knew I'd see her in less than a month and was thrilled to be following behind her. I was only in Singapore a few days before I left again for my final vacation. My bags seemed heavier as I carried them through security. The plane's takeoff wasn't as exciting anymore. I rarely thought of my map. On this flight, I felt weary of travel and tourism. Looking out the plane window, my eagerness to settle down and be on land weighed on me.

For three years, I'd wanted to go to the Angkor Wat temples of Siem Reap, Cambodia. Though the temples were some of the most exquisite I'd ever seen, it was hard for me to enjoy the trip. My mind was in another state, far from that of a laid-back tourist. I was thinking about my family, my career, and the adjustment back to Columbus, Ohio. I was thinking about saying good-bye to my Lydia and Jessica, Kimura-san and Maeda-san, Singapore and India. I tried hard to take in the history and architecture of Cambodia, to soak up the experience, but I couldn't.

I had twelve days left to enjoy my life abroad when I returned to Singapore. Twelve days to take in the best of what it had to offer and bid farewell on a positive note. Lydia and I arranged a going away party for ourselves at one of our favorite outdoor bars. I wished we could have seen all the people we'd known through the years there, but many were gone permanently or out of town. In the end, about thirty friends came to say good-bye.

No one likes saying good-bye, but I despise it. It was hard not to get emotional seeing friends show up in support of my decision to leave. Between Alexandre, my French friends, Eliot, Hiro—I couldn't help wondering when or if I would ever see my dear worldly friends again. I was scared of losing that support and starting all over again. And I was most upset about losing Lydia, Jessica, and Fabian. They had become my clan, the indispensable friends who knew everything about me.

A lot changes when you live in an ever-shifting expatriate community for three years. People moving in and out of your life numbs you from emotional attachment. However, for my case, this scenario opened my eyes to a value that, although I always had, I'd grown blind to: deep, sustainable personal relationships. I had longed for them in Singapore.

Chapter 48
Please Share Singapore

People kept asking why I wasn't partying and living it up during my final days in Singapore. Instead, I was busy researching, e-mailing, and meeting people to figure out my next step. For three years, I'd reveled in the Singapore lifestyle. There was nothing more I wanted to do that I hadn't already done in the country. I was beginning to feel even more that I was ready to move on.

I had only one week in Singapore left. One night, I met Jessica and her fiancé Owen for the SINGfest concert, where Peter and I had first gotten to know each other three years earlier. Jessica, Owen, and I had a blast dancing and enjoying the music, but I couldn't stop thinking of Peter. Standing on nearly the same patch of grass I'd once sat on with Peter, I couldn't stop thinking about how young I'd been and how much I had grown since then.

It had finally reached my last weekend in Singapore. Hiro and I planned to meet for dinner and then go to Eliot's for a barbeque. Hiro and I hadn't spoken much in the past few months. I had consciously separated myself from him because I could sense strong feelings on both sides but didn't know how to manage them in context. The dinner was pleasant, but slightly uncomfortable. We both avoided eye contact in hopes of evading our physical emotions toward each other.

I was getting tired of going out. Dinners were losing their novelty, and I was yearning for comfort, for a home-cooked meal, and for family. Lydia and my other close friends arrived at the barbeque shortly after Hiro and me. The new condo towered over Marina Bay. About twenty floors up, the barbeque pit sat next to a pool amid a garden of plants and overlooked the Singapore skyline.

There was a beautiful French girl there whom I'd heard Eliot had just started seeing. Gabriel was also there with his new girlfriend. Chitchat and a few drinks only temporarily distracted me from my emotions. I liked both Gabriel and Eliot and felt frustrated that we met just as I decided to leave.

Lydia took my shoulder and turned my back to the crowd. She finally called me out, "What's wrong with you, Hils? You ain't the same."

"No, I'm fine." At this point, I was standing in the corner with my arms crossed, peering onto the crowd. My drink was gone.

"You know I hate that word—fine," Lydia said. I sniffed and chuckled. She always made me laugh when I needed to.

"No really, it's nothing. Just reflecting," I said. I didn't want to ruin her night. It was also her last Friday in Singapore, and we were planning on a big night out.

"Don't reflect now. You're out with your friends. It's not the time or place."

Her reference to friends made it even worse. I began to question if they really were my friends. "They're all moving on with their lives despite us leaving, as if we were never there to begin with." I was saying no to a man who was in love with me and longing for a man who now stood there with his new girlfriend.

"Well, what do you expect of them?" she asked.

"I don't know, Lydia. I just can't do this."

"It's okay. What do you want to do, babe?" She was way too selfless. She should have told me to shut up and have a good night.

We ended up getting food and going home. Looking back, I can't believe I wasted one of our last nights out by sulking. I felt terribly guilty although Lydia kept insisting not to.

On Saturday morning, I went to a baby shower for Alvin and his wife, to celebrate their first baby girl. Alvin had invited me before I'd left Toyota, so I felt like I should go since I was still in town. When I walked into the HDB, I found Maeda-san inside. He was sitting on the couch with his two children. Typical of him, he didn't look me straight in the eye. It was awkward. Since I had left the company, it wasn't really appropriate to talk about work, but we didn't have much of a casual friendship like Yoshida-san and I. I also still felt incredibly guilty for leaving him. He was returning to Japan at the end of the year anyway, but he had wanted to use that time to finish the project with me. I had taken that from him.

To try and lessen the discomfort, I began speaking to Maeda-san's children. I introduced myself, asked their names and about their school. Maeda-san opened up a bit and took part in the conversation. He adored his children and respected me for speaking with them. The children of Japanese expatriates often have poor English skills, so their parents appreciate when others help.

The moment I saw Alvin's new baby girl, I knew exactly why I had to go home. I wanted to be a part of my family's lives, particularly my nephew's. Also, I wanted my own children someday. I didn't want to be in

Asia through all of my twenties. I wanted to meet a husband and have a family of my own.

I got ready with Lydia for our official last night out. I had let go of my concerns and decided to just let it be. This night included only my close friends—Lydia, Jessica and her fiancé Owen, Fabian, and a couple others. We decided to go to Clark Quay, the tourist hub for nightlife, just because it was where people started when they came to Singapore.

We didn't get serious or talk about Lydia and me leaving. We didn't discuss work or love or any other somber life issue. We danced and laughed and had fun. It was like any other night out.

That night, I remembered why such a small group of people had become my best friends. It had taken a long time to find them, but they were the best of the best. They were real, sincere, caring, and loving, and I got along with them naturally. They taught me how true friendships were supposed to function and grow. They showed me that, even coming from multiple continents, we had commonalities that related us, and that, nationalities aside, we were all pursuing the same objective in life: happiness.

We continued our party into the next day—this time, with my French friends—the ones who had really showed me how to party. The beach club at Sentosa had transformed over the years from the rustic Km8 to a plush bar called the Tanjong Beach Club.

The conversations at Tanjong Beach Club were short but kind. Many people thought I'd already left. "Yes, I keep rescheduling my flight—I just can't leave!" I joked. It had been a month since I'd left Toyota, and I couldn't believe how quickly time had passed.

Monday brought me to a much deeper awareness of the time and reality. My final weekend in Singapore was coming to an end, and I had only hours left in the country. Ironically, that Monday was Singapore's National Day. It was as if everyone was celebrating the glories of my experience in this country with me. I saw differently that day, taking pictures of everything from taxis to locals on bicycles to the HDBs that stood so tall and strong. I was afraid of forgetting.

There were still several bags of random things that I couldn't fit in my luggage. Most of them were old clothes. I took them to my Chinese doctor who always did my massages. She always sent her earnings home to her family and spent it on her son. She reminded me of my mother and how she rarely did anything for herself. Unfortunately, the doctor wasn't there when I dropped by, but I left two bags with a note that said, "Have fun!"

Lydia had to work until her very last day, so I was still alone on Tuesday and for the rest of my weekdays. It was amazing how time-consuming and confusing packing was. How do you fit three years of life into two bags?

That night was my last night to meet Kimura-san. We were going to dinner at the Japanese restaurant where he had taken my mom.

"The office is the same. I hope the change in scenery will help, but I am not sure," Kimura-san said.

"Yes, I'm sure it will, but maybe only temporarily," I said. The real problem was that many of the staff didn't feel valued, mostly because of their salaries, but also because they didn't feel empowered.

I feel so fortunate to have served in a position where I knew I was valued—although it took many mistakes to learn and see this—but my opportunities were given to me as a way for me to grow. I could have never achieved as much in the other routine jobs.

I often told people that I probably wouldn't have lasted as long in Toyota if I had been in a different position. I adored doing kaizen. As much as I complained, I loved the business trips and working on the front line with the staff.

"Toyota needs to learn to adapt to all, not just Japanese way. We are not in Japan. This is Singapore," Kimura-san said.

"Like Nakamura-san said, TMAP is a young office. I guess it must take some time to learn to adapt," I responded. We stayed at dinner from the time the restaurant doors opened to the moment they closed, talking about work.

"You know, Pong-san didn't want to hire you. Vijay was afraid you came with a boyfriend to Singapore. Pong-san was afraid you were too young."

My jaw dropped. "What? Boyfriend! I didn't have a boyfriend."

"Yes, I know."

"But no one asked me. How did you know?" I tried to keep my voice low in the quiet Japanese restaurant.

"I could sense it. Your reason for applying to Toyota was not in desperation. You had every intention and strong desire to work with the company. I could feel it in the interview."

I didn't know what to say. "I could have never had this if it weren't for you. This entire story could have been nonexistent if it weren't for your one decision to say yes instead of no."

"It wasn't a hard decision. I saw it as an opportunity."

"Thank you. Thank you."

"Thank you, Hilary. You proved that my decision to follow my instincts was right. I couldn't have been happier. I've learned so much more in the past three years than I can track in my career. I'm different now because of you."

I couldn't stop smiling. What if, I kept thinking, what if he hadn't hired me? I simply didn't have any clue where my life would be.

Kimura-san asked what my next step was. Toyota people always wanted to know the next step.

"I have some ideas, something in the pipeline," I said, "but I honestly just don't know yet. I need time to reflect and think about all this."

"I have no doubt in my mind you will do whatever it is," he said.

When we departed the restaurant, words were completely inadequate.

"I owe you my life, Kimura-san."

"No, I owe you mine."

Kimura-san had met my family and my best friends, seen me at some of my weakest points and some of my strongest points.

Only twenty-four hours remained. I waited until the last day to visit the office for my final parting. I wanted to say good-bye when it felt like it was a true good-bye, when there wasn't any more time to postpone it.

I visited TMAP that Wednesday in the late afternoon before my final dinner with my best friends — this one really was the last. Visiting late gave me a reason to keep the conversations short. I didn't want to end up in tears or in any awkward conversations. I quickly found my closest friends, Kom-san and Yoshida-san, and my best girlfriends and lunch buddies, Ein Ein, Ruth, and Yui.

"We thought you left!" Ein Ein said.

"Nope, I've just been on holiday in Thailand and Cambodia. And then taking some time to enjoy my final days in Singapore."

"Wow, how nice."

"When is your flight?" Ruth asked.

I could barely even spit it out in my own disbelief. "Tomorrow afternoon."

"You really are leaving."

"Yep, I really am leaving."

Then Ruth asked me something that I would never forget. "It is kind of weird," she said, "you being the only white girl here. None of us think about it anymore, but it must have been hard. Of all the things, what do you think was your biggest challenge?"

Without even thinking I knew the answer, "Friendships." I'd learned so much about relationships and understanding people by living in an international context.

It was strange and sad to be in the office not as an employee. As much as I had become weary of my job, it was sad that it wasn't a part of my life anymore.

When we met for coffee on one of my last days, Amanda's mother said, "The drive that brought you here is the drive that's bringing you home. Toyota was good for you then, but not now."

Her comment put everything into perspective as I stood watching the staff slave away in loyalty to their work. There was nothing I owed Toyota.

I'd already given them hard work and commitment during my time as a kaizen leader.

During one of our final coffee meetings, Kimura-san once said, "It is not about thinking positively about the company as much as thinking deeply about the situation and realizing it's not about the company. It's about you."

On my way out of the office, Yoshida-san and I took a picture together in front of the famed red block letters of TOYOTA. For a long time, I had taken pride in working for the world-renowned and well-respected company. I vowed to always speak highly of it.

When the elevator door closed, I stared at my reflection in the mirror. I'd finally said good-bye for the last time.

I met the clan at Jumbo Seafood on the Singapore River for our final supper. It just made sense to eat seafood for our last meal, since it would be the last time we could get the country's specialty for so delicious and so cheap.

"Would y'all just leave already — this is an emotional rollercoaster!" Jessica joked.

We ate scrumptious chili crab and butter crab and drank cold beer. Jessica and Fabian presented Lydia and I each with a photo album of our adventures. I couldn't read their notes until later because it hurt too much. I felt so loved. They were some of the best friends I've ever had.

I thought hard about what to get Lydia and ended up making her a shadow box with items from some of our fondest memories, including the original train map she'd used when she first moved to Singapore.

She gave me a card that made me cry again. "You're going to mess up your mascara, Hils!" she yelled at me.

"Then don't get so emotional on me, Lyds!" I yelled back.

We were tired and stuffed with good food, but we continued on to Lydia's favorite bar in Clarke Quay. It was a Wednesday night, but there was still a good crowd. Lydia, Jessica, and I found ourselves on the dance floor singing "Sweet Home Alabama."

We all squeezed each other into a big hug. "I will never forget you guys," I said to them both.

"Me neither!" they insisted.

We had danced. We had cried. It was finally time to say good-bye.

There is something about traveling that changes your view of good-byes. It doesn't have to be sad. It's a reflection on the past, on fond memories, on laughter and learning experiences. It's a tribute to growth in our lives. And it's a sign that we will never forget the people who helped us through each stage. And that, if we want them to, the people we are saying good-bye to will come back into our lives again.

One White Face

Lydia was meeting me at the apartment during her lunch break to ride in the taxi with me to the airport for my 2:00 p.m. flight. The feeling I got when I thought about leaving Singapore reminded me of the day I found out John got engaged. I was numb, not really sad, but prepared, having given myself the adequate time to do so. I wanted to soak in the remaining few hours I had left. It was fascinating how everything grew more significant as time shortened.

I walked across the street to the new HDB that had been under construction since I first moved into the Tanjong Pagar neighborhood. Tanjong Pagar was in the middle of the city, but up until that time, very few expats lived there. What was significant about this building was not only it's sophistication but its size. It consisted of five towers; all connected by a running path and a sky pier on the roof that charged people for access if you were not a resident. Lydia and I had planned to go to the top for the longest time but never gotten around to it. That morning, I decided to go.

It was a sudden decision, but within moments, I had crossed the busy Cantonment Road, the noise of which kept me up plenty of nights, and found the guard office of the new HDB. An Indian man sat behind a glass window with a tiny hole engraved in it. He had lighter skin, probably from sitting in the office all day.

"I'd like to visit the sky pier," I said.

"Sure, it will be ten dollars."

"Ten dollars?" I didn't know it would cost so much and had already exchanged my money to US dollars. I explained my predicament to him and was surprised when he agreed to let me up anyway.

"No problem. Just don't tell anyone," he said. This was incredibly abnormal in Singapore. Workers usually followed the rules.

The man walked me to the dark, silver-plated elevator, let me in, and pressed the button for sixty-five.

"Wow, that is high," I said.

"Yes, Ma'am. Sixty-five floors. Enjoy," he said. "Thank you, Sir."

The door opened and air gushed past my face like the first night I arrived in the country and waited for my ride at the airport. This time, I was enveloped in daylight. I stepped onto the pavement with a fresh view of Singapore. The pier overlooked Chinatown's red roofs merging into the financial district. Blue skies hovered over the Indonesian islands in one direction, and the rural tropical forests of Singapore in the other. It reminded me of my view from my first apartment in Tanjong Pagar, just next door, but over three times higher. I had never seen anything like it.

The sky pier had plastic furniture in morphed shapes like they were made of clay. Whoever designed them hadn't realized how hot they would get that close to the Singapore sun. Moving from one seat to another, I found one that was shaded by the air-conditioning units on the roof. As I sat there, I thought about how I had first envisioned my final day in Singapore. I'd thought I would be a mess of nostalgic tears — distraught, torn, and confused. However, in the final two weeks prior to departure, I had only cried twice. I remembered Ranju's comment during our lunch, "To discover, one must depart the near shore." My new voyage had begun, and I was equipped to go.

Like in my interview long before with Toyota, I pictured myself on a world map, on which Singapore is rarely even marked. I was a miniscule speck of humanity, a pinprick on one of the landmasses stretching across the planet. Zooming in closer and closer to the region, to the country, to the city, and to the building, a woman sat in reflection on her life — a life that would never be the same.

Had this transient lifestyle numbed me? I had traveled nearly every weekend and could pack necessities in ten minutes flat. I'd become the maestro of efficient airport logistics. My standard introduction included my name, home country, how long I had been in Singapore, and how long I planned to stay. Everything was associated with time and movement. This transience had also affected my relationships, which now seemed so fleeting and temporary. Just like a settled lifestyle, it had both pros and cons.

I called my mom from the top of the HDB. She was getting in bed for the evening.

"Oh, what a stunning sight it must be," she said after I described the blue skies, hovering skyscrapers and vast ocean. The sky pier had still been under construction during her visit.

"You will never forget what Singapore has done for you — I know it," Mom said.

I shook my head. "It's far beyond me. I'm not sure how to comprehend it."

"You don't have to. It will forever be a part of you and that alone is all you need to acknowledge."

"Will I ever be the same?" I asked, although I knew the answer.

"No — but your soul is. It's just the external that has changed, blessing you with a portfolio of experiences to speak to."

"I love you, Mom. I'm ready to come home."

I still remember the first time I desired an adventure and learning about the world. It was the summer of 2001, before my junior year of high school, waiting for a return flight home from architecture camp. I was sitting in an airport chair at the gate and drawing a floor-level perspective of people's feet moving in the direction of their destination. In wanderlust, I daydreamed about each passenger's final port and reason for traveling there. Now, that desire for travel had been fulfilled, it has forever changed my identity.

After all my frequent flying, and bringing Mom and Ariana to Asia, I had just enough miles to redeem a one-way flight home on Singapore Airlines. This time, I didn't need to sell my Jeep to fund the ticket.

It was nearing noon when I finally made my way off the sky pier. The time had come to gather my belongings and head for the airport. Lydia would be home soon to meet me.

The apartment was silent. The walls stood brisk white, missing the photos and decorations all packed away in Lydia's boxes. I pulled my two suitcases outside the entrance of our apartment. There was no way they were within the limit of fifty pounds. I was thankful for having gold status so the airline wouldn't charge me. I closed down my computer, looked around my bedroom one last time, and stood waiting for Lydia on our balcony. It hurt too much to wait inside amid all of her boxes.

"I'm home!" Lydia came in yelling.

I immediately hugged her. "Thank you so much for being one of the best friends I've ever had."

"Oh, don't get sad on me, Miss Corna!" She was always so strong. "We will see each other soon." We had plans to meet in a few months, so there was something to look forward to, but those plans didn't make up for me losing my best friend, my rock.

The room had become even more cold and barren, nothing in it but a few pieces of furniture.

"Can we get out of here?" I asked. "I hate to see the place like this."

As we left, I held the heavy oak door open for a moment to see the apartment for the last time. That door had welcomed us home after many nights of laughter and nights of sorrow. It was the place where I had contemplated my future with Lily over tea, grew older and wiser on my birthday, and cried over relationships with guys. It represented my final few months of exploration and decision-making in Singapore—much different from my first apartment—it was my haven for reflection.

"Hils, the elevator is beeping!" Lydia said.

I let the door fall shut and met Lydia in the elevator. We didn't speak much during our drive to the airport.

"I feel like we've had fifty good-byes," she said laughingly.

"Seriously. We've basically been celebrating our farewell since April, just not really knowing it."

"How are you feeling?"

"I just feel like I'm going on another business trip."

"You're not."

Just as she said that, I looked back. We were driving on the bridge that ushers airport visitors into the city. It was almost unrecognizable from the day I'd arrived. New buildings had reshaped the skyline. Centennial

Tower stood powerfully at the entrance of the city, and peering up, I could almost pinpoint my office floor.

"So many hours, memories, thoughts took place there — highlights of my time and the lowest lows I could have ever known," I whispered softly to Lydia.

"You have done so much, Hil. You should be proud. It will always be a part of you."

That was one of the final times I cried.

"I can't forget, Lydia. I must not forget."

The taxi approached the departures drop-off. I paid the driver SG$25. "This is too much, Ma'am," he said. I had saved only the amount I needed for the taxi.

"Please, take it, Uncle. Thank you for sharing your home with me."

Strangely, he didn't look at me like I was some crazy foreigner. His cheeks creased in a smile. "You are welcome. Don't be sad. This is the story of life."

I stood for a moment in a profound sense of relief. I wasn't alone, although I had felt very much so only seconds earlier. I turned around to find Lydia with all my things unloaded and in one of the free carts the airport offered. She looked gorgeous as ever in her black cap-sleeved dress. A tear broke and fell down my cheek.

"I'm so proud of you, Hilary," she said.

"I'm proud of you, Lyds. Know that I wouldn't be here right now without you. I will be forever indebted to you."

"Oh shush, Hil. You are amazing. You will be wherever you need to be. I have no doubt of that. Now get going."

I took a few steps forward and she boarded the taxi. I felt like my energy was being cut in half and driven away. Once again, I stood alone. An intense flash of memory took me to other times in my life when I'd felt the same: my last day in high school, saying good-bye to my mom at college, the day I bought my ticket for Singapore. These were all significant points where it was up to me to move forward, no one else.

When I entered the airport and checked my phone, my inbox was full of texts from friends saying their final good-byes.

My dear friend Kirk said, "Remember that you are an inspiration to Gavin and me. You deserve the best in adventures, love, and life. We know you will achieve everything you dream of in all three."

Another friend wrote, "You're an amazing woman, Hils. Never settle for second best in life and keep shooting for the stars."

Finally, one friend said, "I love it how you manage to find the bright side of everything and are so intrigued by the seemingly most mundane things."

274

I left the hot, humid Singapore air for the last time and entered the air-conditioned airport. I would not breathe fresh air for another thirty-six hours. My hands shook as I handed the airline agent my ticket. I moved slowly and was caught in a gaze, realizing this would be the last time I checked in. I wanted to soak it in.

"I actually wanted to inquire about upgrading to business class. Are there seats available?" I asked the airline agent. It was purely for entertainment and out of curiosity that I inquired — not really with the intent of spending the extra money.

"You are all checked in. For your business class query, please walk to desk at the end of the aisle," she said. "Have a wonderful flight."

My bags disappeared on the belt. I quickly prayed that they would make it home in one piece and then walked to the desk she had pointed to.

So how does one get upgraded to business class? I found the answer: to live abroad for three years and then tell the airlines staff all about it on your return flight home. Also, be sure to lose your boarding pass.

When I realized there was only one person at the desk, I thought I would try to schmooze the lady for a free upgrade. It was unheard on Singapore Airlines, but I had to try.

"Good afternoon . . . Sally, is it?" I said, reading her name tag. She was very sweet looking, short and petite with a round face and beautifully sculpted brown hair. I could tell she was Filipino from her facial features and accent, and the way she kept calling me "Ma'am."

"Yes, Ma'am. Good afternoon," she said. "What can I help you with?"

"You know, I am flying back to the United States for good after living in Singapore for three years. I wanted to just go ahead and see what kind of cost it would be to upgrade to business class."

"Wow. That is a very long time to be away from home. Sure, I can check that," she said. I handed her my ticket and we continued chatting while she looked up the flight.

"So why are you leaving Singapore, Ma'am?" she asked. "Don't you like it here?"

"You are too sweet," I said. "I know! Don't remind me. I love it here. It's just that I've been here for three years, and it's a long time to be away from home."

"Very long time, Ma'am. What did you do?"

"I worked for Toyota."

"To-yo-ta!" She annunciated each syllable the Filipino way. Each Asian country said it slightly different, and they often didn't recognize the name if you said it wrong. "That is a good company."

"Yes, very good company. May I ask, I think you are Filipino?" I said. She hunched over in shyness and giggled, holding her hand to her mouth.

"Yes, how did you know?"

"My project was in the Philippines, so I traveled there for over a year. "

"Wow, did you like it?"

"Yes, I love the Filipino people. They are all so caring and loving."

"Thank you, Ma'am. Well I'm sorry but there is no upgrade available."

"That's okay," I said.

"You have a wonderful story. Please have a safe trip back and share Singapore with your friends and family."

"Thank you. I will."

I said goodbye to my new friend and got in line at the immigration desk. The sun was shining through the tall glass windows of the airport. An hour later, I walked onto the plane. Later during the layover in Hong Kong, I lost my boarding pass for the first time in three years. When I approached the airline desk for a reprint, the clerk handed me a business class ticket.

One of my favorite parts about flying is the takeoff. Every flight I take, I get a rush of adrenaline as the nose of the plane catches air, the wheels lift, and the pressure of momentum and velocity launch a new journey. The challenge of a takeoff is not dealing with the momentum, but making the decision to board the plane in the first place.

I'd boarded a lot of planes over the past three years, but this one was the hardest. I leaned my forehead against the window and my tears smudged the glass. Turning from the businessman next to me, I pulled my arms and legs in a ball against the wall of the plane and stared off at the Singapore landscape for the last time. The nose of the plane lifted, and I gasped for air.

It was mid-afternoon. I could see the skyscrapers downtown and imagined my friends going about another day in the office. They were moving on with their lives, as was I.

The plane turned, and I saw one last glimpse of sunlight reflecting off a glass tower, then gauzy, cloudy white. On the map of the world, I was a yellow dotted line, arcing over the Pacific toward America, toward new adventures, and home.

One White Face

Hilary Corna

Ren & Me

Hilary Corna

ACKNOWLEDGEMENTS

Publishing a book never claimed a line on my list of personal goals. When I returned home with yet another budget and timeline (both well surpassed in the end), my family openly welcomed my ambition. This book, and my sanity, was cared for not just by me.

Adrienne, my big sis, you not only lent me a free room for a year in your new home to write this book, you did even more. You consoled me on lonely Saturday nights of writing and defended my ability to achieve my new goal to the world. You never ever stopped believing in me.

To my phenomenal editor, Laura Snider, for giving up time with her new daughter to take on this project and for pushing me farther than I could've imagined. The feeling of getting a ripped apart sentence so right that you could not say it any more perfectly has become one of my favorite feelings in the world. Even moreso, my sudo-phschologist, your questions prompted emotion and reflection that I otherwise would not have felt.

Kasey, Matt, and Amanda, my editing interns, y'all were prompt, responsible and intuitive. Our editing cycles are what kickstarted this story to come to life.

To Kato-san, for being the closest thing to a father I've ever had. You took a risk. You gave your word to my name, and never let go. To Komatsu-san, for the books, the lunches and the coffees, the inspiration, the push, and for launching a standard of management style in my career that helps me help others. And for *not* believing that I had followed a boyfriend to Singapore. To Ishikawa-san, for showing me that people are people, for giving me one last chance to learn. And Furukawa-san, you always helped me keep a smile on my face.

To AJ, for saying no, and letting me see what I needed. I would not be here without you. To Michelle, for giving up your best friend for three years so she could pursue her dreams. To my other Michelle, for sharing a story with me that only we will ever fully know and never ever forget. Mr. Skinner and Mr. Simpson, as housing me, you became enablers. To Vlad, you taught me some of the strongest lessons of friendship.

My dear Timmy, you showed me the most fervently romantic love I've ever known. To Ramesh, for being my bodhisattva. Jodie, "Jo-day!", and smiling Kate, you showed me how to have fun. To Sue, for being a relentless optimist and sparing thirty minutes to listen. My dear Tap, you enabled a "free-spirited" woman to fly.

At the end of the day, I could not have shared this story without my parents. To my father, for showing my mother the love that she infused into her children. To my mother, for loving your five kids and teaching them the true meaning of survival by illustrating the resiliency and determination we need to succeed instead of survive.

Writing *One White Face* was harder than getting a job in Asia. It's the hardest thing I've ever done in my twenty-six year old life. Since the first visit home when multiple people suggested that I write my stories down, I laughed out loud. Actually, the process of writing was excruciating for my personality type. I don't like to be alone physically, much less with just my thoughts in a cold Ohio home.

Something else pushed me, not my own interests, like a calling from something bigger out there, to the point where I had no choice but to write *One White Face*. Then, after many discussions, I realized the tremendous amount that could be learned by society if even slightly exposed to these stories, and a compelling duty to share them came over me.

Many people think, "Why would anyone want to hear my story?" I believe that no matter who you are, there is someone that can relate to your story and improve their own life from it. If that's the case, we have a responsibility to share them to help others, thus supporting the growth of humanity. I dare you to share. I dare you to discover.

One White Face